8/23

£3:00

(R)

Military Rebellion in A

C000025436

Military Rebellion in Argentina

Between Coups and Consolidation

Deborah L. Norden

University of Nebraska Press
Lincoln and London

The paper in this book meets
the minimum requirements of
American National Standard for
Information Sciences—Permanence
of Paper for Printed Library
Materials, ANSI Z39.48-1984.

Library of Congress
Cataloging-in-Publication Data
Norden, Deborah L. (Deborah Lee)
Military rebellion in Argentina :
between coups and consolidation
/ Deborah L. Norden.
p.   cm.
Includes bibliographical references
(p.   ) and index.
ISBN 0-8032-3339-6 (cloth : alk. paper). —
ISBN 0-8032-8369-5 (pbk. : alk. paper)
1. Argentina — Politics and
government — 1983–   . 2. Civil-military
relations — Argentina — History — 20th century.
3. Argentina — Armed Forces — Political activity —
History — 20th century.
4. Conspiracies — Argentina — History — 20th century.
5. Morale.
I. Title.
F2849.2.N67   1996
322'.5'098209045 — dc20
95-32285
CIP

Contents

Illustrations

Acknowledgments

The number of people who have contributed to this project is by now so extensive that thanking them all is virtually impossible. I would, however, like to express my appreciation for the support and comments of Edward Gibson, Wendy Hunter, Ollie Johnson, Gerardo Munck, Tim Scully, Mina Silberberg, Sam Fitch, and Deborah Yashar; to my dissertation committee at the University of California, Berkeley: David Collier, Robert Price, and Tulio Halperín; and to Sonia Nazario, for her generosity with her research materials when I first began this project. I would also like to thank Aldo Vacs, William Smith, and an anonymous reviewer for their very thoughtful and useful suggestions for the final version. The University of California, Berkeley, Center for Latin American Studies and the Organization of American States made the project possible by financing my research.

In Argentina, I owe extensive gratitude to a great number of individuals and institutions—first to Atilio Borón and the researchers of EURAL for their kind hospitality. The staffs of the Círculo Militar library, Servicios Históricos at army headquarters, and the Press office at the Ministry of Defense offered help and a welcome far beyond anything I might have hoped for. Beyond those mentioned here, I wish to thank the many Argentines, both military and civilian, who unselfishly shared their time and experiences with me.

During the final stages of this project, I have had the good fortune to be on the faculty at Colby College. While a number of Colby's superb staff members have aided me in the past months, special thanks go to Grace Von Tobel for her dedication and competence in getting this into its final form. My students at Colby have also been wonderfully understanding and patient; and my research assistant, Inés Velasco, has been outstanding.

Finally, I wish to thank my parents for their lasting support, and Frank Bright, for always giving me the encouragement I need.

Military Rebellion in Argentina

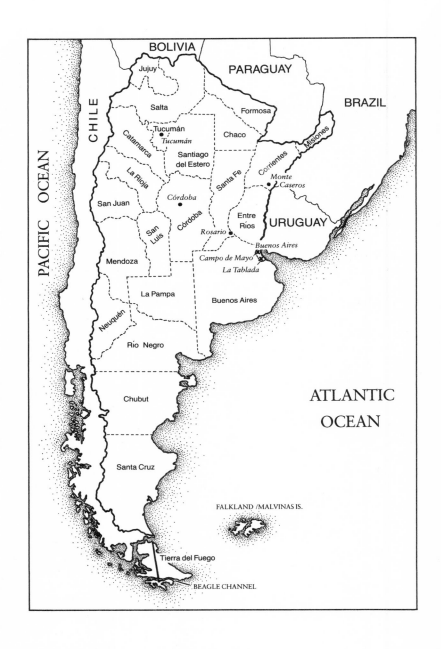

Map of Argentina

1

Democracy and the Armed Forces

Introduction

In Argentina, as in much of Latin America, politics have long appeared as a virtual tug of war between military rule and democracy. Democracy presumes the military's absence from politics; military rule forbids open democratic competition. Yet somewhere between military coups and democratic consolidation are a variety of political alternatives that may collide with expectations of democracy, but that nevertheless fail to trigger its collapse.

During transitional periods, these alternatives represent both the hopes and fears of democratizers. Adjusting the armed forces to the new political order reveals the fragility of the new regime. Military rebellion, in which rebels use the threat of force to pursue institutional interests, provokes particular concern, dramatically brandishing the specter of political reversal. Argentina's military rebellions from 1987 to 1990 demonstrated that such events do not necessarily signal a return to authoritarianism. Even so, rebellions indicate a lack of political control over the armed forces, which may be further diminished in the process. Military rebellion can thereby obstruct the process of democratic consolidation.

Given the importance of military rebellion, discerning its causes and implications is a critical (and largely neglected) task. Why do military officers rebel? In particular, why do they choose this mode of expressing dissent with political decisions, rather than either coups or political lobbying? How do traditions of military interventionism, recent experiences of the armed forces, and the government's military policies affect the likelihood of rebellion? Why do military rebellions succeed or fail? How does the incidence of military rebellion affect the probability of future rebellion, or even direct military intervention?

Democratization in South America

Through much of the 1960s and 1970s, authoritarianism predominated in Latin America. Paraguay preserved the remnants of traditional authoritarianism, with a dictator controlling the government for decades. In other South American countries, including Argentina, Brazil, Chile, and Uruguay, more modern forms of authoritarianism prevailed in which professional military institutions became integrally involved in political rule.

In the 1980s, as the Cold War melted and idealists lauded the purported "end of ideology," Latin America rediscovered democracy. Either the authoritarian regimes collapsed or their leaders chose to extricate themselves from power voluntarily before the choice could be snatched from their control. By the end of 1990, South America's embrace of constitutional democracy was virtually complete. Yet the new regimes still faced numerous challenges before democracy could truly be said to govern Latin America. Traditions of authoritarianism and military rule do not disintegrate the moment elected leaders enter governmental palaces. In conjunction with the challenge of establishing the rules and practices of democracy, the new constitutional leaders would be forced to confront frequently inauspicious legacies left by the prior regimes. In other words, elections represented a first step toward stable democracy rather than its culmination.

The Challenge of Democratization in Argentina

In Argentina, the military's infamous chronic interventionism further complicated the consolidation of democracy. Whereas in neighboring Uruguay and Chile the military regimes of the 1970s could be seen as exceptions within otherwise democratic trajectories, Argentina's problems with the armed forces have been endemic. Since 1930, Argentine history has been punctuated by frequent military coups, creating a virtual pendulum between civilian and military regimes (M. Diamond 1983). Military intervention also intensified during those years, evolving from brief departures from constitutional government to prolonged periods of military rule in 1966–73 and 1976–83. Thus, rather than merely reequilibrating a previous pattern of democratic politics, Argentina's elected leaders needed to establish an entirely new pattern of democratic stability.

The difficulty of democratizing Argentina was further exacerbated by the high levels of state-directed political violence during the 1976–83 period of military rule, among the worst in the region. For many sectors of civil society, institutionally subordinating and incorporating the armed forces would not suffice. They demanded more: that those members of the military community who had authored and implemented the intense repression of the 1970s be brought to justice. Only then, they argued, could the Argentine community cease to be haunted by the "culture of fear" created by prolonged authoritarian rule (Corradi 1987; see also Malamud-Goti 1991).

However, the pressures to avoid an explosion of retribution were equally compelling. The armed forces seemed unlikely to passively accept a virulent attack against their members for having committed what they perceived as justified acts carried out in the context of war. Furthermore, the literature on civil-military relations and democratic transitions is filled with dire predictions of what could occur should the military's prerogatives be threatened (Stepan 1988). Even cutting the military budget has often been portrayed as an excessively risky move.

The government of Raúl Alfonsín (1983–89) largely ignored these warnings. While neighboring postauthoritarian leaders remained cautious, Argentina's government not only made significant budget cuts but even prosecuted military officers in civilian courtrooms in South America's most dramatic attempt at demilitarization. Largely as a consequence of these policies, an important organized opposition began to form within the armed forces. In April 1987, this sector—known as the *carapintadas* [painted faces] for the camouflage makeup they wore—carried out the first of three major military uprisings endured by the Alfonsín government. A fourth uprising followed in 1990, during the presidency of Carlos Saúl Menem.

These uprisings critically delayed democratic consolidation in Argentina by postponing the shift from government-military opposition to the military's institutional incorporation into the state. Yet, significantly, the rebellions never entirely hurdled the boundaries of intramilitary conflict. Despite the important political aspects of the uprisings, no military coup d'état shattered Argentina's latest democratic experiment. On the contrary, in 1989, Argentina witnessed its first relatively smooth electoral transition between freely elected civilian presidents of two different political parties.

This study seeks to explain the advent and development of these military uprisings, as well as the constraints that kept organized military opposition from transcending the boundaries of protest. I argue that the emergence and evolution of rebellion constitute separate phases of military protest that respond to different dynamics. The cleavages that emerged within the army during the uprisings in large part reflected divisions inherent to the military bureaucracy. These lines were converted more explicitly into potential sources of division during the military government of 1976–83, particularly during the 1982 Falklands/Malvinas war with Great Britain. Finally, the confrontational policies of the Alfonsín government served as a catalyst, setting the military crisis in motion.

The emergent rebel movement began as little more than an amorphous reaction to the immediate conditions faced by the armed forces. However, by the end of Alfonsín's administration and the early stages of Menem's presidency, the movement had taken on a more organized and independent character. Rather than remaining essentially a reflection of tensions and cleavages within the armed forces, the movement had become a proto-organization with goals and interests of its own (particularly survival). Yet eventually this process of organizational development proved detrimental to the rebels' ability to generate support within the army. In fact, the very developmental process that initially fortified the movement finally caused its demise within the military.

The story of the Argentine military rebellions helps reveal important aspects about dynamics of military insurrection. Most importantly, military rebellions and military coups cannot be explained or understood merely through external factors, such as the civilian government's military policies or economic crisis. Other factors, including turmoil within the armed forces and prior experiences with military insubordination, influence who within the armed forces is likely to support further insurrection. This study thus focuses on dynamics and experiences within the armed forces, rather than on the broader context or alliances with civilians. With a series of rebellions, as in Argentina, each incident strengthens the resolve and organization of the movement's leaders, but also strengthens the opposition. Ultimately, whether the rebels appear to voice the concerns of a large enough constituency beyond their immediate followers determines whether they succeed or fail.

Overview

This study is concerned with the relations between constitutionally elected regimes and postauthoritarian militaries, focusing on the organization of military opposition movements. The first chapter deals with some of the conceptual issues concerning the relation between democracy and military insurrection, as well as the military's range of political expression, from political lobbying to military uprisings and direct intervention. Chapter 2 turns to the case of Argentina and its long battle with recurrent military intervention, beginning with the 1930 civil-military coup and Perón's polarization of the political system. Attention focuses on previous cases of attempted democratic consolidation, from which I draw some early conclusions regarding the determinants of military behavior in the postauthoritarian period.

Chapters 3 through 6 look at the antecedents and dynamics of military decision making during the recent postauthoritarian period in Argentina. Chapter 3 analyzes the internal legacies of the period of military rule from 1976 to 1983, especially the effects of the "countersubversive" war, the exercise of government by the military, and the Falklands/Malvinas war. Chapter 4 turns to the military policies of the Alfonsín government, tracing the process through which those policies evolved and exploring some of their implications. Chapter 5 looks specifically at the cleavages within the army that differentiated the two major factions in the April 1987 military uprising. Chapter 6 discusses the evolution of the military movement generated by this uprising, from its inception in 1987 through the climactic uprising of December 1990. The chapter explores the increasing independence of the rebel movement as it began to develop an organizational character of its own.

The overall model of causality underlying the analysis thus presumes that important changes may occur through a series of steps, rather than either abruptly or so gradually that sources of change cannot be identified. Minor decisions may redesign the context of decision making and change the path of future events, often in unanticipated ways. As Terry Karl and Philippe Schmitter explain, "Small differences and minor choices, whose relevance is often unknown to those experiencing them, may be capable of producing major effects and channelling a system in quite different and lasting directions"

(1991:270). Each rebellion in Argentina, and each reaction of the government to the rebellion, created a new context.

The final section of the manuscript addresses broader questions regarding military interventionism, military rebellion, and civil-military relations in transitional regimes. Chapter 7 deals with the dilemma of intransigent military interventionism in Argentina. Chapter 8 compares the transition to democracy in Argentina to other South American cases—Chile, Brazil, and Uruguay—and focuses on the kinds of conditions and inheritances that might alternately facilitate or hinder the peaceful subordination of the armed forces. Finally, in the conclusion, I consider more specifically the dynamics of coalition formation and their relationship to organizational evolution.

Data and Method

The analysis presented here is drawn primarily from research conducted in Buenos Aires, Argentina, from September 1988 to August 1989, with follow-up trips in September 1991 and August 1993. Information has been culled from periodicals, military journals, military bulletins (the official publications of the Argentine armed forces), and rebel publications, as well as secondary sources.

Another crucial source for this study has been interviews with military officers and politicians. The interviews probably contributed the most interesting details and insights into the issues. However, they also engendered their own methodological problems. Given the sensitivity of the issues and the Argentine context, obtaining a random sample of subjects and carrying out a structured survey was essentially impossible (and probably of limited utility). Argentina's history of internal violence meant that for the right and left alike, a stranger posing questions could only be greeted with distrust. Officers in the postauthoritarian period were well aware that granting a candid interview meant taking a risk. Nonetheless, I did attempt to assure some representation from different ranks, specializations, and factions in the army, and was surprisingly successful in doing so. Whenever possible, I sought to verify information from another source. On other occasions, it was necessary to rely on my own assessment of the informant's credibility, using such criteria as whether or not it appeared to be in an individual's interest to portray a particular image.

Defining Democracy

By the end of the 1980s, democracy had emerged from the pack of conflicting political models as the virtually uncontested paradigm. The possible merits of various forms of authoritarianism or revolutionary socialism fell from popular debate, replaced by debates about competing versions and definitions of democracy. The democratic model may have triumphed, but it remained an ambiguous, amorphous conceptualization of the political process, with the label frequently applied (or denied) as much on the basis of normative criteria as objective observation. Such perspectives alternately point to rebellious militaries as largely irrelevant to categorizations of the political system, or as virtually nullifying democracy. In contrast, I argue that democracy, when defined in a meaningful manner, is an ideal that military rebellion severely injures.

The most commonly agreed upon meaning of democracy is "rule by the people." Yet, in modern societies, it is impossible for all members of democratic communities to directly participate in all phases of decision making. Thus, some form of representation is generally also incorporated into definitions of democracy. Taking into account the political conditions that allow formal representation to be meaningful, the following factors seem to compose the essence of political democracy (Dahl 1971, 1989; Diamond, Linz, and Lipset, 1988; O'Donnell, Schmitter, and Whitehead, 1986; Karl 1990; Linz 1978):

   1. *Electoral competition.* Political leaders are chosen through open, competitive, and regularly occurring elections.

   2. *Associated political rights.* All citizens enjoy the freedom to express different political perspectives, present them as alternatives, and organize to promote those alternatives.

   3. *Accountability of elected leaders.* This implies that the system includes some mechanism by which elected leaders are compelled to continue recognizing the demands and needs of citizens or, at the extreme, face the possibility that their position may be revoked. Regulations for impeachment fulfill this criteria.

   4. *Universal inclusion.* All adults subject to the rules of the polity may vote and run for office, thereby helping to form those rules.

In most fully consolidated and functioning democratic political systems, these factors constitute the most recognizable components of democracy. In Latin America, however, these conditions have rarely sufficed to ensure that the state responds to the demands and interests of the people. The frequency of military intervention, and the less noted but equally prevalent autonomy of the armed forces, the police, and the intelligence agencies, cause an important gap between the input of the people and the output of the state. The citizenry may determine who governs, but those who govern cannot necessarily control the institutions responsible for carrying out their policies. In many cases, those policies cannot even be initiated without taking into consideration potential risks from unincorporated sectors of the state. Thus, some authors have opted to include a further criterion for democracy:

> 5. *Responsiveness of state institutions (such as the armed forces, police, and intelligence services) to the government* (Rueschemeyer, Stephens, and Stephens 1992:43; S. Valenzuela 1992; Schmitter and Karl 1991).

This criterion recognizes that form is not necessarily enough to guarantee substance, and that relations of power must at least minimally support the formal structure for it to be viable.

Applied strictly, the definition elaborated above probably would allow few countries to adopt the label "democracy." However, I must emphasize that this is a *model*; it represents the essential qualities of a political ideal type. Even some of the political systems most universally described as "democratic" may not completely comply with all criteria. For example, political alternatives perceived as revolutionary, "antisystemic," or in violation of pluralist norms are sometimes prohibited from competing in otherwise relatively open systems. It is particularly complicated to assess whether these prohibitions are "undemocratic" when the excluded political groups are themselves exclusionary, such as those that discriminate against other races or religions.

Universal inclusion is perhaps even less frequently achieved in its totality. In many cases, the criteria for exclusion would probably be unlikely to call into question the regime's level of democracy. For example, individuals are commonly prohibited from participating on the basis of citizenry (noncitizens cannot vote) or for violating the rules of the society, as in the case of convicted criminals. However, other bases of exclusion, such as literacy, ownership of property, religion, race, or gender, more obviously construe limits to the degree to which democracy has been achieved, even though all of these have been common historical constraints on participation.

Recognizing gradations of democracy also implies recognizing the possibility of *change*. Such an approach seems essential for the study of democratic transitions and democratic consolidation. Transitions to democracy create the incipient structures for political democracy and subsequently transfer control from the prior authoritarian rulers to a democratically elected government. As O'Donnell and Schmitter emphasize, the entire process is inherently uncertain: "It is characteristic of the transition that during it the rules of the political game are not defined. Not only are they in constant flux, but they are usually arduously contested; actors struggle not just to satisfy their immediate interests and/or the interests of those whom they purport to represent, but also to define rules and procedures whose configuration will determine likely winners and losers in the future" (1986:6).

O'Donnell and Schmitter portray the subsequent stage, democratic consolidation, as relatively less uncertain. Theoretically, democratic consolidation entails institutionalizing the rules established during the transition, thus stabilizing the new political order. According to Samuel Valenzuela, "A democracy is consolidated when elections following procedures devoid of egregious and deliberate distortions designed to underrepresent systematically a certain segment of opinion are perceived by all significant political forces to be unambiguously the only means to create governments well into the foreseeable future, and when the latter are not subjected to tutelary oversight or constrained by the presence of reserved domains of state policy formation" (1992:69). Valenzuela's definition thus places the end of the consolidation process at the point where full procedural democracy obtains some degree of legitimacy.

Yet the stage of establishing rules and procedures, and the analytically subsequent stage of institutionalizing and/or legitimizing them, need not be temporally separate. Realistically, these processes occur concurrently, at least to some extent. At the moment that an authoritarian ruler passes the presidential sash to an elected president, many of the rules of political democracy have yet to be established. Those rules that have been implemented are still quite feeble, and their viability is yet untested. Furthermore, the creation of institutions not only follows democratic procedures, but also helps establish them. In sum, the process of democratic consolidation is probably much more dynamic than transition-focused analyses might suggest. Thus, I propose looking at the concept of political democracy as a process, with variation along different dimensions, rather than as an absolute standard that actual democracies (particularly those in transition) rarely match.

Militaries and Democracies: Variations in Military Behavior

Coups command attention. Their apparent obverse, institutionalized military subordination, encourages tranquil disconcern—a disconcern that many individuals in less stable environments energetically covet. Yet, the lines between subordinated and unsubordinated militaries are far less distinct than they might appear. There is a range of alternative military behaviors or roles filling the continuum from unconditional subordination to military government, often with a good deal of blurring in the middle.

Subordinate and insubordinate military behavior can be differentiated by two key variables: the kinds of issues that stimulate a reaction, and whether the threat of violence or direct intervention is explicit, or even implicit, in the means that military actors choose in order to express their position. A military epitomizing institutionalized subordination theoretically would concern itself with only the bureaucratic needs of the organization. It "lobbies as do other parts of the government; seeks to carry out a relatively specific set of policy objectives; and employs channels of decision-making within the military that do not breach its integrity as an institution" (Welch 1976:2). At the other extreme are those militaries or military sectors that use violence to obtain control of government and thereby implement the political programs of their choosing.

Nonetheless, some semblance of political awareness pervades all actual militaries. As Claude Welch explains, "Armed forces are never totally apolitical, given their role in national defense and security, their quest for professional autonomy and budget resources, and their historical roles in many states as leading agents of governmental personnel and policy change" (1987:12). Identifying which issue areas fall outside of the military's legitimate concerns may thus be rather complicated. Even though only such bureaucratic concerns as budget allocations and organizational autonomy reside clearly within the domain of the armed forces' institutional interests, one would expect the military leadership to at least be aware of international alliances and tensions—areas that could provoke war and influence how it might be carried out. At the same time, efforts to actively interfere with the conduct of foreign affairs violates the boundaries between those responsible for making policy and those charged with carrying it out. Along another vein, interpretations of security that incorporate such nondefense issues as education and economic development also blur the lines between military and nonmilitary roles.

Nevertheless, due to the innately political nature of military concerns, the means of expression tends to serve as a more revealing indicator of the relative level of subordination. At one end of the spectrum, armed forces responding to civilian control "engage in bureaucratic bargaining, provide expert advice, and accept overall policy direction from government officials, under whose auspices military prerogatives and duties are established" (Welch 1987:13). In other words, military leaders might not opt for silence, but they do recognize the ultimate authority of the government.

At the other end of the spectrum, interventionist militaries or military sectors may assume a variety of roles far beyond those representing subordination. Eric Nordlinger identifies three such interventionist roles, of varying intensity: rulers, guardians, and moderators (1977:22). The "rulers" category is self-explanatory: government by the military.[1] On the other hand, guardians and moderators both have the *potential* to become rulers. According to Nordlinger, "Moderator-type praetorians act as highly politicized and powerful pressure groups in relation to the civilian incumbents, sometimes backing up their demands with explicit threats of a coup. Where necessary, they may carry out a displacement coup" (22). In other words, moderators carry out an *oversight* role, but without assuming power themselves. In contrast, guardians may carry the oversight function somewhat further. "[G]uardians are often no different from moderators in wanting to stave off political change and maintain political order, except that guardians are convinced that these goals can best be realized by controlling the government themselves" (24).

Such extremes do not, however, exhaust the range of behavioral options. Between political subordination and the distinctly interventionist "ruler" and "oversight" roles, there are at least two intermediate categories of military behavior, which might be referred to as independent political participation and aggressive institutional advocacy. Each of these modes of military action oversteps the boundaries of one criterion discussed above. In the case of independent political participation, military officers may form political parties that, despite their origins, compete democratically (as Argentine rebel Aldo Rico did in 1990). In these instances, sectors of the armed forces overtly concern themselves with noninstitutional issues, but without using or threatening the use of violence. This mode of behavior certainly violates Samuel Huntington's conceptualization of "objective subordination," but does not necessarily destabilize the political system.

On the other hand, aggressive institutional advocacy may prove destabilizing, and may generate more directly interventionist behavior. Aggressive institutional advocacy refers to those actions such as *planteos* [uprisings] in which the perpetrators threaten violence but attempt to constrain their demands to institutional issues. These actions most resemble military versions of strikes; however, since these groups' refusal to work would engender minimal costs for the military command or the government (given the armed forces' non-economic function), the "striking" sectors use a somewhat different arsenal. Not all uprisings fit into this category—many (if not most) do involve political issues, and some lack even the pretense of an institutional orientation. Others, though, do purport to limit their protests to institutional concerns, despite frequently dubious definitions of what that entails.

In many respects, these intermediate categories constitute the most intriguing forms of military behavior, and the most important during transitional periods. Militaries that have recently governed seem unlikely to immediately slide into a completely subordinate relationship to the newly elected government; thus, the crucial question is how they opt to express their beliefs and demands. Direct political organization and participation may provide relatively "safe" outlets for discontented sectors to express their views, thereby facilitating the consolidation of constitutional rule. On the other hand, choices that threaten or utilize violence may generate potentially destabilizing dynamics by magnifying the degree to which the armed forces act (or are perceived as acting) as a political competitor instead of an essential sector of the state. The kinds of intermediate behaviors that are selected, and the dynamics through which they develop, help determine the degree to which sectors of the armed forces move toward either renewed interventionism or long-term subordination.

Explaining Military Insurrection

The image of political democracy has long pervaded Latin American ideals, while eluding Latin American reality. Pervasive military intervention has prevented many countries from sustaining—not to mention intensifying—democracy, even in some of the most economically advanced countries of South America. Not surprisingly, military coups, the most dramatic and identifiable hindrances to democracy, have drawn the most attention from analysts. Many such studies have focused on the context of military coups, looking at such factors as the social, economic, and political roots of the breakdown of democracy and somewhat neglecting military behavior per se. Others, however, have placed more emphasis on the military institution, thus providing potentially useful insights about a range of military behavior, including both coups and military rebellion.

Society-Oriented Explanations

Military intervention has frequently been explained in either *functionalist* or *instrumental* terms. In the former, the military is perceived as acting in response to the needs of an inadequate or malfunctioning state. Military intervention would thus be expected to occur when a weak political system or inadequate economic system require it (O'Donnell 1973; M. Wallerstein 1980; Huntington 1968). In contrast, the second perspective portrays the armed forces as largely *instrumental,* operating as the servant of an undemocratic, or democratically uncompetitive, right.

While informative, both of these approaches have their limitations. Perhaps the most common criticism of functionalism is that it imposes a post factum logic on social events and an overall order that do not necessarily exist. Outcomes occur to serve systemic needs. In many instances, however, the outcome did not serve the posited need. The armed forces have succeeded only rarely in instituting adequate economic reforms and have frequently generated economic programs significantly less orthodox than those expected.[2] Militaries have been even less effective in substituting for the usual political party duty of aggregating and representing interests.

Instrumental depictions of the military tend to portray it as the virtual pawn of the right. The military is again perceived as filling particular needs, but these are more likely to be the needs of the elite, rather than the overall system. For example, according to Torcuato Di Tella (1972), Argentina's oligarchic elite have historically lacked the political base to compete electorally. The right, therefore, has found it necessary to resort to an alternative source of political power—the military. From a slightly different perspective, Guillermo O'Donnell and Philippe Schmitter identify an important (if not definitive) role of the military as the "prime protector of the rights and privileges" of the bourgeoisie in *Transitions from Authoritarian Rule* (1986:69).

The argument that the military acts at the behest of, or at least in the interest of, the right (or, more specifically, the oligarchy, bourgeoisie, or the status quo) has enjoyed persistent popularity for fairly obvious reasons. Democratic regimes frequently collapse when the interests of those sectors are threatened; thus, it would be logical to conclude that the military acts on their behalf. Yet how then does one explain such cases as Peru's progressive military government of 1968–75, or the alliance between Argentine officers and members of the middle-class Radical party in 1943? These exceptions would encourage some skepticism about the nature of the link between the military and the right.

Most important for our purposes, while both functionalist and instrumental interpretations of military behavior may contribute to explaining the fragility of democratic political systems, they cannot explain many facets of military behavior—including many aspects of military intervention. Both approaches tend to depict the military as a relatively unified entity, merely reacting to external conditions. Yet this is clearly not the case. As Arturo Valenzuela writes: "It is . . . misleading to continue to assume that the military is merely a symptom of underlying political difficulties, a neutral force which mechanically moves into the political sphere when a vacuum is created.

The fact is that the armed forces are powerful political actors (sometimes working at cross-purposes with each other) with interests and stakes of their own, operating either individually, or in concert with other actors in society" (1985:140). Understanding military intervention and its alternatives thus requires looking inside the military institution.

Military-Oriented Explanations

If military intervention can be only partially explained by the surrounding context, what factors *can* explain variations in military behavior?

The military is undeniably a unique form of public organization. Unlike other branches of the federal bureaucracy, the armed forces have a physical prowess (guns, tanks, and the ability to use them) that permits the military to transcend its assigned role within the political system. Yet not all militaries exploit this power, and even in those that do, such efforts only very rarely obtain unanimous adhesion within the armed forces. Among the most important factors that help explain the *why, whether, how,* and *who* of military intervention are (1) professionalism, socialization, and training; (2) bureaucratic organization; and, perhaps most importantly, (3) the relation between these two in the armed forces.

Within the armed forces, profession and organization merge in a complex, and at times uneasy, manner. Modern militaries require intensive training, much of which may occur within relative isolation from civilians. This distinct training, along with the concommitant socialization and ideological formation of the armed forces, is commonly portrayed as creating a virtual enclave—an organized sector of society with norms and ideas distinct from those of the larger community in which it exists.

Some of the most interesting and important debates within the literature on civil-military relations have occurred among those who share this basic perspective but who are at odds on the meaning and implications of this separation. The fundamental concept of *professionalism* has formed the core of this debate. Among the authors who have argued that differentiation, when occurring in the form of professionalism, may enhance military subordination rather than prohibiting it are Samuel Huntington (1957) and Samuel Finer

(1962). After posing the argument that military officership *should* be considered a profession, due to such essential characteristics as expertise, corporateness, and responsibility to a client, Huntington offers two different conceptualizations of professional subordination: "subjective" and "objective" civilian control.

According to Huntington, "subjective civilian control achieves its end by civilianizing the military" (1957:83). In other words, it does so by decreasing military autonomy and professionalism in order to maximize the parallels between civilian and military thought. The bias toward subjective control sprang from the belief that the more developed and autonomous the armed forces, the more likely they would be to incite the utilization of their skills, conceivably plunging the country into war unnecessarily. As is discussed in chapter 4, subjective control has also been advocated by policymakers concerned about clashes between the armed forces and their own population. From this perspective, militaries that share values and beliefs with civilians would be expected to be less prone to both intervention and repression.[3]

In contrast, Huntington argues that civilian control of the military is actually achieved most successfully through "objective" means, in which the military's autonomy and professional divergence from civil society are encouraged. According to Huntington, objective control is achieved when the military is made "politically sterile and neutral" (1957:84).[4] As Finer explains, "the greater the professionalism, the more immersed does the officer become in his own technical tasks, and the less involved in any policy issues that do not affect them" (1962:21). Thus, these authors would assert that the more "militarized" the military, the less likely it is to be politicized. Professional armed forces would therefore be less prone to influence political decisions about security, both outside of the country and within it, as well as being less likely to take over the government directly. As the present study demonstrates, impediments to the professional goals of the military can encourage insurrection even without the conditions for a coup.

It is at times difficult, however, to differentiate which goals and concerns can be considered professional. Professional goals at times merge with institutional concerns, which leads to officers defending established prerogatives rather than protecting the essential efficacy of the armed forces. This tendency has been underlined in Alfred

Stepan's *Rethinking Military Politics* (1988). Stepan suggests that the issues most likely to induce a military reaction during the period following a military regime concern the withdrawal of military prerogatives. The relative levels of political stability versus fragility are therefore presented in terms of the balance between military "prerogatives" and military "contestation" as those prerogatives are challenged.

A similar broadening of how professionalism is interpreted has, in other contexts, essentially reversed the relationship between military professionalism and intervention posited by Huntington. This was demonstrated by the puzzling appearance in the 1960s and 1970s of military regimes in the South American countries with the most highly professionalized armed forces. According to Stepan, this new breed of military intervention can be explained by shifts in military doctrine. In "The New Professionalism of Internal Warfare and Military Role Expansion" (1973), Stepan suggests that these shifts toward a more encompassing conceptualization of security altered the meaning of professionalism in Latin America. As security came to be defined in terms of a broad conjunction of social, economic, and strategic factors, with particular attention to domestic affairs, military perceptions of their appropriate roles expanded correspondingly. Responsibility for security thus came to include (rather than *pre-*clude) concern with politics. These concerns provided a "professional" justification for military intervention, yet with a form of professionalism that went far beyond the technical proficiency implicit in a more narrow definition of the term.

Nevertheless, professionalism in whatever form is somewhat limited in its ability to explain the *who* of military insurrection. Militaries are diverse, complex organizations in which individuals act according to their positions. They are, however, distinct from other bureaucracies. As Claude Welch explains, "Though armed forces have features common to bureaucracies everywhere—for example, hierarchies of position, sociological roles that are defined within these positions, criteria for advancement, different levels of responsibility for separate positions—they are unique in their centrality to the state and their relationship to violence" (1987:9–10). The particular nature of the military role thus lends a somewhat different character to its bureaucracy. Politically, the positions that particular officers take tend to reflect not only their hierarchy but their military functions. Officers from the army infantry and officers from the navy frequently take very different stances in moments of crisis.

Another major difference between military officers involves their perceived "place" in a war—behind a desk or on the front lines. According to Morris Janowitz (1961), militaries have evolved in this respect. He argues that militaries gradually progress from a warrior emphasis (in which the norms of the armed forces diverge considerably from those of civilians) toward more technocratic, managerial roles very similar to those found in civilian bureaucracies. However, within most militaries, warriors and bureaucrats coexist. In Argentina, the tension between these two groups emerged as one of the major sources of factionalism in the late 1980s.

In sum, both professional and bureaucratic factors influence how militaries may divide and how they are likely to interact with civilian governments. As is discussed in chapter 5, however, this is not necessarily an easy coexistence. The combination of the bureaucratic hierarchy with professionalism may actually create an additional source of difficulty.

Conclusion

Variations in military behavior thus have a range of different causes. Undeniably, the militaries of some countries have a higher tendency to intervene in politics than those elsewhere. That tendency, which I refer to as "chronic interventionism," can be explained by some of those factors that shape and affect the military as a whole. From within the institution, this includes socialization; with respect to external factors, chronic interventionism may be encouraged by such factors as an inadequate political system or a lack of legal costs.

However, explaining more specific variations in military behavior, particularly those alternatives that fall somewhere between subordination and interventionism, requires more attention to the complexities of a combined professional and bureaucratic organization. Bureaucracies demand functional divisions among their members; these divisions, in conjunction with a historically developed ethos of interventionism, may be exacerbated by more contextual complications to provoke sectors of the armed forces to step outside of their institutional role. In fact, I would argue that in even the most unified examples of military intervention, such factionalism deserves serious attention. In these cases, coups succeed at least in part because of particularly extreme political conditions, or because of the ability of coup leaders to use shared concerns to unite an otherwise diverse group. The natural hierarchy of the military bureaucracy may facilitate this process, but only if some semblance of consensus is achieved at the very top of the organization. Military uprisings, such as those that occurred in Argentina, reveal even more clearly the importance of factionalism. These divisions shape the way in which such intermediate strategies emerge and develop, as well as contributing to their eventual outcome.

Successful democratic consolidation requires that the military relinquish strategies that either threaten violence or interfere with the decision making of elected officials. Yet the path between military rule and democratic consolidation is inherently complicated, with numerous twists and turns, and with no guarantee of reaching the desired destination. The emergence of military rebellion can be a critical obstruction to that goal.

2

The Political Roles of the
Argentine Military:
Historical Overview

In a history plagued with profound conflict and political instability, Argentina's armed forces have unquestionably played a primary role. The military's appearances have nonetheless varied vastly, both in form and content. After early appearances as the "watchdog" against corruption and guardian of the constitution, military leaders increasingly began to impose their own rules and standards on the political system until, eventually, the armed forces became that system's most powerful player. Democratic government became the exception; military rule became the virtual norm.

For much of the twentieth century, Argentine political leaders sought the elusive formula that would secure and stabilize democratic rule. Argentina's 1983 transition to democracy was by no means its first: prior postauthoritarian governments also struggled with militaries only recently out of the presidential palace. Subsequent to the militarization and Peronist polarization of the political system in the 1930s and 1940s, Argentina swung fairly regularly between military and civilian governments. Twice after Perón and prior to 1983, civilian governments confronted the challenges of postauthoritarian rule: the Unión Cívica Radical Intransigente (UCRI) government of Arturo Frondizi, 1958–62, and the Peronist government (Hector Cámpora, Juan Domingo Perón, Raúl Lastiri, María Estela Martínez de Perón), 1973–76. Between these two governments, civilian president Arturo Illia (1963–66) also faced daunting military oversight, despite different antecedents. Nevertheless, none of these governments succeeded in consolidating constitutional rule. The pattern of military interventionism thus was fortified rather than reversed.

The Militarization of Argentina:
The 1930 Civil-Military Coup

Despite their many differences, all of Argentina's democracies have shared the legacies of militarization and political polarization. These core characteristics of post–World War II politics in Argentina originated in two key periods respectively. The first critical period was the 1930 military coup, which launched the military into the political arena and thereby set the stage for the institutionalization of chronic instability. The second formative period surrounded the emergence of Juan Domingo Perón in the mid-1940s. The events surrounding Perón's rise to power formed the parameters for Argentina's major political conflicts in the decades to come.

Of all Argentina's military coups, the 1930 overthrow of Hipólito Yrigoyen was undoubtedly the least "military." The actual participants numbered only around 1,500 (Potash 1969:42). According to David Rock, "Most of those who marched from the Army garrison at Campo de Mayo to take possession of [the] Government House, the Casa Rosada, were junior officer cadets. They completed their task swiftly, with little bloodshed, and against only token resistance" (1987:215). Furthermore, the coup resulted in only a relatively brief occupation of the government by military leaders; less than two years later, a civilian president again headed the Argentine government. Nonetheless, the events of 1930 launched the military's trajectory, originating its subsequent defining role in the Argentine political system.

Hipólito Yrigoyen's 1916 election to the presidency marked the first expansion of Argentine democracy from decades of symbolic, elite-dominated democratic rule. Yrigoyen's Radical party, Unión Cívica Radical (UCR) began to challenge the restricted, fraudulent nature of the system toward the end of the 1800s (under the leadership of Leandro Alem), with actions ranging from attempted revolution in 1890 to "intransigent" refusal to participate in the largely meaningless elections. In 1912, however, conservative president Roque Saenz Peña initiated a law that temporarily ended the Radicals' abstention.[1] The law included several important electoral reforms, the most important of which were universal male suffrage for native

Argentines eighteen and older, and the implementation of the secret ballot. Voting was also made mandatory, controlled by the lists used for military conscription (Rock 1987:189).

The expansion of the political system destroyed the rural oligarchy's political monopoly, permitting the more middle-class party of the Radicals to achieve dominance. Yrigoyen was replaced in 1922 by another Radical, Marcelo T. de Alvear, only to be reelected in 1928. Throughout this period, many displaced conservatives continued to chafe at the new political environment. During Yrigoyen's second presidency, the combination of a changing context and the deterioration of Yrigoyen's leadership exacerbated this discontent. On the one hand, Yrigoyen had the obvious misfortune of governing at the time of the Great Depression, which significantly restricted his administration's capacity to utilize public spending to buy support (Rock 1987:212; Potash 1969:42). Yrigoyen was also becoming increasingly senile. According to some accounts, certain associates of the president began to take advantage of the situation, manipulating his decision making by providing him with specially formulated news reports.

Yrigoyen's management of military affairs also directly antagonized the armed forces. The government's military policies were characterized by widespread infringements on military professionalism. Salaries and pensions did rise during this period, but not sufficiently to compensate for the less auspicious treatment of the military institution (Potash 1984:56). According to Miguel Angel Scenna, the government delayed ordering promotions, "the military budget diminished, . . . works in progress were suspended, [and] armament purchases ceased" (1980:155). Yrigoyen also fostered the politicization of the armed forces by introducing personal and political criteria into military promotions and appointments (Potash 1969:36–37; Scenna 1980:155). Thus, by 1930, many officers still unaccustomed to military intervention were sufficiently disillusioned by the Yrigoyen government that they opted to stand by passively while a limited number of their colleagues removed the president from office.

Despite the military's relatively short tenure in office, the impact of the coup was quite extensive. Argentina's newly expanded democratic system was yanked away, replaced until 1943 by a system of fraudulent, elite democracy in an attempt to replicate the political system prior to 1912. More importantly, following the 1930 coup, the armed forces incorporated the supervision or guardianship of the political system as an accepted role. That role gradually expanded, from monitoring the system to directly governing the system, with little reversal. Half a century later, the armed forces still had not recovered professional neutrality.

The Rise of Perón and the Polarization of Argentine Politics

The militarization of Argentina was facilitated and exacerbated by the polarization of the country's politics in the mid-1940s. At the middle of this conflict stood Juan Domingo Perón. An army officer, Perón forged a new political doctrine in which a progressive working-class orientation merged with an emphasis on industrialization and a conservative, essentially Catholic vision of the social order (Lubertino Beltrán 1987; Rein 1993:101–7). This complex amalgam of elements, combined with Perón's increasingly authoritarian and provocative behavior, succeeded in rending the fabric of Argentine society into two distinct halves: intensely loyal supporters of Perón and equally adamant opponents.

From Conspirator to President

Perón's ascent to power began quietly. In the 1943 coup that ended the "infamous decade" of fraudulent conservative rule and that eventually provided the vehicle for Perón's rise, Perón remained primarily a background figure. The coalition that carried out the coup was composed of a diverse conglomeration of frustrated Radicals, a few senior army and navy officers,[2] and a more substantial group of mid-level and junior army officers (captains to colonels). A group of mid-level officers who had secretly organized as the GOU [Group of United Officers] formed the heart of the movement.[3] Yet rather than claiming the presidential sash for their own, the officers of the GOU (captains to colonels) wisely left formal leadership of both the coup and the subsequent de facto government in the hands of the generals, as the proximity of these individuals to the pinnacle of the military hierarchy facilitated the process of gaining support (Perón 1982:89). As commonly occurs in such situations, the revolutionaries primarily shared their opposition to the incumbent regime, temporarily leaving aside particular motives.

As the government began to take shape, these issues began to come to the fore, and the ideological foundations of the coup coalition became increasingly important. In particular, the primacy of the GOU in the coup of 1943 was undeniable. According to Robert Potash, members of the GOU were actually the original organizers of the movement, and the principal founder of the GOU was, in turn, Juan Perón (1969:184–98; 1984). The ideology and intentions of the GOU remain vague, however, possibly by deliberate design of its leaders. Potash writes:

> In working to persuade their fellow officers of the need for a special organization, Perón and his associates of this inner group played on a variety of themes: the need to guard against a Communist upsurge; fear of involvement in [World War II] as a result of external, especially U.S. pressure; the sense of solidarity within the officer corps; and resentment at the intrusion of politics into the Army. To cast aside any suspicion of ulterior motives, the promoters of the GOU insisted on their absolute lack of personal ambitions. . . . Their only interest, they claimed, was the welfare of the Army and the Fatherland. (1969:186; see also Scenna 1980:189)

Thus, in their efforts to gain support within the military, the leaders of the GOU focused on concerns shared by many within the officer corps, in the same way as later efforts to gain support from civilian sectors focused on shared opposition to the Castillo government of 1940–43.

Nonetheless, the orientation of the inner circle of the GOU was strongly nationalist. According to Felix Luna, the group was characterized by "its sympathy for the Axis, its fundamental nationalism and its mistrust of democracy, at least the democracy that had been practiced up until then" (1972:19).[4] The GOU was also concerned with issues of social justice, and inclined toward an increased role of the state both in fostering economic distribution and in managing politics (Potash 1984:188).

By 1945, the founder of the GOU, Juan Perón, had emerged as the coalition's most powerful member. A secondary position in the Ministry of War had been supplemented with control over the National Labor Department, virtually ignored up to this point. A shrewd politician from the beginning, Perón turned this ostensibly unimportant position as Secretary of Labor into a surprisingly powerful political weapon. The urban working class had been largely neglected by other Argentine political leaders. In contrast, Perón began directly appealing to these sectors, attempting in particular to coopt union organizations. Perón's approach to existing organized labor was relatively straightforward: union leaders who could be seduced were given positions in the Labor Secretariat. Those who refused, such as the socialists and communists, found their unions under severe attack. Competing unions were formed, and only those unions loyal to Perón were granted official recognition (Potash 1969:227; Luna 1972:23). Gradually, Perón managed to organize the majority of Argentine labor unions into a powerful confederation, answerable to him.

Perón versus the Military

In February of 1946, Juan Perón was elected president of Argentina with 54 percent of the popular vote (Rock 1987:260–61). He had succeeded in avoiding his opponents' efforts to dislodge him, using an overwhelming display of popular support on 17 October 1945 to consolidate his position. Yet Perón had made many enemies during his climb to power, including members of the Radical party who were disappointed that the coup had not led to their expected revival and members of the rural elite, the group most threatened by Perón's urban industrial focus. As Perón's incumbency continued, however, an even more dangerous opposition group began to develop closer to home—within the very organization from which Perón had emerged.

The rift between now General Perón and the army had a multiplicity of causes, having to do both with Perón's politics and with his personal life.[5] On the political side, Perón's cultivation of the working class was probably the least important issue. As will be recalled, the military had only recently supported the overthrow of the conservative regime; arguments that the armed forces were merely the pawn of the upper classes thus fall rather flat. Of greater consequence were Perón's personalistic treatment of the armed forces and the increasing authoritarianism of his government. In regard to the latter, Perón clearly used the reins of government to enhance his personal power. His efforts to gain control of the union movement were followed by attempts to use this control over the unions to extend the government's domination to a greater number of Argentine workers. Freedom of the press was also increasingly restricted, as the government's tolerance for dissent and diversity gradually diminished.

Perón's interaction with the armed forces was similarly authoritarian, and reminiscent of Yrigoyen's efforts to coopt supporters. Although the government did offer certain professional benefits to the military, such as improved equipment (as long as these purchases could be afforded) and expanded control over manufacturing, the majority of Perón's policies toward the armed forces contradicted norms of professionalism. Perón sought personal loyalty, rather than institutional obedience. By 1949, Perón had begun overtly attempting to incorporate the armed forces into his political movement (Potash 1980:107). By 1951, "Loyalty tests were imposed in army promotions; *doctrina peronista* was added to the required courses of the military academy, the *Escuela Superior de Guerra*. Two top-ranking military adherents of the regime . . . were assigned to monitor the troops for any indications of disaffection" (Rock 1987:305). Even more controversial, members of the armed forces were expected to be devotees not only of Perón but of his wife, Eva Duarte de Perón. On the whole, rather than rewarding political neutrality, Perón choose to penalize it.

Nevertheless, Perón probably antagonized the greatest number of people (both within and outside of the military) by his conflicts with the Catholic Church (Potash 1980:171–78; Rock 1987:314–15; Luna 1972:82–84; Ejército Argentino 1958). Argentina has always been an extremely Catholic country, and the armed forces even more so. In fact, much of Perón's appeal undoubtedly derived from the strong parallels between the ideas he espoused and Catholic social doctrine. This was not, however, sufficient to prevent the clash between the church and Perón. As the government became increasingly authoritarian, Peronism appeared to be advancing on church territory. According to Rock, "The Church was affronted by the government's political exploitation of organized charity and by Perón's designation of *justicialismo* as a 'doctrine,' its adherents as 'believers,' and himself on occasion as its 'apostle'" (1987:314). The church began to demonstrate growing discord with Peronism. In turn, Perón eliminated authorization for questioned Catholic organizations, ceased funding to Catholic schools, closed a Catholic newspaper, arrested several dissident priests, and legalized divorce and prostitution (315).

The burgeoning conflict between Perón and the Catholic Church was the final straw for many members of the military, energizing an opposition movement that had begun to emerge some three years earlier.[6] Finally, in September of 1955, Perón was forcibly removed from the presidency.

Shortly after the coup, the Tribunal Superior de Honor [Military Tribunal of Honor] produced a scathing document assessing Perón's behavior and justifying his discharge from the armed forces (Ejército Argentino 1955). According to the tribunal, Perón's membership in the armed forces obligated him, as any officer, to conform his conduct to the "ethical norms" of the military. "In the transitory functions of public life and in private life, his conduct should reflect the same sentiments and the same moral principle" (1). The charges against Perón included the following infractions: "Sowing hatred in the Argentine family and inciting violence and crime," a charge that encompassed "attacks on the Catholic religion"; "Failure to comply with the oath to respect the national constitution"; and "Lack of loyalty to the [military] institution" (2–12). The tribunal found Perón unworthy of military standing, and voted accordingly. The army's most prominent representative had become not only a disappointment but, in the eyes of many, an embarrassment.

Peronism's Polarization of Argentine Politics

Argentine politics became polarized for decades to come around the figure of Perón. However adamant his opponents, the general's advocates were equally devout. Despite his frequently authoritarian tactics, Perón was a hero to many. The reforms of his government included limits on the length of the workday, limitations on child labor, "subsidized housing and legal services, vacation resorts, [and] full legal status for trade unions" (Rock 1987:262). The government also made a practice of important symbolic gestures, such as distributing cider and fruitcake for the Christmas holidays. Many workers felt, for the first time, that someone was looking after them. Finally, Perón's government at last extended the vote to Argentine women.

For decades following the 1955 overthrow of Perón, the military sought to eradicate Perón's influence. Upon leaving power in 1958, the commanding officers of the Revolución Libertadora [Liberating Revolution] chose to prohibit Perón or any Peronist party from participating in the political system, rather than risking a return to Perón's dominance. This prohibition remained for the following two periods of civilian rule and was not withdrawn until the 1973 elections, following a seven-year episode of military rule. Again, the political party with the greatest popular support could not compete.

Frondizi (1958–1962): Constraints and Concessions

The government of Dr. Arturo Frondizi began its tenure under much less than ideal circumstances. The proscription of Peronism seriously limited Frondizi's legitimacy and consequently his ability to govern. In addition, Frondizi himself elicited significant distrust from much of the armed forces. His predominantly concessionary policies toward the military only weakened his position further. Eventually, Frondizi too became an unacceptable president in the eyes of the military leadership.

The Precarious Transition to Partial Constitutionalism

The presidential election of February 1958 developed into a contest between two factions of the UCR (Unión Cívica Radical), now legally separated into the UCRI (Unión Cívica Radical Intransigente) and the UCRP (Unión Cívica Radical del Pueblo). The outgoing military government forbade participation by the Peronists as well as collaboration with them by other parties. Yet, as Guillermo O'Donnell (1973) has argued, the rules imposed by the military virtually doomed the experiment in partial constitutionalism from the start, converting the electoral competition into an "impossible game." With the largest proportion of the electorate backing a proscribed candidate, the participating parties were faced with a dangerous dilemma. Whichever candidate managed to acquire the support of the Peronists was likely to win the elections. Yet appealing to the Peronist leadership would inevitably generate a resounding veto by the game's ever-vigilant armed authors. In sum, the very existence of open competition between two parties within a larger context of limited competition created an unworkable system.[7]

Each candidate chose his own means of confronting this daunting scenario. The UCRP's leader, Ricardo Balbín, emerged as essentially the "official candidate," following the anti-Peronist dictates of the military government. According to O'Donnell, "the Radicales del Pueblo's campaign was a 'crusade for democracy' against 'the new demagogue,' and to save the country from the nightmarish evils that would be suffered if the Peronista-supported Radical Intransigente candidate won the election" (1973:184–85). Balbín enjoyed several advantages that allowed him to take this potentially unpopular position, including strong supporters within the government, considerable prestige as a longtime UCR leader, and the support of the core UCR leadership (Potash 1980:261; Rouquie 1975:50–55). Furthermore, an earlier election for the Constituent Assembly had already indicated that with the Peronists casting blank ballots, Balbín's party would be able to defeat the UCRI (Rouquie 1982b:144).

Hence for the UCRI candidate, Arturo Frondizi, coopting the Peronist sectors became a tactical necessity, as well as fitting conveniently with his more substantive goals. Frondizi thus adopted an explicitly pro-Peronist stance, advocating the legal and active reintegration of the Peronist sectors into the national political arena. As early as 1956, Frondizi began to get substantial publicity and soon not-so-subtle endorsements from the weekly magazine *Qué* (edited by Rogelio Frigerio, an ally of Frondizi), which was designed for a Peronist readership (Rouquie 1975:48). Eventually, entire supplements began to be dedicated to promulgating Frondizi's ideas. For example, the first such supplement, published in February of 1957, contained exclusively an essay by Arturo Frondizi on "Argentine Industry and National Development," which emphasizes the crucial role of both organized labor and private industry and argues as well that improved economic conditions for workers would be beneficial for the overall economy. Combined with a cover promising "well-being to 20 million Argentines," the publication of the magazine was clearly designed to enhance Frondizi's popularity among the Peronist working class.

Frondizi also sought the endorsement of Perón himself, perhaps the only certain way to ensure the adherence of his followers. From these efforts emerged the exceedingly controversial and still unconfirmed "pact" between Frondizi and Perón (see Cooke and Perón 1972). In a copy of the alleged document (the original was never found), Frondizi reportedly agreed, among other things, to eliminate all "political persecution," restore powers to the CGT (the Peronist union organization), and lift the restrictions against the Peronist party. In return, the Peronists pledged to withdraw any Peronist candidates from other political parties and "leave the Peronist mass freedom of action to vote in the form that best expresses their repudiation of the military dictatorship" (San Martino de Dromi 1988a:106). Approximately a month later, in February 1958, Perón explicitly ordered his supporters to vote for Frondizi.

In June 1959, more than a year after the agreement was formulated, Perón finally decided to make the text public, asserting that Frondizi had not fulfilled his commitments (Rouquie 1975:96). Nonetheless, Frondizi continued to deny that any such document was ever signed, emphasizing instead an informal accord between the two parties.[8] Whatever the true nature of the accord, Frondizi's maneuverings succeeded in winning him the presidency in the elections of February 1958. Retaining the presidency was a different matter.

Legacies of the Revolucíon Libertadora

The greatest threats to Frondizi's government derived from the legacies of the preceding military regime. In addition to stipulating the rules for the transition, the leaders of the Revolucíon Libertadora maintained active oversight of the new "democratic" government. The anti-Peronism that first stimulated the 1955 coup and that was then expanded and elaborated during the years of military rule stimulated a context in which Frondizi's every action was immediately subject to evaluation.

The military government of 1955–58 moved rapidly from moderation to vehement anti-Peronism. General Eduardo Lonardi, the first president, adopted the creed of "neither victors nor vanquished" in regard to the Peronists (Rouquie 1982b:123). Yet less than two months after Lonardi took office, he was supplanted by General Pedro Eugenio Aramburu, dramatically changing the tenor of military rule. Aramburu sought to "destroy the Peronist political apparatus," prohibiting known Peronists from participating in politics, declaring even the printing of Perón's name illegal, and directly intervening in the Peronist union organization, the CGT (Potash 1980: 228). The harshest purge, however, took place within the military itself, particularly following an attempted coup in June of 1956. According to Potash, "Over the next three days, despite the removal of the death penalty from the code of military justice, 27 individuals, eighteen military and nine civilians, were shot by firing squads" (233).[9] The executions were followed by the increased use of political criteria in promotions, the retirement of large numbers of nationalist or politically suspect officers, and the reincorporation of previously retired anti-Peronists into the active armed forces (Rouquie 1982b:138–39). Thus, by the time of the 1958 elections, few active officers remained with even minimal tolerance of Peronism.

Frondizi's impending presidency consequently became increasingly controversial. Some within the military adamantly opposed allowing him to take power. Not a few perceived Frondizi to be a communist sympathizer, a reputation not at all alleviated by the support of the communists during his campaign. General Alejandro Lanusse writes: "During the government of the *Revolución Libertadora,* Frondizi was seen as he wanted to be seen: a persistent member of the opposition . . . there were even those who maintained that he was a marxist and a great political speculator" (1988:145). In fact, ever since the UCR split, navy leaders had advocated postponing the transition until the resurgence of Peronism ceased to be probable (Scenna 1980:253; Rouquie 1982b:150).[10] Rumors of the "pact" with Perón bolstered their position.[11]

Others, however, including President Aramburu, steadfastly defended the need for constitutional rule in Argentina and for the military to avoid prolonged interference in the political system. In the end, the transition to civilian rule was allowed to take place largely due to Aramburu's considerable personal authority.

Nonetheless, the contested transition meant that sectors of the military had pledged themselves to constantly monitor Frondizi's rule, and that discord continued to exist within the armed forces. General Tomás Sánchez de Bustamante explained: "When Frondizi took charge, he had two structures, two armies, two tendencies. One that intended to continue participating in the administration of the government . . . , [especially] decisions that had to do with Peronism. And another that understood that the armed forces had fulfilled their commitment, had completed their task, and should leave the government alone, *barring some catastrophe which would obligate their intervention.*"[12] In other words, even those officers advocating "continuismo" retained some reservations about allowing the new government complete autonomy.

Military Policies of the Frondizi Government

Frondizi chose to confront the continuing power and autonomy of the military by, in essence, not confronting it. According to the former president, this was not a priority. "I did not have any plan to impede the intervention of the Armed Forces. I concerned myself with applying my overall government plan, which collectively included social, economic, political, international parts, etc."[13] Overall, the military policy of Frondizi's government can best be defined as one of concessionism, with the armed forces being granted both material benefits and considerable autonomy. Similarly, Frondizi tended to deal with his military opponents (who came to be many) by granting their demands, rather than attempting to thwart them.

Perhaps the one area in which Frondizi asserted some independence was in his ministerial appointments. Although he did consult with Revolución Libertadora leaders and attempted to select relatively uncontroversial candidates, Frondizi did not necessarily appoint those the military hierarchy would have preferred.[14] In particular, Army Chief of Staff Hector Solanas Pacheco was apparently nominated largely due to his personal relationship with Frondizi. Frondizi also risked military disapproval with his decision to restructure the top military command, merging the military secretariats with the positions of army, navy, and air force commanders-in-chief (Potash 1980:276; Scenna 1980:254).

Frondizi did, however, bow to Revolución Libertadora priorities by scrupulously avoiding appointments of individuals likely to be suspected of having communist or Peronist sympathies.[15] Once in office, the president explicitly honored the leaders of Revolución Libertadora by initiating legislation to promote General Aramburu and Admiral Rojas to the highest rank possible in their respective services (Potash 1980:282).

The Argentine military was also granted increased professional autonomy and authority during the Frondizi years. In particular, toward the end of 1959 and the beginning of 1960, the security functions of the Argentine army expanded dramatically. As in many parts of Latin America, the Cuban revolution stimulated substantial concern by members of the military with the threat of communist insurgency. In conjunction with a noticeable growth in terrorism and widespread strikes, the development of protoguerilla organizations encouraged the government to institute the Plan Conintes, or Plan de Conmoción Interno del Estado [Plan for Internal Upheaval of the State], (Rock 1987:340; Rouquie 1982b:156–57). As Potash explains, "this was a state of emergency that assigned to the armed forces direct responsibility for repressing terrorism, subordinated provincial police forces to their authority, and gave military courts jurisdiction over civilians accused of participating in or fostering subversive acts" (1980:322; see also San Martino de Dromi 1988, 1:144–49). The Plan Conintes was placed in effect in March 1960. By late 1961, the armed forces had formally begun training for counter-revolutionary warfare (Rouquie 1982b:159).

Collapse of the Constitutionalists

Frondizi's generosity toward the armed forces did not succeed in bolstering military support. In total, the government of 1958–62 has been estimated to have endured more than 30 *planteos* and uprisings (Scenna 1980:259). Rather than risking overall defeat, Frondizi regularly opted to succumb to his challengers' demands. This demonstrated that the tactics could be effective, and only minimally risky. Initially, only the most conspicuous of Frondizi's military opponents were forced to retire. As the period progressed, even the most egregious offenders remained and prospered.

The most important series of incidents involved General Carlos Severo Toranzo Montero. After Solanas Pacheco's resignation on 30 June 1959, Frondizi appointed retired General Elbio Anaya as the new army secretary (Potash 1980:314). Anaya brought in Toranzo Montero as commander in chief, despite Frondizi's reservations. Before long, Toranzo Montero succeeded in raising Anaya's suspicions as well and was removed from his position. This provoked the first serious rebellion, which concluded with Anaya's retirement and Toranzo Montero's reinstatement. Victorious, Toranzo Montero began pursuing his own agenda within the army, eventually seeking control of the government as well. This objective was hindered through the efforts of Anaya's successors, Generals Rodolfo Larcher and Rosendo Fraga. Finally, in March of 1961, Toranzo Montero offered his resignation, after failing to obtain the support of Fraga and other army leaders for a proposed coup. Nevertheless, Frondizi's inability to contain and subjugate Toranzo Montero and his reluctance to take the kinds of measures necessary to assert his own control seriously eroded the president's authority.

Frondizi confirms that: "At no time did I order the repression of rebellious groups; I was opposed at all costs to bloodshed."[16] What may have been a moral stance became interpreted as weakness, however. An officer active at the time explains:

> Frondizi began with a certain—I wouldn't call it support of the armed forces—but with a certain respect by the armed forces for the constitutional regime. Such that the armed forces did not want the president to be overthrown. He did have a few enemies. But, as I said to Frondizi, [at first] he had 2,500 officers prepared to defend legality. As he never [took a stance], there came to be 250. And the next time, only 25 of us would remain with him in favor of legality. We were going to lose.[17]

Frondizi ceased to command sufficient support to confront his increasingly entrenched opposition. Thus, even though Frondizi avoided threatening the armed forces' institutional interests, he sufficiently alienated the constitutionalists as to have no bulwark against the activist opposition.

The Final Defeat

Throughout 1961, the economic and political difficulties confronting the Frondizi government increased. Despite some advances in production (especially of petroleum), the country continued to rely heavily on foreign investment, and the debt began to take its toll (Rock 1987:341). The CGT, responding to government attempts to economize, sponsored a series of lengthy strikes.

In regard to foreign affairs, the Cuban question caused particular tension between the government and the military. Despite Argentina's close relations to the United States, for nationalist reasons, Frondizi leaned toward tolerance of the Cuban revolution. In August of 1961, Frondizi chose to meet secretly with revolutionary leader Ernesto "Che" Guevara, at the time, Cuba's minister of industry (Potash 1980:338).

Some months later, in January of 1962, an Argentine delegation to the Organization of American States spurred further military protests, arguing that expelling Cuba from the OAS would only deepen that nation's ties to the communist bloc (Luna 1972:136; Potash

1980:342–45). After a series of confrontations with the armed forces and repeated denials of communist sympathies, Frondizi finally ended diplomatic relations with Cuba in February 1962 (Rock 1987:342).

Nonetheless, the final straw for the Frondizi government involved not Cuba but, once again, Peronism. In March 1962, tempted by Alliance for Progress funds and overconfident about the popularity of his political party, Frondizi decided to allow the Peronists to participate in congressional and provincial elections. As the elections grew closer and the Peronists' campaign advanced, the wisdom of this decision began to appear questionable. Anticipating the repercussions of the elections, Frondizi practically encouraged the military leadership to "force" the proscription of Peronism; the military refrained (Potash 1980:357).

The Peronists swept the elections, winning in "ten of the fourteen provinces in which elections were held, including the province of Buenos Aires" (Rock 1987:342). In response, the military demanded that the national government intervene in seven provinces, launch "a direct assault against communism; and [proscribe] Peronism, its emblems, and its activities, direct or indirect" (Potash 1980:362). Frondizi partially acquiesced. He placed five provinces under federal control, a decision toward which he had appeared inclined even prior to the elections (359). Rather than ameliorating tensions, the apparent compromise effectively consolidated opposition. To the hard-line anti-Peronists, it was insufficient; to the constitutionalists, it was excessive. As the pressure increased, Frondizi made further concessions to the military. By now, though, it was too late. The military opposition would accept only his resignation as sufficient.

Even toward the end, many in the military resisted overthrowing the government. Yet these sectors found themselves in a rather weak position. In many respects, Frondizi's tolerance for both Peronism and Cuba had managed to unify an otherwise divided military (Potash 1980:335). During the final stages of the Frondizi government, concern over these issues was sufficient to convince all three commanders in chief—General Raúl Poggi (Toranzo Montero's replacement), Admiral Agustín Penas, and Brigadier Cayo Alsina—that overthrowing the president was unavoidable. Nonetheless, even if military oversight had been incorporated into military role beliefs, military rule had not. Frondizi was detained and imprisoned (following procedures he himself had designed), after which military leaders immediately arranged for a civilian successor.

Illia (1963–1966): The Struggle to Survive

Despite the collapse of the Frondizi government, a year later the experiment with limited democracy was repeated. Again, the Peronists were excluded, leaving the competition between the two Radical parties. This time, however, the Peronists withheld their support from both candidates. Dr. Arturo Illia of the Unión Cívica Radical del Pueblo (UCRP) emerged as a weak winner, with only 25.8 percent of the vote; in second place were the blank ballots (19.2 percent), followed by UCRI candidate Oscar Alende with 16.8 percent (Rouquie 1982b:225). A rural doctor without much of a national political reputation, Illia was not expected to win. Military oversight had furthermore become increasingly entrenched. All in all, Illia faced a daunting scenario.

Political Inheritances

Along with the political constraints of restricted democracy, Arturo Illia's civilian government of 1963–66 inherited a military just emerging from one of the most internally convulsed periods ever. Following the coup of 1962, José María Guido assumed the presidency through the constitutional rules of succession. Guido remained "notoriously subordinated to the military command," however, unable to reclaim the executive power that should have accompanied his presidential sash (Luna 1972:149). The armed forces neither ruled nor returned to the barracks.

The military's political involvement provoked serious internal tensions within the institution. The armed forces divided vertically into two major factions, the Azules and Colorados, based on their attitudes toward Peronism. In both September of 1992 and April of 1993, hostilities between these groups reached a stage of virtual war. Ships began moving toward Buenos Aires, fighter planes bombed tank regiments, mines were laid, and more than one soldier was killed in the fight over control of the armed forces (Castello 1986a: 259–71; Rouquie 1982b:211–12; Sánchez de Bustamante 1962–63; Verone 1985: chapter 4).

The question dividing the armed forces concerned the political participation of the Peronists. The Colorados strongly opposed permitting them any political space, given their perception of Peronism as "a sectarian and violent movement that [would] allow communism" (Rouquie 1982b:213). The Colorados appeared to have few compunctions about intervening politically to ensure Peronist exclusion. Few Azules supported Peronism, either; however, they tended to see it as a national movement that could *prevent* communism through its absorption of the working class (213). The Azules thus came to be seen as the more legalist and more professional faction of the armed forces.

By the time Illia took office, the military had overcome much of the fragmentation of the Guido period. In addition, control of the army had shifted from the Colorados to the Azules. Conditions remained difficult, however. To begin with, the UCRP had previously allied themselves with the Colorado faction, leaving the Azules uncomfortable allies, at best (Rouquie 1982b:228). Secondly, the resolution of military factionalism left the man credited with resolving those tensions, General Juan Carlos Onganía, with exceptional authority within the armed forces—certainly more than the government. Finally, even the Azules were far less devoutly legalistic than many have asssumed. According to a member of the Azul leadership, General Tomás Sánchez de Bustamante, as early as October 1962 the Azul leadership had committed themselves to putting in place a "political plan . . . with the objective of achieving a return to a constitutional regime as rapidly as possible, *anticipating the possibility of having to take charge of the government with a political plan of concrete and defined period.*"[18] Illia's continuity would by no means be easy.

Policies of the Illia Government

Despite his weak beginning, Illia's policies toward the armed forces were much more assertive than those of Frondizi. Unlike Frondizi, Illia did not allow rebels to succeed (Kvaternik 1990:76). The growing cohesion of the army under General Onganía (the commander in chief) in some ways facilitated this task, as Illia confronted fewer challenges than his predecessor. At the same time, though, Illia sought to limit political intervention in the military institution, hoping to thereby avoid the reverse phenomenon. Thus from the beginning, the government agreed to accept the leadership of Onganía and the Azules and to respect military autonomy in such areas as promotions and assignments (83).

Yet, the military continued to see Illia as ineffective (Rizzi 1990: 146). As General Sánchez de Bustamante explains, "he was not a man of rapid decisions . . . so much so that his enemies ridiculed him, saying he resembled a tortoise."[19] After years of active surveillance of government policies, and in the context of an expanding conceptualization of the military's role, the armed forces were concerned with much more than just his treatment of the institution. Furthermore, Illia ran into some important difficulties in areas that the military considered critical for national security—internal order and the economy.

Illia began his government with moderate economic success; within two or three years, however, the economy no longer acted in his favor. Argentina was graced with very successful harvests during Illia's first few years in power, a critical issue in a country that has always been highly agricultural. By 1966, however, the yield had fallen (Luna 1972:175–76). After canceling contracts with foreign petroleum companies, the government also confronted high costs from reinbursing companies and declining petroleum production (173).[20] Perceptions of economic crisis were further augmented by growing inflation and frequent devaluations (176).

At the same time, a highly militant labor movement created a sense of disorder. Because of the UCRP's history of antagonism toward Peronism, the unions were predisposed to condemn Illia. When the government did not react to the extensive demands of the Peronist CGT union organization, they responded by carrying out a *"Plan de Lucha"* [battle plan]. This meant widespread strikes, factory occupations, and even taking hostages. This disruption was certainly sufficient to support the military's image of an ineffective government (Castello 1986b:9; Kvaternik 1990:30; Luna 1972:174–75).

Collapse

By the end of 1965, relations between the government and the military had deteriorated even beyond their questionable beginnings. The government's decision not to send forces to join a regional force occupying the Dominican Republic—after having indicated other intentions—conflicted with the military's conception of the appropriate course of action (Castello 1986b:10; Luna 1972:179). Not long thereafter, in November of 1985, Onganía resigned under pressure from the government (Castello 1986b:12). Finally, like Frondizi before him, Illia crossed the ultimate barrier by permitting Peronist participation in congressional elections. Again, the strategy stimulated a military coup.

The resulting military government proved to be far more extensive than any previous experiment. Rather than a relatively limited, interim period of de facto rule, General Juan Carlos Onganía and his allies sought an extensive and prolonged role in restructuring the political system. Guillermo O'Donnell defines this system of government as "bureaucratic authoritarianism," a system characterized by government by the military institution, strong reliance on technocrats, and the deliberate political exclusion of certain mobilized social sectors (1973, 1988). Onganía himself governed only until 1970, at which point a subsequent coup placed General Roberto Levingston in the presidency. The bureaucratic-authoritarian system continued, however, even as the presidency was transferred first to Levingston and finally, in March 1971, to General Alejandro Lanusse —perceived by many to be the true force behind the movement from the beginning.

The Return of Peronism (1973–1976)

Under Lanusse's leadership, the military government opted to permit the reestablishment of constitutional government—this time with far fewer restrictions. Yet, far from the aspired constitutional normalization, the ensuing period of Peronist rule evolved as perhaps the most complicated, unstable epoch in Argentine history. Four presidents governed during this period: Hector Cámpora (a stand-in for Perón); Raúl Lastiri; Juan Domingo Perón; and, finally, María Estela (Isabel) Martínez de Perón, Perón's third wife. By the time the government collapsed, no one appeared to actually rule.

Legacies of the Military Regime of 1966–1973

In some respects, the Peronist government initiated in 1973 inherited a much more promising situation than the preceding civilian governments in Argentina. In particular, the threat of military intervention seemed to have decreased, due to a combination of factors. The interim of military rule had diminished expectations of political efficacy by the armed forces. Yet, the period of military government did not generate substantial internal disruption within the armed forces themselves—at least not on the scale of the early 1960s or late 1980s. Finally, the degree of repression incurred by the military regime was sufficient to stimulate some distrust of military rule (and to feed the flames of the incipient guerrilla movement), but was not sufficient to provoke any unified civilian retaliation, as would occur in 1983.

ECONOMY

According to William Smith, the military government of the Revolución Argentina [Argentine Revolution] of 1966–73 instituted "a far-reaching plan of state economic intervention," aimed at facilitating capitalist accumulation (1989:50). During the first few years, the government achieved notable success, implementing a primarily export-oriented economic plan. Inflation declined, accompanied by significant industrial growth (Rock 1987:348). The trade-off, however, was an increasing foreign debt. The costs of servicing this debt soon began to surpass the profits from exports (Smith 1989:151). At the same time, the government faced an increasingly powerful reaction from those sectors excluded from the benefits of the economic plan—in particular, the organized working class—which eventually forced a revision of some policies (O'Donnell 1988:264–65; Perina 1983:95–129). The combination of these and other factors stimulated a discouraging reversal in the economy from 1969 on, evident in a declining GNP and a rising inflation rate. By the time the military government left power, memories of the early triumphs had long faded.

UNITY AND DISSENT

Nonetheless, the armed forces were able to avoid some public accountability for the economic troubles through their leaders' efforts (in particular, Onganía's) to limit the military's political participation. Throughout the military regime of 1966–73, civilians dominated the administrative structure of the government. The number of military cabinet ministers never surpassed 25 percent, and was usually significantly lower, and the total number of military officers in the top strata of the government remained around 11 percent (Ricci and Fitch 1988:table 1). Thus, actual military participation was low enough to moderate the stigma of the regime's failures.

The military government's relative moderation in incorporating officers into political and administrative positions also diminished the divisiveness of military rule. Overall, the armed forces appeared more united than in 1958, at least partially due to Onganía's efforts since 1962 to achieve internal discipline. With less internal division, the number of potential sources of political opposition was also reduced correspondingly, even though the possibility of more unified threats certainly had not been eliminated.

During Lanusse's government, the newly forged military unity began to show some signs of wear. Lanusse inspired dissent from two sectors, the more nationalist (or, at least, less liberal) groups among the army and some apolitical, professionalist sectors. Most active resistance to Lanusse came from the nationalists, exemplified by a group of nationalist colonels—Peronist sympathizers—caught organizing the overthrow of Lanusse in 1971. Finally, in October of 1971, Lanusse faced an organized uprising from a group of nationalists in the military garrisons of Azul and Olavarría (O'Donnell 1988:244).

Other sectors of the military criticized Lanusse's behavior from a professionalist perspective, claiming that the general was becoming too politicized. Others reacted to more specific aspects of his comportment, for example, excessively favoring personal allies and members of the cavalry (the branch to which he belonged) in promotions and assignments (Fraga 1988:33). The most controversial aspect of Lanusse's behavior, however, was his increasingly apparent political ambition (O'Donnell 1988:252–53; Rock 1987:357). Nearly two decades later, Lanusse would still be derided by military officers as "a politician."

Nonetheless, the organized opposition to Lanusse appears to have been limited to a small, if active, minority (R. Fraga 1988:27). According to Lanusse, "We [the leadership of the armed forces] had all reached the same conclusion. We had to finish with the military government. We had to dedicate special attention to the recuperation of constitutional normality." Resistance, he claims, was minimal.[21]

Shared threats began to supplant mutual antagonism. Anti-Peronism still prevailed, yet it had been surmounted by the fear of communism. The gradual expansion of guerrilla activities through the 1960s and early 1970s had contributed to increased unity within the armed forces and had moderated fears of electoral Peronism, no longer seen as the most dangerous alternative. Peronists began to be perceived as potential allies in the battle against the guerrilla groups.

REPRESSION AND RESTRAINT

In the meantime, the military government was unable to postpone or dissipate active opposition enough to avoid confronting it. During the Revolución Argentina, the increasing violence was exemplified by the *Cordobazo*, a clash in May of 1969, primarily in the province of Córdoba, between university students and organized labor (particularly auto workers) on the one side and the police and military on the other (Anzorena 1988:55–69; O'Donnell 1988:149–60; Rouquie 1982b:283–86; Smith 1989:129–61). The violent protests and harsh repression marked an important turning point in the military regime. From this point on, the government began to question whether it could effectively rule, spurring various policy shifts and the significant weakening of Onganía's position. From the outside, the repression lent significant fodder to the incipient guerrilla movement.

Reports of excessive government repression in less public domains also began to surface. The military and the police were accused of "arbitrary arrests, the torture of suspects, [and] the pure and simple disappearance of leaders of the extreme left" (Rouquie 1982b:292). Nonetheless, in contrast to the subsequent military regime, the government's mode of combatting guerrilla warfare remained primarily legal and nonviolent. Legislation included a National Defense Law, passed in October 1966, that emphasized internal security and outlined the Argentine version of the "national security doctrine," and laws passed in 1967 and 1969 that made the propagation of communist ideology punishable by imprisonment.[22]

In addition to these laws, some of the most important legislation focused on facilitating the arrest and trial of suspected guerrillas, which thereby lessened the likelihood that harsher methods would be employed. As early as July of 1966, a law was passed that authorized the security forces (Gendarmería and Prefectura Naval) and the federal police to "conduct raids and arrests when strong indicators or convincing [*semiplena*] proof of guilt existed" (San Martino de Dromi 1988, 1:370). In May of 1971, a new decree-law provided for the creation of a federal court capable of dealing with criminal acts throughout the country, in contrast to Argentina's standard regional system of courts (388). This procedure, deliberately designed to combat guerrilla organizations, allowed the judiciary to aggregate information and charges from different regions. According to General Díaz Bessone (who firmly believed that police actions were insufficient in these cases), "In two years of work, close to 600 guerrillas were condemned and hundreds more were put on trial" (1988b:15). While all of these laws undeniably violated certain civil rights, as well as principles of ideological freedom, those violations nonetheless remained contained—suspects generally went to prison, rather than to their death.

Overall, by the end of this period, the armed opposition that arose as a reaction to the military regime (as well as being a function of the times) appeared considerably more violent than the military. In fact, in some respects, the violence of the guerrillas—including the brutal torture and assassination of former military president Pedro Aramburu—probably strengthened the military's standing within civilian society. The armed forces and the police undeniably did resort to some violence in their efforts to suppress the guerrilla (or "subversive") activities. Yet the primarily legal, nonviolent methods they utilized left the military with some legitimacy within Argentina, or at least without the threat of unified civilian reprisals.

The Transition

By 1973, the military government faced enough internal opposition and external tumult that a timely exit seemed advisable. At the same time, these conditions had not disrupted the military enough to force an uncontrolled retreat.

In planning the transition, Lanusse sought to use his position to turn the situation as much to his advantage as possible. Initially, this included not only assuring a continuation of the military's oversight role but maximizing Lanusse's personal power as well. According to one anonymous informant, Lanusse hoped to demystify Perón in order to eliminate his political power. Lanusse and General Tomás Sánchez de Bustamante (then the vice-president of the Círculo Militar) reportedly planned to create the public expectation that Perón would return, despite a private assessment that he actually would not. Perón would then be politically destroyed, allowing Lanusse to emerge as the political beneficiary. Ideally, the legal restoration of the political parties in 1971 (shortly after Lanusse assumed the presidency) and the subsequent Gran Acuerdo Nacional [Great National Accord] would lead to the choice of Lanusse himself as a compromise presidential candidate (O'Donnell 1988:238–41; Rock 1987:357).

It soon became evident that efforts to destroy Perón's mystique were in vain—Perón was unlikely to be defeated. Nonetheless, the outgoing military leaders were able to impose certain conditions on the transition. The electoral rules, for example, required that all candidates had resided consistently within Argentina from August 1972 until March 1973, the date of the elections (San Martino de Dromi 1988, 1:508). According to Liliana de Riz, negotiations between representatives of Perón and Lanusse also resulted in Perón's agreement not to present his own candidacy and to withdraw any support from the guerrillas (1981:33).

Nonetheless, the most critical limitations on the new government did not come specifically from the military government but from the army hierarchy as a whole. In a document entitled Los Cinco Puntos [The Five Points], military leaders specified their expectations of the incoming government (Lanusse 1977:319–22; R. Fraga 1988:34–38, 49; San Martino de Dromi 1988, 2:102–3). In addition to demanding compliance with the constitution, laws, and "republican institutions," the document warned against "the application of indiscriminate amnesties for those who are on trial or condemned for having committed crimes associated with subversion and terrorism" (R. Fraga 1988:49). The Document of the Five Points also states that the army "cannot permit . . . the return to unacceptable political practices that resort to imposing tyranny through apparently democratic forms" (clearly in reference to early Peronism), demands that all "legal recourses" be taken against "subversion and terrorism," and strongly discourages dramatically altering the military hierarchy (Lanusse 1977:320; R. Fraga 1988:35). All active-duty generals signed the document, symbolizing their shared determination to continue overseeing the policies of the subsequent government (Lanusse 1977:319; 1988:222).

At the same time, the military was incapable of unilaterally imposing the rules of the transition. Some concessions were made by Lanusse's side as well. For example, the electoral rules also forbade Lanusse from competing for the presidency, through the stipulation that any top authorities (including the president, commanders in chief of the armed forces, cabinet members, and top provincial authorities) who remained in office after 24 August 1972 were disqualified (San Martino de Dromi 1988, 2:507). Furthermore, the military appeared unable or unwilling to enforce some of the conditions they had designed, conditions that were soon challenged by the Peronists. Perón's designation of Hector Cámpora as the Peronist candidate directly conflicted with residency rules. Nonetheless, in the end, Cámpora's campaign was allowed to proceed.

Chaos and Collapse: The Peronist Debacle

Peronism's 1973 revival brought neither political reconciliation nor stability to Argentina. Instead, the regime seemed doomed by a series of mistaken decisions and unfortunate circumstances, regardless of the role of the military. Within a short three years, four individuals held the Argentine presidency, and at least one other intermittently executed the presidential functions. Furthermore, little or no political consistency was maintained from one presidency to the next. Political tendencies swung dramatically from the left to the right, from sympathy for the armed left to the rejection of political violence and, finally, to support for the armed right (both within and outside of the state).

Having avoided a preemptive military veto, Dr. Hector Cámpora became the first president of the 1973–76 constitutional period. To the degree Cámpora was known, it was for his blind devotion to Juan Perón. Nor was it ever assumed that Cámpora would govern as anything more than Perón's stand-in. Peronists openly proclaimed their motto: "Cámpora to the government, Perón to power" (De Riz 1981:55). On 13 July 1973, less than two months after taking office, President Cámpora and Vice-President Vicente Solano Lima resigned after Perón expressed his dissatisfaction with his representatives (San Martino de Dromi 1988, 2:7; Rock 1987:360). Two months later, new elections were held—Perón emerged triumphant with approximately 60 percent of the vote (Rock 1987:360) In the interim, the presidency fell to Raúl Lastiri, president of the House of Deputies, after the president of the Senate (constitutionally the third in line) added his resignation to the pile.

When Perón finally assumed the presidency in October of 1973, Argentines entertained the short-lived hope that the period of chaos and violence would finally end. Perón stood out as the only president truly elected by popular vote in nearly two decades (since the end of his last presidency). Memories of his earlier reign remained sufficiently strong to encourage the hopes of the excluded working classes and to potentially facilitate the reincorporation or isolation of radicalized sectors of the political community. At the same time, the years had faded memories of Perón's excesses enough for even some of his former enemies to greet him with tolerance and guarded hope. Perón had become more moderate, they would say; he had "matured." Yet Perón had also aged.

On 1 July 1974, Perón died, leaving the presidency of this still chaotic and traumatized country in the hands of his third wife, María Estela (Isabel) Martínez de Perón. A far cry from the dynamic—if controversial—Eva Duarte de Perón, Martínez de Perón had little political vocation or experience. Apparently, the possibility that the vice-president actually might assume the presidency had not been considered. In the period that followed Martínez de Perón's donning of the presidential sash, "la Presidenta's" mysterious, extreme-right adviser, José López Rega, managed to usurp much of the true power of the presidency. Vice-president Ítalo Luder also played an important role during the Martínez de Perón presidency, particularly during the would-be president's periodic absences.

GOVERNMENT POLICIES AND THE GUERRILLA WAR

During the early 1970s, any long-term goals of democratic consolidation were dwarfed by the need to reign in the rampant political violence. From the military perspective, national security was at stake, thereby mandating that the government employ all possible methods to reestablish order in the country. Thus, for the armed forces, the most important criteria for differentiating between the different presidencies concerned how these leaders dealt with the problems of guerrilla warfare, terrorism, and "subversion."

CAMPORA

In this respect, Hector Cámpora's term proved far more critical, and far more destructive, than one would suspect from the length of his incumbency. Cámpora's association was with the more radical, leftist sectors of Peronism (De Riz 1981:57). Pressured by these groups, Cámpora issued an extensive political pardon to imprisoned guerrillas (Decree 2, República Argentina, *Boletín Oficial,* 4 July 1973:4). By the following day, Congress had lent its support to the pardons, through an amnesty law (Law 20.508, República Argentina, *Leyes Nacionales,* 27 May 1973). In one dramatic gesture, the amnesty eradicated the results of the legal battle against guerrilla warfare. The guerrillas were back on the streets, free to resume organizing. From the perspective of the military, Cámpora's decree had demonstrated police actions to be insufficient in combating terrorist or guerrilla actions. Only by permanently eliminating perpetrators could the military be sure of having terminated the formers' activity.

During his two-month presidency, Cámpora also presided over the most dramatic outbreak of political violence the country had yet experienced. The occasion was Perón's return to Argentina on 20 June 1973. Thousands of Perón's supporters, including Peronist guerrillas (Montoneros), converged on Ezeiza airport to welcome their leader. Before the reunion could occur, the celebration had been transformed into a bloodbath, with numerous people—some estimates went as high as four hundred—left either injured or dead (Anzorena 1988:257–59; Díaz Bessone 1988a:187–90). Perhaps the only aspect of the Ezeiza violence that was truly clear was, as Rock writes, "Cámpora's inability to control the movement and to hold at bay its contending forces" (1987:360). Thus, not only were Cámpora's political leanings inherently suspect for the armed forces, but his government could not protect the most important military priorities—order and security. Perón's instructions were sufficient to remove Cámpora from office, thereby dispensing with the necessity for a military end to his disastrous government. After Raúl Lastiri's brief visit to the presidency, Perón himself finally returned to power.

PERON

Juan Perón offered a far more promising scenario than either of the opening acts for his presidency. Whatever his position may have been previously, the events at Ezeiza had underscored the dangers presented by the extremists within (and outside of) his movement. Perón's sympathies notably shifted toward legality, with a hint of conservatism. In a speech during February of 1974, Perón proclaimed: "Our Armed Forces are and will be a chief support of national institutionalization. Their duty affirms it and their honor guarantees it. Neither the ultraleft nor the ultraright have a place in

Argentine reality, whose people have already decided the path they want to follow" (Perón 1988:35). Along the same lines, one of the key initiatives of Perón's third term in office was a law increasing sentences for those convicted of guerrilla-related activities (Law 20.642, República Argentina, *Leyes Nacionales*, 25 January 1974:591–95). On 1 May 1974, Perón further illustrated his impatience with the Peronist left in a dramatic confrontation with the Montoneros guerrilla organization from the balcony of the presidential palace. Perón evicted the Montoneros from the Plaza de Mayo and, by implication, from the Peronist movement.

MARTÍNEZ DE PERÓN

The government of Martínez de Perón also demonstrated hostility toward the armed left. Yet an important difference characterized this period. The Martínez de Perón administration tended to emphasize combating violence with violence, rather than with legal prosecution. The military was given the authorization to launch a full offensive against the guerrilla movement (see chapter 3).

Paramilitary groups of the extreme right also contributed to the growing violence. The Triple A (Alianza Argentina Anticomunista), purportedly under the leadership of López Rega, began employing methods at least as brutal as the guerrilla organizations, if not more so, to combat the influence of the left. According to David Rock, "in the latter half of 1974 the Triple A murdered some seventy of its opponents, mostly prominent leftist intellectuals or lawyers; by early 1975 they dispensed with leftists at the rate of fifty a week" (1987: 363). In sum, while Martínez de Perón's government did grant the armed forces the degree of autonomy they would consider desirable in the countersubversive war, in other respects, the government appeared to facilitate the escalation of anarchy. The obvious power vacuum helped obliterate any tolerance that the armed forces might retain for the government of Isabel Martínez de Perón.

POLICIES TOWARD THE MILITARY INSTITUTION

The policies of the Peronist presidents toward the military varied somewhat less than their policies specifically concerning the guerrilla issue. Each leader's military policies nonetheless paralleled his or her specific political tendencies.

For example, during the Cámpora government, military leaders with Peronist sympathies were clearly favored for the top positions within both the armed forces and the Ministry of Defense (R. Fraga 1988:22). With Perón's approval, General Jorge Carcagno—seen as a populist general—was named head of the army (San Martino de Dromi 1988, 2:104). Under Cámpora's leadership, Carcagno directed Operación Dorrego, an experiment in public works that combined the efforts of the army and the Peronist Youth (R. Fraga 1988:70–71). Political objectives therefore eclipsed professionalism, and military policies reflected the concerns of the Peronist left.

Once Juan Perón came to power, the Peronist left had distinctly lost its favored status. The general's decisions on military appointments seemed calculated to minimize potential conflict. While he did avoid choosing only known political sympathizers to head the armed forces, he also avoided choosing officers who were sufficiently distinguished to be able to present a challenge (Terragno 1974:75). Leandro Anaya, who replaced Carcagno as head of the army, had the reputation as a professional, but not really as an important leader within the institution (R. Fraga 1988:113–15; San Martino de Dromi 1988, 2:105; Terragno 1974:75).

One of the more important aspects of Perón's policies toward the armed forces was, however, also one of the most subtle. Perón had always been a master of symbolism, a skill that he used deftly in his dealings with the military during this period. Laudatory speeches and dramatic gestures, such as his ostracism of the Montoneros, were key elements of his arsenal. Perón also made an effort to elevate the prestige of the armed forces. After being readmitted into the army, he donned his uniform for his first public reappearance (Terragno 1974: 74–75). While irritating to many die-hard anti-Peronists, the gesture did indicate respect and pride in the Argentine military. As Terragno writes, "he caused the uniform to be applauded in the Plaza de Mayo" (75). As prestige and symbolism have frequently tended to be more important to the armed forces than concrete benefits, a tendency that would be clearly illustrated in the post-1983 period, such policies significantly enhanced Perón's standing with the military.

Of the Peronist presidents of this period, Martínez de Perón seemed the most inclined to appoint military leaders on the basis of their political positions. General Anaya was replaced by General Numa Laplane, described as "a supporter of 'integrated professionalism,' a doctrine that committed the institution to the government's politics" (De Riz 1981:133). Intense pressures from all three branches of the military eventually forced Martínez de Perón to request Laplane's resignation, and she replaced him with a more traditional professionalist, General Jorge Rafael Videla (134).

Development of the Coup Coalition

The military coup of March 1976 surprised no one. Nonetheless, certain particulars about the event should be mentioned. To begin with, the 1976 coup was the most clearly *professionalist* instance of military intervention in Argentine history. The organizers were the leaders of the three armed forces, not members of less-favored factions competing for a share of the power. They thus acted according to military norms of hierarchy, thereby facilitating the task of achieving a following. The leaders also represented the political center of the armed forces, rather than either the left or the extreme right. Finally, the leaders of the coup—General Videla, Admiral Emilio Eduardo Massera, and Brigadier Orlando Ramón Agosti—reportedly were reluctant to instate a military government, despite the encouragement they were receiving from various members of the political community. The coup coalition was consolidated only after various members of the military were thwarted in their efforts to provoke impeachment proceedings.

Could this outcome be predicted from the inception of the government? For the most part, it would seem that it could not. Of all Argentina's transitions to constitutional rule, this case most resembled what Terry Karl and Philippe Schmitter (1991) refer to as a "pacted transition," considered the most propitious condition for a transition to a stable democratic regime. The military remained intact but was unable to unilaterally impose its conditions on the incoming regime. In effect, the fact that the Document of the Five Points was so quickly challenged, and without engendering a prompt military veto, indicated that the armed forces were perhaps not in a position to maintain the oversight role they had promised. Yet, at the same time, the government was certainly not in a position to risk direct provocation of the armed forces, particularly given the situation of generalized violence.

Another difficulty in arriving at a post factum "prediction" derives from the composition of the coup coalition. These were not the same individuals who had overseen the transition and authored the Document of the Five Points. Videla, for example, was an infantry officer and by no means from the same cavalry cohort from which most of the former army aristocracy—including Lanusse and Onganía—had emerged.

Yet some legacies of the preceding military government did color the military coup. Most notably, the emphasis on professionalism and the unification of the armed forces were certainly reflected in how the coup was organized and carried out. The institutional cohesion of the armed forces somehow remained predominant, despite the obviously politicizing effects of the Peronist period.

Some Tentative Conclusions

The events between 1930 and 1976 form an important part of the backdrop for the subsequent evolution of Argentine politics. The military's eruption into politics in 1930, Peronism's virtual reformulation of Argentina's political forces, and the institutionalization of military rule that occurred in the 1960s and 1970s helped mold the political context of 1983. Any subsequent democratic regime would be forced to shoulder the political rivalries of the past, as well as confronting the tradition of military interventionism.

Argentina's earlier civilian regimes—especially the Frondizi and Peronist periods—help clarify the nature of the challenges faced by the 1983 democratic regime. Four factors have been considered in this analysis: the legacies of the military regime; the context of the transition; the strategies of the transitional civilian government; and the development of coup coalitions.

Each of these factors plays an important role in determining the outcome of transitional democracies, although none serves as a "sufficient" cause of either consolidation or collapse. It is, however, possible to assess the relative *weight* of the different factors. In particular, the character of the transition itself appears to have been seriously overestimated in studies of democratization. While the character of the transition is important, it is largely a "symptom" of the preceding period. More information about the legacies inherited by the newly founded regime can be derived from studying the antecedent period of military government than by studying the transition itself. For example, the 1973 transition appears to be a case of pacted transition, with the military carrying somewhat disproportionate weight in the pact. Yet a look at the previous period indicates that while members of the military were perhaps sufficiently unified to present a joint statement, they were not strong enough to impose it. Any agreements were therefore valid only in determining the rules of the transition itself; the resultant government faced no preestablished norms. Nevertheless, the collapse of the Peronist government resulted not from the violations of the military's rules but from the government's blatant inability to carry out basic functions of government—in particular, providing some kind of order and stability.

In the case of the Frondizi regime, the character of the transition appears to have been more important—but again, due to the nature of the preceding regime. The military government that relinquished the presidency to Arturo Frondizi in 1958 was in a much stronger position than the government of Lanusse. The military was thus able to impose severely restrictive rules on the electoral game, including the exclusion of its most important player. Nonetheless, it is notable that when one of those rules appeared to have been violated *even before* the actual elections (in the case of the Frondizi-Perón agreement), the military leadership did not act to impose its rules. In the end, the critical factor in this case appears to have been Frondizi's policies toward the military. Frondizi's persistent "concessionism" allowed an antigovernment coalition to consolidate and eventually take control.

What conclusions does this analysis allow us to draw? The legacies of the military regime, as well as the more general historical legacies, contribute to forming the context in which a transitional democracy initiates its incumbency. In particular, those legacies determine the degree to which the military is likely to act in a cohesive manner, the amount of power it retains to impose its demands, and the kinds of issues that the military leadership will consider to be relevant. The military policies of the new government interact with that inheritance, challenging it or maintaining it. In the end, transitional democracies seem to have the best chance of success if their governments act to incorporate the military institution into the state, neither accepting nor encouraging politicization and simultaneously refraining from threatening professional roles and capacities.

3

Disappointments of Military Rule, 1976–1983

The military regime that preceded the constitutional period of 1983 deeply traumatized Argentina's armed forces. The seven-year military government achieved few of its stated intentions, failing bitterly at efforts to achieve legitimacy or economic success and even immersing the country in a devastating war with Great Britain. The one major goal that the government did reach was the elimination of guerrilla warfare; however, that also traumatized the military. Overall, Argentina's military regime of 1976–83 appears to have been the least successful experiment in bureaucratic authoritarianism in South America. Brazil and, in particular, Chile could claim some economic success to help even the score card, and Uruguay at least balanced limited success with somewhat more moderate repression. Argentina's authoritarianism had no such balance.

The Initiation and Goals of the Military Regime

The coup d'état that overthrew the government of María Estela (Isabel) Martínez de Perón in 1976 was far from an improvisation. A committee composed of representatives from each of the armed forces met for months prior to the event, drafting and redrafting the political plan of the Proceso de Reorganización Nacional (PRN) [Process of National Reorganization] and deciding on such critical details as who would become the minister of economy (Fontana 1987a: 71, 89). Finally, on 24 March 1976, Isabel Perón was removed from office and replaced by a military junta consisting of General Jorge Rafael Videla (army), Admiral Emilio Eduardo Massera (navy), and Brigadier Orlando Ramón Agosti (air force). In contrast to both the violently chaotic social context in which it occurred and the large-scale repression that followed, the coup was a surprisingly peaceful event.

Shortly after the junta took control, the new government published a formal statement of its goals and objectives. Above all, the document emphasized the guerrilla threat and the need to combat that threat through an integrated, multifaceted approach. Somewhat more subtly, the statement reveals an ontology that focuses on ideological forces in an essentially bipolar world. According to the document's authors, the government's objectives included the following:

> Reinstitute the essential values that serve as the foundation of the integral leadership of the State, emphasizing the sense of morality, propriety and efficiency, indispensable to reconstruct the content and the image of the Nation, eradicate subversion and promote the economic development of national life based on the equilibrium and responsible participation of different sectors towards the end of assuring the later installation of a republican, representative and federal democracy, suited to the reality and the demands for solution and progress of the Argentine people. (Verbitsky 1987:145)

The document then proceeds to elaborate these general goals. Along with emphasizing the reestablishment of internal order, certain other points stand out. First of all, the tract strongly emphasizes moral issues. Point 2, in particular, argues for the protection of Christian values and "national tradition." Point 8 indicates the government's intentions to actively intervene in the education system (146). In part, this undoubtedly reflected simple concern with the long-term development of the country. Yet the issue was somewhat more complex than this. At the time, many of Argentina's universities had become highly politicized centers of leftist activity, a condition that probably did interrupt the process of education. From the perspective of the armed forces, however, limitations on students' learning possibilities were less critical than the possibility that the universities could be used to disseminate what the military interpreted as subversive ideologies. Correspondingly, the government's subsequent education policies largely involved modifying the ideological and moral formation of students (Spitta 1983).

Secondly, the PRN document explicitly states the government's intentions to ally Argentina internationally with the "Western and Christian world." This point is closely related to the famed U.S.-orientation of the relatively internationalist "national security" doctrine. In some respects, the American and Argentine versions of the doctrine coincide, particularly with regard to the perception of the world as distinctly bipolar, divided between East and West. Yet, the U.S. version of the cleavage emphasizes different economic systems: communism and capitalism. In contrast, the Argentine version appears to place more emphasis on value systems, for example, criticizing the atheist definition of the Soviet state and lauding the perceived Christian base of American society (Verbitsky 1987:146).

The stated objectives of the PRN do support capitalism, but with a more nationalist thrust. Thus, point 5 proposes the

> definition of a socioeconomic situation that assures the capacity of national decision making and the full realization of the Argentine man, in which the State maintains control over areas vital to security and development and offers the conditions necessary for fluid participation in the process of national exploitation of resources to private, national and foreign initiative and capital, neutralizing all possibility of their interference in the exercise of public power. (Verbitsky 1987:146)

The document then declares that the government would promote "general well-being" by encouraging "fruitful work, with equality of opportunity and an adequate sense of social justice" (146). Again, reiteration of Argentina's allegiances in the bipolar world are accompanied by more subjective elements ("the full realization of the Argentine man"). At the same time, however, the authors implicitly promise economic growth and development, national autonomy, and a reasonable standard of living for all. It would not be an easy promise to fulfill.

In sum, the military junta initiating the Proceso de Reorganización Nacional proposed to eliminate the roots and acts of guerrilla warfare (subversion), institute a traditional code of morality, and boost the economy. A subtle tension between liberalism (free market policies and a close political alliance to the West) and the army's more common nationalist tendencies pervaded the plan. The repeated references to Christianity and morality reflected the nationalist tendencies, as did the declaration of the need for some measure of continued statism. The varying degrees to which these policies were implemented, taken in conjunction with their outcomes, significantly influenced later orientations within the armed forces.

From Defense against Terrorism to War against Subversion

The junta's preoccupation with combating insurgency represented the culmination of years of theoretical and practical preparation for domestic conflict, similar to trends throughout Latin America. It also marked a critical turning point in the military's approach to that conflict. From initially defensive and largely legal counterguerrilla tactics, the armed forces passed to a much more extensive, offensive strategy in 1975. With the military takeover in 1976, the intensity of repression escalated dramatically, and the armed forces definitively relinquished legal boundaries.

Foundations of the Countersubversive War

The Argentine military to some degree had been preparing for the possibility of guerrilla warfare since the late 1950s. Military journals stemming back from the late 1950s and early 1960s are replete with articles on counterrevolutionary warfare, many of these authored by French advisers drawing on their experience in Algeria. For example, in December 1958, an article appeared in *Revista de la Escuela Superior de Guerra* by French Lieutenant Colonel Patricio de Naurois, entitled "Subversive War and Revolutionary War."[1] The article emphasizes the moral and mass foundations of revolutionary or subversive warfare and, corresponding to the national security doctrine, the need to combat it with combined "political, administrative, economic, social, cultural, and military means" (695). Finally, the author warns readers of Mao Tse-tung's plan for the step-by-step communist takeover of the world. The implicit meaning was clear: the Argentine military should prepare to combat revolution.

During the next few years, planning for counterrevolutionary warfare in Argentina advanced. As elsewhere in Latin America, Fidel Castro's 1959 triumph in Cuba made communism appear much less abstract and much closer to home. However, the most vehement reaction seemed to come from the United States, which, under the leadership of John F. Kennedy and Robert McNamara, began to encourage Latin American countries to expand their notions of security in order to protect the West from communism (Stepan 1971:126–33; López 1987; Nogues 1962:27). This emphasis merged well with concepts of national security already developing in Latin America, particularly in Brazil. The idea also had resonance in Argentina. By January 1962, the Argentine Army General Staff had already begun to elaborate military doctrine on counterrevolutionary warfare (Nougues 1962:33). In 1964, General Juan Carlos Onganía delivered a speech at West Point that became the public symbol of the military's shift toward an internal security orientation (López 1987:174–77; Wynia 1992:80).

The Guerrilla Offensive

By the time of Onganía's speech, it was beginning to appear that the military might be justified in its preparations. According to General Ramón Genaro Díaz Bessone, Argentina's first guerrilla group (which demonstrated Peronist sympathies) appeared in 1959. In 1961, a second group was founded, this time Trotskyite in orientation (1988a:80).

The guerrilla organizations made few inroads during this period, however, at least partially because of their frequently misplaced orientation. At the time, most guerrilla efforts tended to concentrate on stimulating a rural-based revolutionary movement (Wynia 1992: 64). Argentina's lack of a numerically significant peasantry and its still relatively high general standard of living reduced the impact of these efforts.

In the years following Onganía's 1966 coup, would-be guerrillas were finally given a more marketable purpose: to end military rule (Anzorena:1988). The Montoneros (the armed branch of the Peronist youth), Ejército Revolucionario del Pueblo (ERP) [People's Revolutionary Army—a Trotskyite group], and Fuerzas Armadas Revolucionarias [Revolutionary Armed Forces] began to organize. However, for most members of the military, the real beginning of guerrilla activity is marked by the 1970 kidnapping and murder of former military president General Pedro Eugenio Aramburu.[2]

Aramburu's death indicated the degree to which guerrilla attacks tended to point directly at military and police personnel, both active duty and retired.[3] For the left, this emphasis constituted popular retaliation for the military and security forces' recurrent interference with political freedom. Yet, by concentrating on these targets, the guerrillas magnified the military's perception of the extent of the threat. Even in Tucumán, where the guerrilla threat appeared most convincing, the size of the movement remained limited. According to

Martin Andersen, "Arrayed against 5,000 army troops, the ERP guerrillas never succeeded in putting more than 120 to 140 combatants into the field, and that only for less than two weeks" (1993:125). However, the much larger military is also in some ways a small cohesive organization. The assassination of members thus generated a very real panic among the remaining officers. A naval officer told of having his wife stand at their apartment window with a rifle to guard him each morning as he drove away. Others recounted their constant fear and insecurity, never knowing when they or a friend might be the object of an attack. If the guerrillas wanted to assure that the military took them seriously, they certainly succeeded.

Nonetheless, military repression initially remained fairly limited, as well as largely legal and overt. As table 1 indicates, during the years 1969 to 1974, deaths attributed to "subversion," or guerrilla actions, were actually higher than the number of deaths attributed to the military (the "disappeared"). The military's apparent restraint was particularly remarkable in that guerrilla violence had already become quite significant (120 people killed through terrorism in 1974) and focused against the armed forces.

Evolution of Counterinsurgency Tactics

In 1975, military repression began to surpass the violence of the guerrillas, although the armed forces still remained primarily within the boundaries of legality. On 2 February 1975, Isabel Martínez de Perón's constitutional government issued a secret order to the military to "execute the military operations necessary to neutralize and/or annihilate the action of subversive elements acting in the province of Tucumán," thereby initiating "Operation Independence" (Asociación Americana de Juristas 1988:15). Eight months later, the internal role of the armed forces expanded further, with Martínez de Perón's order to pursue the same goal throughout the entire country (15).

Along with constitutional authorization for states of seige (Loveman 1993:290), the armed forces considered Martínez de Perón's decree sufficient to legitimize extensive action against terrorism, even after constitutional government had been interrupted. However, after the 1976 coup d'état, the form in which the armed forces opted to combat terrorism changed considerably. Rather than concentrating exclusively on armed combatants (terrorists or *guerrilleros*), the

Table 1

Casualties of the Argentine "Dirty War," 1969–1983

Year	Deaths Caused by Guerrillas	"Disappeared" and Military Presumed Responsible	Civilian Deaths in Confrontations
1969	1	—	—
1970	4	—	—
1971	24	6	—
1972	26	5	—
1973	49	18	—
1974	120	46	—
1975	179	359	564
1976	293	4,105	1,277
1977	70	3,098	555
1978	18	969	63
1979	7	181	3
1980	—	83	—
1981	—	19	—
1982	—	12	—
1983	—	9	—
Total	790	8,910	2,462

Source: Asamblea Permanente por los Derechos Humanos, 1982:32.

armed forces broadened their scope to include "subversion," the purported ideological or cultural sources of revolutionary activity. According to the military's perspective, any small core of ideological dissidence could represent a potential source for terrorist or revolutionary behavior.[4] As Jack Child explains: "Using the biological metaphor, the internal enemies of the organic state are envisioned as malignant cells that have gone bad and are attacking their host. The military attempts, first, to contain these cancerous cells through therapy and repressive means. If this should fail, then the ultimate draconian step of surgical removal (extirpation) may be necessary" (1990: 144). In Argentina, eradication came to be perceived as the only solution to the perceived subversive threat. Thus, by early 1976, the term used by the military to describe the conflict, Guerra Contra-Subversiva [Countersubversive War], became chillingly accurate. Workers, students, intellectuals, psychiatrists, and others suspected of challenging the government were seized from their homes, were taken to clandestine detention centers, and, finally, "disappeared" (CONADEP 1986:296). Some were affiliated with the guerrilla organizations; others were not.

The Level of Military Involvement

The question remains as to how many members of the military actually did participate directly in the illegal aspects of the war. Eduardo Luís Duhalde writes that "the Grupos de Tareas [Task Groups] had their permanent personnel, but in each of these, in order that the blood pact was not only binding for a few officers, but for the totality of officers of the armed forces, the periodic intervention of all active duty officers in the capture, interrogation, taunting, and assassination of prisoners was arranged by means of permanent rotations of military personnel, complementary to the fixed, specialized teams" (1983:95). Duhalde's assertion gained further plausibility after two navy officers testified before the Senate in October of 1994 that torture had been a standard form of interrogation during the military regime.[5] This would imply that not only were all officers aware of the methods being used, but all took part.

However, other evidence suggests that involvement may have been more restricted. Those estimates place the number of military personnel who were directly involved in the repression at anywhere from slightly under 900 to around 1,300 (Varas 1989:58–59).[6] According to the Comisión Nacional Sobre la Desaparación de Personas (CONADEP) [National Commission on the Disappeared], the repression did not implicate all members of the military or the security forces, due to the need for secrecy (CONADEP 1986:65–66; also see Buchanan 1987). Although this topic was clearly a difficult one to broach in interviews, and even more difficult to verify, at least one interview supported the position that participation was not universal. In this particular case, an army major related in June of 1989 that in 1976, he was about to be transferred to a post in which his principal duty would be interrogation. After being informed by a friend that "strange things" were happening in the interrogations, he requested to be sent to a different post. The request was granted.

Such a request probably represented the maximum dissent an officer could express, however. Moving from asking for a different as-
signment to either openly opposing the repression or aiding suspects
constituted a rather dramatic escalation of risks. Any member of the
repressive apparatus who attempted to cross that divide could be
gambling with his own safety (CONADEP 1986:294).

Legacies of the Repression within the Military

Despite the different roles that officers took, in one sense, the countersubversive war did lend an element of unity to the military. Several
officers made unsolicited comments to me that they had participated
in one form or another (either actively or from a desk) and that they
still felt that their actions were essential. When asked exactly what
percentage of the army had participated in the antisubversive war, an
active-duty general replied in a June 1989 interview that practically
all officers and noncommissioned officers (NCOs) had taken part in
some way, even if supervising travel, and that in Tucumán, even soldiers (draftees) had participated.[7] Similar to other officers, the general explained the brutality of the repression by the combination of
the extensiveness of terrorism, the lack of a legal framework for that
kind of problem, and the inevitability of "excesses" in any war.
Along the same lines, a lieutenant colonel explained in a November
1988 interview that the military's refusal to accept the human rights
trials did not imply a denial that excesses had been committed. Instead, the reaction emanated from the common belief that a greater
end was at stake, which justified the use of even cruel and drastic
means. "Beyond excesses," he argued, "the republic was saved from
a totalitarian regime." More than a decade passed before the military
institution, beginning with Army Chief of Staff Martín Balza, would
openly condemn the repression.[8]

Yet, the relative unanimity that existed in the early 1980s with respect to the ethicality and necessity of the countersubversive war
could not completely overcome the divisions that it produced. Instead, the varying modes and degrees of participation generated related differences in prestige, along with the predictable accompany-
ing rivalries.

Perhaps surprisingly, part of the internal turmoil seems to have
emanated from the enhanced status attributed to those who had par-

ticipated more extensively in the especially disagreeable aspects of the war. By 1978, there were two hierarchies: legal and illegal. A major who had remained with the legal branch of the army complained in a June 1983 interview that those who had participated in the illegal repression became arrogant. Those forming part of the illegal structure gained a certain prestige primarily for two reasons. First, the nature of their activities granted them a certain degree of autonomy from the formal command structure. Secondly, these individuals were also perceived as laudable for their willingness to take responsibility for unpleasant tasks that many believed essential but few wished to carry out.

Closely related to the enhanced status of members of the illegal apparatus was the loss of prestige by the high command. Writing orders and directives for the repression was simply not equivalent to physically dirtying one's hands. As a middle-level officer indicated in a July 1989 interview, "the generals had the Swiss bank accounts, and we were left with the blood." According to CONADEP, this attitude was not unique. During their investigation, they received various voluntary testimonies from officers who had participated in the repression. The cooperation of these people generally was not due to any repentance for their actions but, instead, came from their feeling of "'having been abandoned by their own leaders,' after 'having contributed to the antisubversive war in some cases losing their career or risking their own life, while they contemplated their leaders' enrichment, the generalized corruption in the ranks, and the loss of the objectives which had been denoted as the motivations for the fight'" (1986:254).

In sum, while the countersubversive war did leave a legacy of shared experiences and, at least at the moment of the 1983 transition, a shared perception of success, it also contributed to two overlapping cleavages: between bureaucrats and warriors and between high-ranking and middle-ranking officers.

The Military as Government

In contrast to the reactions to the countersubversive war, military reactions to the institution's attempts at government during the period of 1976 to 1983 were decidedly negative. Not one, whether from within the military government, from the upper echelons of the post-Proceso active-duty military hierarchy, or from the middle ranks in the post-Proceso period (captains, majors, and lieutenant colonels), would claim that the government had been a success.[9] Above all, criticisms of the government centered on two issues: corruption and the economy.

The existence of corruption within the military government came as a shock to the military. Not only did it destroy the perceived moral authority of the organization both internally and externally, but for members of the middle and lower ranks, it stimulated both shame and resentment. Most middle- and even upper-level officers active in the period of 1984–89 had not participated directly in the government. Yet, since they were members of the institution, the activities of their superiors nonetheless reflected on them. Several years later, one of the lieutenant colonels leading the rebellions of 1987–89 expressed his resentment of this situation (as he perceived it) in a letter to a leading newspaper:

> This leadership, of course, gave responsibility exclusively to the military sector for the management of government. In the shade of this management, by complicity, by irresponsibility or by the impotence of those who exercised control of the government, the world hegemonic interests carried away a large part of the Argentine patrimony. They did this through the intervention of their agents, Argentines, of course. The diverse crimes that might have been committed in this time were never seriously investigated, much less convicted. Even more, those superior officers with government or military responsibility that warned of the dispossession and dared to denounce it or oppose it were relieved of their posts. The disastrous part is that without distinguishing responsibilities or authority, all the armed forces, especially members of the army, were blamed. (León 1988:9)

How Military Was the Military Government?

The high degree to which the military institution participated in the government made it particularly difficult for officers to avoid blame. The Argentine leadership also did not attempt to separate military and political hierarchies, a move that helped protect the Chilean armed forces from the divisive effects of governing. According to María Susana Ricci and J. Samuel Fitch, of all ministers during the period, 49 percent were military officers, with a high of 76 percent military ministers during the Videla government of 1976–80 (1988: table 1).[10] "Each service had its 'feudal domains' and active duty officers were appointed to a much wider range of subordinate posts, as commanders of the federal police, intervenors of the central labor federation and key unions, and heads of the major state enterprises" (60). Military control, furthermore, also penetrated the provincial level, dividing governorships between the different branches, and at times reached down even as far as local government (see Castiglione 1992).

Yet one of the military's principle reasons for overthrowing the Martínez de Perón government and placing significant proportions of the state apparatus under the direct control of military officers was their belief that the armed forces were not subject to the same kind of corruption that seemed to plague political leaders. Where, then, did they go wrong?

Corruption and Politicization in the Military Government

A central problem of the military government involved the organizational politicization of the armed forces. In any organization, there exists a natural competition for resources among different bureaucratic units. The military is no exception. Yet, in the attempt to minimize interservice rivalries, the Proceso managed to exacerbate the problem. Every level of the government was to some degree divided between the three branches of the military. A three-man junta, initially represented by Videla, Massera, and Agosti, controlled the presidency. The junta also divided the ministries, allocating the Ministries of Labor and the Interior to the army, Foreign Affairs and Social Welfare to the navy, and the Ministry of Justice to the air force. Only the Ministry of Economy was left entirely under civilian control, although Videla's sponsorship of Minister José Martínez de Hoz did implicate the army in the running of this area as well.

In sum, the government was structured in such a way that the competition between branches of the military for resources would likely be compounded by competition for positions of power, and interservice rivalries would almost inevitably interfere with the formation of a coherent government. To many members of the military, the kinds of political interests that developed under this system were a far cry from their honor-bound ideal of the armed forces, in which God and country are the only truly legitimate focuses of military concern.

Yet most examples of corruption within the military government concerned the use of political positions for personal, rather than organizational, gain. One of the most overt and widespread examples of this was the legalized practice of taking home multiple salaries. As Arnold Spitta explains,

> The military officers that fulfilled the duties of a position in the public administration—whether as governor, provincial or national minister, or as ambassador, municipal superintendent, intervener or director of a state enterprise or in another function (there were thousands of positions to cover)[—]had [received] for all this time double salaries: their income as an active or retired officer and those of the civilian position, both functions with the later right to retirement and respective pensions (1983:89).

By 1981, this had come to the public attention, and in an attempt to appease a dismayed citizenry, the military leadership made some efforts to revise the situation.

Corruption did not stop here, however. Some military officers took further advantage of the situation to obtain private low-interest loans from abroad, using only their positions as collateral. According to Michael Monteon, this money was used primarily for financial speculation rather than productive investment (1987:26). Finally, in addition to these forms of corruption, the military government also was tainted by various episodes emanating more directly from the battle against subversion, that is, extortion and looting.[11] All in all, quite a few members of the armed forces emerged from the period of military rule in significantly better financial shape than they had been in before, and not merely due to increases in salaries. The military institution, however, paid.

The Economy of the PRN

As a whole, the country was far from having obtained an economic bonanza from the 1976–83 period of military government. The economic policies of the regime, designed largely by the Proceso's first minister of economy, José Martínez de Hoz, generated a mixture of intentional and unintentional costs. The plan instituted by Martínez de Hoz was, above all, a plan to liberalize the Argentine economy. Import tariffs were to be reduced, along with taxes on agricultural exports and certain governmental subsidies. The government also attempted to diminish the size of the state, primarily by eliminating significant social services and "rationalizing" or privatizing state enterprises (Buchanan 1987:357). For example, data on personnel employed by state enterprises demonstrate a progressive decline, from 424,923 individuals employed in 1975 to only 291,832 in 1982 (Ministerio de Economía 1983:77; 1982:58).

The reduction of state-provided national benefits and the elimination of employees from the public payrolls were not the only ways in which workers suffered under the military government's economic plan. According to Paul Buchanan, the plan also sought to "reduce real wages by at least 40 percent relative to those of the previous five years" (1987:357). The government succeeded in reaching this goal. An index of worker's participation in the national income indicates a drastic drop from 129.7 in 1975 to 85.0 in 1976 and 81.1 in 1977 (see table 2). Perhaps the only area in which the government explicitly attempted to protect workers was in regard to unemployment levels. Unemployment rates actually diminished during this period, reflecting the government's very reasonable fear that higher numbers of unemployed might provide a new recruitment pool for the guerrilla organizations (Rock 1987:369). Overall, however, whether the government sought to break the power of the unions, as some have argued, or whether the economic team was more concerned with attacking hyperinflation and the balance of payments deficit, the working class suffered the brunt of the Martínez de Hoz economic plan (Rock 1987:368: Buchanan 1987:360).

For a brief period, however, the attempt to achieve a more liberal, growth-oriented capitalist economy did seem to pay off. Inflation rates dropped to 50 percent, and foreign loans seemed to pour in (Monteon 1987:26). Furthermore, as David Rock describes, "export earnings increased by 33 percent, imports fell by 20 percent, and the previous year's $1 billion payments deficit became a surplus of $650 million (1987:368). Thus, at the macroeconomic level, things looked promising.

Nonetheless, optimism proved tragically short-lived. By April 1980, banks had begun to fail, initiating a much more generalized

Table 2
The Argentine Economy, 1973–1989

Year	Gross Domestic Product (Million $U.S. 1980, Deflated)	Total External Debt (Million $U.S.)	Current Account Balance (Million $U.S.)	Index of Worker Participation in National Income	Unemployment (%)
1973	72,015	6,429	711	123.4	5.6
1974	73,094	6,789	118	124.5	3.4
1975	75,705	8,171	-1,287	129.7	2.3
1976	75,517	9,880	651	85.0	4.5
1977	80,476	11,445	1,126	81.1	2.8
1978	77,793	13,276	1,856	83.7	2.8
1979	82,295	20,950	-513	86.3	2.0
1980	84,989	27,157	-4,774	89.5	2.3
1981	79,805	35,657	-4,712	—	4.5
1982	74,516	43,634	-2,353	—	4.8
1983	76,475	45,920	-2,436	—	4.2
1984	78,297	48,857	-2,495	—	3.8
1985	74,862	50,945	- 952	—	5.3
1986	79,350	52,450	-2,859	—	4.4
1987	81,020	58,425	-4,235	—	5.3
1988	78,719	58,706	-1,572	—	5.9
1989	75,238	64,745	-1,205	—	7.3

Sources: Gross Domestic Product from Wilkie and Contreras (1992):1368; Index of Workers' Participation in National Income from Caputo (1983):136; Unemployment from Wilkie and Contreras (1992):378; Current account balance from IMF, *International Financial Statistics Yearbook* (1994): 190–91.

economic collapse. During the next year, one bank after another toppled, and Argentines rushed out of the country whatever money that remained, as their fragile confidence in the national economy rapidly disintegrated. By the end of 1980, the current account balance had plummeted from minus $513 million in 1979 to minus $4,774 million in 1980 (see table 2). The Gross Domestic Product (GDP), which had climbed during most of the Proceso, began to fall, dropping from $84,989 million in 1980 to $79,805 million in 1981. By the beginning of 1982, the collapse of the military government seemed to be only a matter of time.

The Falklands/Malvinas War

However they may be evaluated, both the war against subversion and the governmental experience of the Proceso had increasingly drawn the armed forces away from traditional military roles and, consequently, further away from conventional sources of prestige and honor. The military government could not demonstrate that their economic policies had rescued the country from some dramatic security threat; on the contrary, Argentine economic conditions had become significantly more precarious.

On the other hand, the countersubversive war did provide an identifiable threat to security that the armed forces had undeniably conquered. However, the manner through which the war was implemented denied the military any public claim to battlefield heroism. The dramatic escalation of the repression after the military takeover, the regular use of methods considered unacceptable internationally, and the military's failure to openly declare war on the guerrillas led many to even deny that this *could* be considered a war (Moyano 1991). Thus, when the violence tapered to an end, there were no parades to pay homage to the victors, no public acclaim for acts of heroism. Rather than being honored as saviors of the nation (as they continued to perceive themselves), the armed forces were disparaged as a collection of power-hungry, immoral ogres.

The Argentine military appeared to need a "clean" war, a classical conflict against a foreign enemy that would perhaps help heal the wounds left by the internal conflict. In 1978, Chile very nearly became that enemy. With the enthusiastic encouragement of junta member Admiral Emilio Massera, the longstanding territorial dispute between Argentina and Chile over the Beagle Channel barely missed exploding into a full-scale war (Rock 1987:370). However, the intervention of the pope at the last minute helped Argentine and Chilean leaders reach a diplomatic solution. Armed troops, poised to invade Chile the very next day, were ordered to put down their arms, forget the valiant mission they were about to commence, and calmly return home. For some, feelings of frustration overshadowed feelings of relief.

National Symbolism of the Malvinas

The Falkland/Malvinas conflict provided a useful outlet for that frustration, as well as proving politically expedient, given the faltering Argentine economy and the government's declining legitimacy. As the vast majority of Argentines consider the Malvinas to be usurped national territory (despite the fact that the Argentine occupation of the islands lasted only around five and a half years back in the early 1800s), the restoration of the islands was guaranteed to rally support. Particularly since Perón's rise to power in the late 1940s, Argentines have been taught from childhood that the islands rightfully belong to them. According to Carlos Escudé, "By force of law every map of Argentina, including elementary-school ones, must carry not only these islands but also the so-called Argentine Antarctic Sector, which overlaps with Chilean and British claims" (1988: 160; 1987).

The Falkland/Malvinas Islands thus provided a timely distraction both for a population disillusioned with military government and for a military struggling with its own "dirty war" experiences and an increasingly fragmented institution (Fontana 1984). Efforts to resolve the question diplomatically had not been entirely exhausted, but could not guarantee the Argentines a title to the territory. The English-speaking islanders staunchly preferred to remain under British control; thus as long as the British continued to defend the islanders' wishes, the possibilities of a peaceful transfer of the islands remained slim. Hence, when an excuse for a military offensive emerged, both the military and the nation were inclined to rush in. The opportunity was not long in coming.

The Trigger: The Davidoff Affair

In 1978, a businessman by the name of Constantino Davidoff began to plan a salvage operation in the Georgia Islands, a dependency of the Falklands. Although the contract was signed in September of 1979 and authorities in the islands were notified one month later, the initiation of the project was postponed until December of 1981. At that time, Davidoff made an initial visit to the islands aboard an Argentine ship in order to conduct an inspection, remaining only a few hours (J. Fraga 1983:133). The trip occurred quite peacefully, despite the preparations of a small Argentine naval unit for the possibility of British interference (Comisión Rattenbach 1988:64).

Upon returning to Buenos Aires, however, Davidoff received the first indication of some potential resistance on the part of the British, although it did not seem a particularly strong reaction at the time. The British embassy merely notified Davidoff that, according to established procedure, he and his crew should have presented themselves at the British post of Grytviken before landing. When the Davidoff crew paid a second visit to the Georgias at the end of February (this time on a private Panamanian yacht and without Davidoff's personal presence), they appear to have again bypassed Grytviken, although without provoking a British reaction.

This was not the case in March, however, when Davidoff and his workers next landed on the islands, once again aboard a ship belonging to the Argentine navy. The salvagers had notified the British embassy and provided it with the list of personnel who would be disembarking on the islands, and the certificates ("white cards") used for immigration had been arranged. Yet, on 19 March 1982, when the Davidoff team arrived at Port Leith, Georgia Islands, it again failed to make the requisite stop at Grytviken. From the British perspective, this infringement on the rules was exacerbated by rumors (denied by the Argentines) that military personnel were among those disembarking, and that the Argentine flag had been raised upon arrival, thereby indicating something more than merely commercial interests. British sensitivity was arguably also heightened by the scheduled reduction or elimination of the British presence in the Georgias, which would leave the Argentines in a strategically advantageous position (Gamba 1984:117–19).

Despite the situation, the British reaction still seems to have been inordinately strong. When, on 25 March, the Argentines finally answered British protests with an offer to transport the workers to Grytviken to have their documents (white cards) stamped, the British responded that the workers would instead have to have visas issued on their passports (Anaya 1989). From the Argentine point of view, this was unquestionably not an acceptable solution. As junta member Admiral Jorge Anaya explained, "If I accepted a British passport in the southern Georgia Islands for 41 workers, I was de facto recognizing British sovereignty over the Georgia islands, and this was a legal precedent that I would never be able to deny."[12] After the years of negotiations to attempt to regain that territory, Argentina was not about to sacrifice its ambitions so easily. When, on the same day, Argentine intelligence notified the junta that Great Britain had launched two nuclear submarines headed for the area, confrontation was deemed inevitable.[13]

Operación Rosario: The Invasion of the Islands

Although the British reaction to the Davidoff incident certainly provided an immediate stimulus for Argentine action, it would be misleading to argue that the Argentines were forced into an unwanted war. On the contrary, the invasion of the Falkland/Malvinas Islands, given the name Operación Rosario,[14] had been on the junta's agenda since 12 January 1982, only shortly after Galtieri took power through an internal military coup in December of 1981 (Comisión Rattenbach 1988:46). According to the military's plans, however, the operation was not supposed to occur until the end of the year, and at the very earliest on 9 July 1982 (later pushed up to 15 May), with no less than fifteen days of advance warning (47).

Nonetheless, the occupation of the islands succeeded. While the Argentines did suffer some casualties (three deaths and seven people injured), none occurred among the British (de Martini 1988; Train 1987:40; Comisión Rattenbach 1988:85). The Argentines hoped that by not spilling British blood, they could avoid any severe British retaliation. As late as 2 April 1982, the day on which they invaded the islands, Argentine leaders still hoped to recuperate the Malvinas without escalation into a full-scale war.

As subsequent events demonstrated, this was not a realistic expectation. Despite the distance, expense, and probably limited value that the islands had for Great Britain anyway, Britain launched a very determined and very successful campaign to reclaim the territory. On 14 June 1982, little more than two months after its euphoric conquest of the islands, Argentina surrendered to Great Britain, unable to deny a devastating defeat.

Causes and Effects of Defeat

For at least six years after the surrender, from the moment when crushed Argentine troops returned to their homeland through the day in 1988 when the wartime commanders were sentenced for their performance, the "mission" of both military and civilian analysts would be to uncover the causes of defeat, along with clarifying the reasons that the dispute escalated to such a scale.

From one perspective, the immediate cause of the Argentines' loss was simply the numerical and material superiority of British troops. According to Frederick Turner, at the time of the conflict "both Argentina and Britain were spending 4.5 percent of their gross domestic product on the military; yet, given the larger size of the British economy, total British spending was three and a half times greater" (1983: 60). Both the weapons and number of men available in the two countries reflected these differences. At the time of the war, the number of military personnel in the British forces was nearly double that at the disposal of the Argentines, around 343,600 in contrast to 185,500 (Dabat and Lorenzano 1982:81).

The allocation of resources probably also advantaged the British, as the Argentine military's recent efforts had emphasized counterinsurgency rather than conventional warfare. Much of their training and equipment was thus somewhat inappropriate for this kind of conflict. Furthermore, the distribution of resources among the army, navy, and air force differs considerably between the two countries. At least in part due to geographical demands (Great Britain is a relatively small island nation, while Argentina covers a much more extensive and complex territory and shares borders with five other countries), Argentina's military favors the army much more than do the British forces (Dabat and Lorenzano 1982:181). In an island war, in which air and naval forces are critical, this seems likely to be a disadvantage.

Other factors favored the Argentines, however—in particular, the limited likelihood that the battling countries would make full use of their forces and have them available to do so. The Malvinas conflict was not a total war, fought on home territory and engaging the complete power of both nations' national defense systems. Instead, it was a war fought on and around territory claimed by both but not extensively occupied by either. Despite Britain's prior presence in the islands, its physical distance from the battlefield posed a serious problem. For Great Britain, the time and costs of transporting troops and equipment to this tiny, primarily sheep-inhabited piece of land thousands of miles away were considerably more than those borne by the

Argentines. Consequently, overall, Britain actually employed a smaller number of troops than Argentina, and certainly suffered fewer casualties. According to one estimate, by the end of the war the Argentine army had between 9,000 and 11,000 men present, while the British forces numbered between 3,000 and 4,000 men (Dabat and Lorenzano 1982:190; Goyret 1984:23; Wynia 1992:101). In sum, while differences in training and equipment undoubtedly made a difference, the sheer difference in size of the respective military institutions does not seem to be an adequate explanation for the outcome of the war.

From the perspective of many Argentines, the primary reason for the defeat in the Falklands/Malvinas war was the U.S. decision to support Great Britain, only stopping short of sending American troops to the islands. The United States reportedly aided Britain's intelligence capacities through the use of an American satellite whose orbit was supposedly changed from the Soviet region to the South Atlantic, and facilitated two hundred Sidewinder missiles to the British, which were later considered to have been responsible for a considerable proportion of Argentine aerial losses (García Enciso 1984:8; de Martini 1988). The United States was also reported to have offered Great Britain aircraft fuel and aircraft carriers, had they become necessary.

The U.S. position probably should not have taken the Argentines by surprise. The United States clearly holds important historic ties to Great Britain, as well as being joined through the NATO alliance. In addition, the United States would seem to have a natural interest in supporting the international territorial status quo. Yet the Argentines could also find several reasons to expect the United States to maintain neutrality (Feldman 1985). Relations between the Reagan government and the military junta had been quite friendly. More formally, Argentines could point to the existence of the 1947 Inter-American Defense Treaty, or Rio treaty, which bound members of the Organization of American States to join in the defense of American states against any external aggression. For the Argentines, the war *was* stimulated by British aggression—direct aggression in 1833 and provocation during the Davidoff incident. Unfortunately, the OAS did not perceive the situation in the same way. While no condemnation of Argentina was issued, the OAS remained on what it considered to be middle ground, asking both parties to withdraw.[15]

The other factor leading Argentines to expect at least neutrality from the United States was the latter's dependence on (and obligation to) Argentina in Central America. Practiced in combating communist "subversion" in their own country, the Argentine military had become involved in battling communism in Central America. Much of the training and organization of Nicaragua's counter-revolutionary forces (Contras) occurred under the direction of Argentine officers, thereby helping the United States to keep its involvement out of the public eye. Thus, according to some Argentine leaders, by supporting Britain in the war, the U.S. government would face not only the alienation of its American allies but also a strong domestic reaction to the consequent need of the United States to expand its activities in Central America.

Initially, the junta's gamble seemed likely to pay off. The United States ostensibly assumed the role of mediator, and as prominent a figure as Jean Kirkpatrick openly advocated American neutrality. According to an American officer then working in the Pentagon, the Defense Department had also reached the conclusion that U.S. interests would best be served by not taking sides. Nonetheless, Secretary of State Alexander Haig apparently took a different perspective, and it was not long before the United States had given up its neutral facade.

Planning and Coordination Problems in the Malvinas Islands

Argentina's greatest disadvantage came, however, from its own lack of foresight. As Harry Train writes, "The Argentine invasion plan had been conceived entirely as a short and peaceful occupation of the Malvinas by a relatively small force, not as sustained operations by a large force, preparing for, and ultimately involved in combat" (1987: 49). The Comisión Rattenbach coincides with Train in its assessment that the military command had not taken into account or planned for the possibility that Great Britain might take military action to reclaim the islands. Instead, the initial plan began and ended with Operación Rosario. The plan for the defense of the islands was not generated until 12 April 1982, a full ten days *after* the occupation (Comisión Rattenbach 1988:59).

The military leadership was responsible for other deficiencies in planning and direction as well. For example, the troops sent were certainly not those most prepared to fight. The soldiers still left from the previous year's draft were kept at the Chilean border, while new soldiers with as little as two weeks of training were sent to the islands. Furthermore, cooperation between the army, navy, and air force was extremely poor, in part because of the premature implementation of the invasion plan. In the end, the plans submitted by those officers charged with elaborating strategy for their particular force were approved and executed without ever having been coordinated (Comisión Rattenbach 1988:48). Jealousy and competition between the forces then exacerbated this initial flaw. According to Train, in one instance, the navy actually had to "invade" the headquarters of another force to obtain some essential information (1987:58).

The war in the Falklands/Malvinas Islands helped even more than the military's experience in government and the countersubversive war to provoke the already simmering rupture between commanding and intermediate ranks in the armed forces. Not only did the military leaders steer their people into a war that, however popular, realistically was not likely to be won under the circumstances, but they even implicitly blamed those people for the defeat upon their return. Rather than receiving a hero's welcome, or even returning promptly to their waiting families and friends, the war veterans were temporarily isolated, hidden away from the public eye. For many, it seemed that they had gone from being the prisoners of the British to being the prisoners of their own institution. As a captain expressed in a July 1989 interview, "This event [the Malvinas war], beyond whether it was strategically or politically good or bad, had a terrible effect on the armed forces, because once the war was over, and having lost the war, those that had combatted were received in the country as delinquents, but not by the population, by the very members of the armed forces that were the Proceso de Reorganización Nacional" (also see Ruíz Moreno 1986:430–41).

Along with those at the pinnacle of the military organization, high-ranking officers in the field were also accused of having inadequately led their men. According to Turner, "while some officers fought with dedication (with medals for bravery going to officers at the rank of major and below), many field commanders left their men for the safety of the rear echelons. In many cases, it was the heroism of new recruits, fighting alone, that held off the British as long as possible" (1983:60). While a few of the generals of the late 1980s were recognized by the middle-rank officers of that period as having been good soldiers, many were seen, once again, as bureaucrats who left the responsibility to their subordinates.

Revisions of the National Security Doctrine: The New "Old Professionalism"

After the defeat in the Falklands/Malvinas Islands, the military government quickly moved toward relinquishing their now wobbly seat of power. Under General Bignone, elections for a new—now civilian—president were held, ending the regime. Yet the military government of 1976–83 left armed forces very different from those with whom they had started. The military had failed at government, failed at external war, and failed at convincing the civilian population of the legitimacy of their methods in the internal war. None of the other South American military regimes of this period could boast such a miserable record. An army captain (active in the military rebellions of 1987–90) summed up the situation in the following manner in a July 1989 interview: "Having ended the government of the Proceso, that undoubtedly was a disaster, and that provoked one of the most difficult situations for the armed forces, we found a morally destroyed army, because of the war against the subversion and, fundamentally, because of the year 1982, which produced the Malvinas war."

These combined experiences resulted in the revision of the national security doctrine, as officers reverted to an interest in a Huntingtonian "objective" professionalism. Various officers expressed the sentiment that the military had failed in its attempt to govern and that politics should be left to the politicians. Particularly those officers active in the Malvinas war expressed a desire to end the politicization and bureaucratization of the armed forces and to place a new emphasis on combat and leadership skills. Although many of these sentiments went little further than casual conversation, some indications of this new orientation on the part of the mid-rank and lower-rank officers did begin to appear in the military journals. In 1984, for example, a lieutenant colonel wrote, "The value of the armed forces is given by its effective capacity to support national politics in its obtention of its objectives" (Figueroa 1984:11). In its espousal of military responsiveness, the statement implies that a military that contradicts the national government is of no value whatsoever. In sum, an effective military is a subordinate military.

Another article published in the same journal (*Revista Militar*) in 1983 contains a much more explicit criticism of military politicization and what the author perceives as being responsible for this, the national security doctrine. "To begin with, it is not 'national', in that it is not born within a country, but instead its origin (in the case of America) is the United States, which created this theory to defend its own interests and not ours." Author José Ismael De Mattei continues by arguing that when fighting internal enemies, "the armed forces become transformed into 'occupation troops' of their own countries. . . . Armies employed in this way begin to lose their 'national' character . . . of 'the last moral reserve of the fatherland', to become transformed in a 'party' in that they inevitably become politicized" (1983:82). Although criticizing the military's domestic battles remained not at all common (as discussed above), the call for an apolitical military—reflected in the quote—became much more so. Many members of the armed forces felt that the crises they suffered would not have occurred had the armed forces remained outside of politics.

The national security doctrine was thus significantly revised, if not entirely discarded. In some respects, the emphasis on values (rather than economic factors) in the Argentine national security doctrine may have facilitated its transformation. The military did not relinquish the idea that Argentina had significant potential internal threats to security, but the holistic concept of national defense faded. In other words, while members of the military generally believed that they should be prepared and permitted to fight against internal enemies (ostensibly armed), for the most part they did not seem to believe that controlling the government or the economy was a necessary or functional part of the package. In sum, by the end of 1983, the Argentine military seemed ready for a new and subordinate role within the Argentine state.

4

Quest for Control: Military Policies of the Alfonsín Government

After seven years of military rule, Argentines welcomed the new round of democratic rule in 1983. Yet a rocky path still awaited them. The new government confronted more than the usual tasks inherent in managing a democratic state; officials also faced the highly controversial issue of how to deal with Argentina's violent past. After the years of intense repression, many Argentines saw the transition to civilian rule as not only a chance to reestablish democratic freedoms but a chance to pursue retribution for the state-sponsored violence of the late 1970s.

At the same time, the armed forces, fragmented by their most recent bout with military rule and traumatized by their defeat in the Falklands/Malvinas war, were unable to negotiate a favorable transition. Uruguay's publically approved amnesty and Chile's preservation of the military regime's constitution and political presence were not shields available to the Argentine military. In Argentina, last-minute measures to protect the armed forces from legal retribution soon collapsed, as the outgoing regime had little power to back up its demands. Yet, from a historical perspective, the threat to the military still appeared minimal. In decades of alternating military and civilian rule, no Argentine civilian government had seriously attempted to confront the armed forces.

This time, things developed differently in Argentina. Aggressive policies toward the armed forces left them with decimated material resources and large numbers of officers facing the courtrooms. Before long, some within the military came to perceive Raúl Alfonsín as an extreme leftist, determined to destroy the armed forces and thereby create the necessary context for a communist revolution. By early 1987, sectors of the army had organized to defend themselves, launching the first of a series of dramatic military uprisings. The government responded with various concessions, yet the damage had already been done. Alfonsín and the Unión Cívica Radical (UCR) had been permanently branded as the military's enemies—an ironic twist after decades during which military leaders had sought the democratic defeat of a Peronist candidate.

Foundations of Raúl Alfonsín's Political Position

In the presidential elections of 30 October 1983, few predicted Raúl Alfonsín's triumph. A lawyer and longtime member of the UCR, Alfonsín had eyed the presidency since the previous period of civilian rule. With the 1981 death of the UCR's leader, Ricardo Balbín, Alfonsín's somewhat more leftist Renovación y Cambio [Renovation and Change] faction of the party was finally in the position to lead the party (Rock 1987; M. Acuña 1984). Alfonsín was known and respected, but not necessarily enough so to defeat the Peronist candidate, Ítalo Luder. Despite the Peronists' loss of their own chieftain, Juan Domingo Perón, loyalty to the movement remained high. Furthermore, Peronism had never lost an open presidential election, although the number of times the party had been able to compete was certainly limited. Finally, Luder was probably even more known than Alfonsín, although perhaps somewhat tainted by his position as president of the Senate and interim president during Martínez de Perón's catastrophic government of 1974–76.

The elections revealed an apparent change in the inclinations of the Argentine people: the Peronists lost the election, obtaining only 40 percent of the vote, in contrast to Alfonsín's 52 percent (Rock 1987:389). Explanations for the Radicals' triumph have ranged from concrete changes in the situation of the two parties to more general speculation about their respective images. On the one hand, the death of Perón and the reunification of the Radical party into a reconstructed Unión Cívica Radical were certainly advantages for Alfonsín. However, most explanations have more to do with image than concrete circumstances. The Peronists were, as always, the more dynamic, mobilizing competitors; or, from another perspective, they were the rabble-rousers. With the enhanced utilization of television during this campaign, along with the not-so-distant memories of the catastrophe of 1973–76, this image was particularly compelling. In addition, the Radicals made a concerted effort to enhance perceptions of the potential danger of the Peronists. Most explicitly, the Radicals achieved a significant advantage by reporting a presumed preelection accord between the Peronists and military leaders. Whether or not the agreement actually existed, the rumor was sufficient to antagonize vast numbers of people who were unwilling to see the military escape from retribution for the occurrences of the "dirty war."[1] On the other hand, Alfonsín, a moderately progressive lawyer, portrayed himself as the symbol of democratic procedures, the reinvention of legal boundaries, and, above all, balanced justice. As Wynia summarized the situation, "Most people wanted a respite from militarism, and the unspectacular Alfonsín, known more for integrity than charisma, seemed to offer the best possibility for achieving it" (Wynia 1992:108).

Some of the very reasons the voters chose to back Alfonsín were, for the military, the most threatening aspects of his impending presidency. His dedication to human rights was interpreted by the armed forces as unmitigated hostility toward them. The military policies pursued by the Alfonsín government succeeded only in strengthening that conviction, as well as contributing to suspicions that Alfonsín's politics lay too far to the left.

Fundamentals of Alfonsín's Political Position

Despite a greater emphasis on social issues than has been traditional in the Radical party, Alfonsín's writings do not reveal him to be the devout communist that many within the military perceived him as being. On some issues, his writings do vary through the years, ranging from highly balanced, moderate attempts to isolate the extremists and find a working solution to the ongoing conflicts, to occasional outbursts of frustration and even rage at the interminable obstacles to his political ideals. However, throughout the period analyzed, some clear continuities do exist. Alfonsín consistently demonstrated a high degree of nationalism, a sincere belief in the goals of progress toward social and economic equality, and, above all, an adamant allegiance to democracy (Alfonsín 1981, 1983, 1986, 1987a, 1987b, 1987c).

Alfonsín's nationalism is, in many respects, traditional within his political party, as well as being characteristic of the armed forces.

The primary components of Radical nationalism include: (1) rejecting foreign intervention and (2) advocating extensive government participation in the economy. In the history of the UCR, nationalism began with Radicalism's founder, Hipólito Yrigoyen, and was maintained during later years primarily by the UCRP. During the early years, the central nationalist issues concerned the petroleum industry. In Yrigoyen's era, nationalists fought to eliminate foreign ownership of petroleum companies. Similarly, one of Arturo Illia's (1963–66) most publicized policy decisions was the suspension of concessions granted to petroleum companies during Arturo Frondizi's (1958–62) government (Snow 1971:22–24; Rock 1987:208–10). In Alfonsín's essays, nationalism emerges primarily as a general determination to break away from the hold of international capital and foreign political influences, thereby reasserting Argentina's economic and political autonomy. Such sentiments have frequently been shared by sectors of the armed forces.

However, Alfonsín has also used nationalist doctrine to critique the postures of certain sectors within Argentina. The nation's economic elite are depicted as acting in collusion with foreign economic interests and against the best interests of their own country (1986: 258; 1983:31, 69). Alfonsín even denounced the internationally famous Madres de la Plaza de Mayo [Mothers of the Plaza de Mayo] as "antinational," probably due as much to their harsh criticisms as to their speculated connections to international communism. With respect to the armed forces, Alfonsín cushions his criticism by representing them as more pawns than actual culprits. Thus he portrays the national security doctrine (referred to as the continental security doctrine) as an entirely externally generated orientation that corrupted and seriously damaged the professional capacity of the armed forces (1983:55). He writes: "We have understood—this was our experience for recuperating the exercise of our sovereignty in the Malvinas—that our armies were trained and equipped to preserve a security scheme which we had not conceived. A scheme that looks after the security and interests of others" (52–53). Alfonsín thereby transfers the blame for the military's actions to outsiders. Nonetheless, few within the armed forces responded to his efforts to demonstrate sympathy.

Of more concern to the military was Alfonsín's position on social policies. This is also the aspect of Alfonsín's position that seems to deviate most from the traditional Radical position. Alfonsín openly advocates social democracy, along the lines of some of the Western Europe countries. His writings demonstrate an identification with the poorer sectors of society, criticizing the selfishness of the oligarchy and supporting increased economic distribution.

In certain respects, this aspect of Alfonsín's position was foreign to the UCR, historically considered the party of the middle class, rather than the working class. The middle sectors tend to be most interested in having more voice in government; the poorer sectors are usually more concerned with seeing more bread on their tables. It was Perón who initially responded to these concerns, rather than the UCR, thereby creating a formidable stronghold for Peronism within the working class. Alfonsín's worker-oriented discourse was, therefore, probably as much an effort to eliminate the Peronist political monopoly (concomitantly expanding the constituency of the UCR) as a true reflection of his ideological proclivities.[2]

Regardless of his motivation, Alfonsín's discourse remains moderate. He consistently refuses to accept the arguments of more extremist sectors that might prefer to sacrifice democratic procedures in order to achieve a better standard of living for the lower classes. For Alfonsín, democracy is nonnegotiable. Nonetheless, he depicts more progressive social policies as necessary to safeguard democracy: "One of the causes of Latin American political destabilization is that democracy has not succeeded in satisfying the expectations of the popular sectors, translated in requirements connected to social justice, and, definitely, with the dignity of man" (1983:31). Thus, Alfonsín argues that some shift toward more progressive social policies is desirable, and even essential, to achieve a stable democratic system.

1966–1973: Democratic Intransigence

Many of Radical leader Alfonsín's essays also reflected the traditional commitment of the UCR to procedural democracy, which generally took precedence over substantive issues. During the military regimes of 1966–73 and 1976–83, Alfonsín maintained an unwavering opposition to authoritarian rule. Nonetheless, that opposition did not necessarily transfer to the armed forces per se. Particularly in the earlier stages of this period, Alfonsín deliberately and explicitly differentiated the *military government* from the *military*. He confined his criticisms to the military leadership—those members of the armed forces directly responsible for the initiation and administration of military rule. Furthermore, his writings frequently portray these sectors as little more than unwitting pawns of the oligarchy.

Yet 1966 faded into 1967, 1968, and 1969, and a transition to democracy appeared equally distant. Meanwhile, the government's intolerance with dissent was becoming increasingly evident. In response, Alfonsín's focus shifted, and he began to question the armed forces as a whole, rather than just the leadership (1986:190–92). While he retained his inclination to differentiate levels of responsibility within the armed forces, his frustration with the lack of dissent by the less accountable sectors was also becoming evident.

Alfonsín continued to hope that civilian resistance might eventually force the military leadership to relinquish their hold on power. "Resistance to oppression" he wrote, "is an obligation, not a right" (1986:68). Yet Alfonsín appears not to have been particularly comfortable with violent resistance, either. His obvious preference was that opposition be exercised through words rather than weapons (175). The government's intransigence gradually took its toll, and Alfonsín's tolerance for more active resistance increased. In June 1969, he wrote: "The people [*el pueblo*] are morally obliged to resist oppression and poverty. If not, it would not be honest. Peace cannot be sought at the price of slavery. Many will prefer to lose their lives before losing the dignity of their lives. They cannot—they humanly cannot—discard violence in advance—even though they pray to avoid it—when violence is attacking them from the flanks" (191). Alfonsín remained firm, however, in his opposition to violent revolution. Violence as a defense against state violence may have been considered unavoidable; violence in order to achieve a new socioeconomic order was not.

The "Two Demons": Alfonsín's Preelection Position

Alfonsín's momentary acceptance of more aggressive strategies by the civilian opposition occurred before the height of terrorist activities in Argentina, however, as well as before the full-fledged organization of the countersubversive war. During the ensuing decade, Argentina's bloody 1970s, political violence became increasingly brutal. Correspondingly, Alfonsín's condemnation of the terrorist tactics became increasingly virulent.

Nonetheless, his earliest and strongest critiques were of the military's violations of human rights. In 1972, he described the military's methods of combating the guerrillas as "the whole range of sadism and perversion" (1986:263). A few years later, Alfonsín became a founding member of the Asamblea Permanente por los Derechos Humanos [Permanent Assembly for Human Rights], one of Argentina's principal human rights organizations (Leis 1989:31).

The doctrine that Alfonsín gradually generated to define his position toward the propagators of the political violence of the 1970s came to be referred to as the "theory of the two demons." In brief, the argument sustained that neither the guerrillas nor the military held exclusive blame for the violence. By the early 1970s, it had become apparent that both the military and armed groups of civilians were equally capable of employing excessive and unacceptable force. Alfonsín writes that "the Argentine man was marked and wounded during the last decade by a new type of violence, terrorist subversion, that with a method tending to provoke anxiety and chaos used the most cruel and repugnant methods, thereby demonstrating a total contempt for man and his dignity" (1981:50). Alfonsín thus avoided definitively aligning himself with either extreme of the political spectrum. In 1977, he summarized his position as follows:

> our enemy is not to the left or to the right. It is whoever sustains that the end justifies the means. Those who have thought in this manner are the dregs of history and are the great culprits of the most serious catastrophes of civilization. We repudiate the methodology of terrorism without even thinking about its objectives, but we also condemn those who sustain the convenience of forgetting the respect due to fundamental human values, for the sake of being more effective in the fight. (1987b:301)

Alfonsín's later proposals for dealing with the issue of human rights violations in the 1970s reflect an attempt to balance the distribution of blame. The proposals also exhibit a nuanced perception of culpability *within* the armed forces. Alfonsín distinguishes three groups of actors who had contributed to the countersubversive war: those who gave the orders, defining the tactics that would be employed; subordinates who exceeded their orders; and those who merely carried out orders (1983:148). According to Alfonsín, the first two groups were the ones that should be brought to justice. On the other hand, the last category, assumed to be the bulk of the participants in the repression, was not to be considered responsible for their actions.[3]

In sum, Alfonsín did not intend to condemn the military as a whole, nor to carry out an extensive battle against it. He did hope to permanently subordinate the armed forces to civilian rule and to establish and enforce laws that would deter any recurrence of the past. Yet, the readjustment of the military's position did not occur precisely as Alfonsín might have anticipated. The president's somewhat limited understanding of the military disadvantaged him from the start. This, combined with the actions of other powerful political actors within the decision-making setting, distorted many of his policies in such a way as to create the impression of a much more antagonistic position.

Decision-Making Setting

The military policies of the Alfonsín government emerged as the product of the interaction between the efforts of different members of the decision-making community—in other words, as an effect of all, intended by none. This counters some common perspectives of the all-powerful Latin American presidency. In most respects, the executive branch (especially the president and the Ministry of Defense) does hold primary responsibility for the armed forces. However, the Constitution designates significant powers over the military to the legislature. Furthermore, despite its normally relatively marginal role in military affairs, during the 1983 to 1989 period the judiciary also became quite significant. Finally, perhaps more than any other time in Argentina's history, organized interest groups (in particular, the human rights organizations) were also critical to the development of civil-military relations during this period.

Executive

Despite the many similarities between the majority of Latin American constitutions and the U.S. Constitution, presidents in Latin America tend to be far more powerful than in the United States. The primary cause of this difference lies in the context, which determines how formal rules and structures are implemented. In Latin America, a strong leadership tradition and a persistent situation of crisis have combined in such a way as to enhance the relative weight of the executive vis-à-vis the legislature and the judiciary. Furthermore, when Latin American constitutions differ formally from that of the United States, these discrepancies also tend to favor the executive. As Scott Mainwaring explains: "the vast majority of legislation in Latin American countries is initiated by presidents, and presidents have most of the capacity to implement policy. They can often veto specific parts of bills, while the U.S. president must veto or accept an entire bill. Presidents can push through many bills as 'executive decree-laws', which are automatically approved unless congress specifically vetoes them" (1990:12). In Argentina, as in most other Latin American countries, the ability of the president to discharge these legislative functions is further facilitated by a system of proportional representation that maximizes the control of party leaders over other party members.

Legislature

During the Alfonsín administration of 1983–89, the legislature emerged as the least significant of the three branches of government in regard to civil-military relations, despite its considerable formal responsibility for defense issues. According to Gustavo Druetta, congressional powers include control over the budget and recruitment, authorization of declarations of war, and "exclusive jurisdiction to legislate on the establishment of forts, arsenals, etc." (1988:4). The Senate is also responsible for approving promotions to high ranks within the armed forces (6).

This degree of formal power, combined with the governing party's limited control over Congress, created the possibility for the legislature to challenge UCR policies. The UCR held an absolute majority only in the lower house. In the Senate, the Peronists controlled twenty-one seats, in contrast to the UCR's eighteen, leaving the governing party without even a plurality (Mustapic 1986:17). The Peronists were therefore in a position both to initiate their own legislation and to block that of the Radicals.

Nonetheless, most of the legislature's activities involved acting as merely a rubber-stamp for the president's policies. As Mustapic writes, "Congress continues to be a body with little legislative initiative and poor capacity to react to the policies of government" (18). Overall, of the projects sanctioned by the Congressional National Defense Committee, none emerged without the support of the UCR (Druetta:1988). The one significant piece of defense legislation that was sanctioned at the instigation of an opposition party, the National Defense Law, failed to ever really be implemented, as is later discussed. Perhaps the major role of Congress during this period was therefore that of a forum, a place where dissenting views might be expressed, even if those views could not be easily acted upon. As Congressman Toma expressed with regret: "When there are coups d'état, there is a power that is destroyed, which is the legislative power, a power that becomes conditioned, that is the judicial power, and a power that becomes the core of the institutional system, that is the executive power. In a country that has had more years of dictatorship than of democracy, the executive has become gigantic . . . and there is practically no legislative tradition."[4] When asked about the degree of control that Congress had over the actions of government, Congressman Toma noted: "When they cannot get a law out, they create organisms by presidential decree." In other words, Congress remained highly subordinated to the executive during this period.

Judiciary

In contrast to the Congress, the judiciary emerged as a surprisingly powerful and independent force in the development of civil-military relations during the Alfonsín administration. Formally, the judiciary has little relationship to the issue of defense. Members of the Argentine military have historically been tried in military courts, consequently leaving the civilian system of justice entirely out of the picture.

The expansion of civilian judicial powers over the military in the 1980s emanated primarily from a single decision—the reform of the Código de Justicia Militar [Code of Military Justice]. This reform gave the attorney general the explicit right to initiate proceedings in cases related to the "repression of terrorism," along with limiting the amount of time the Consejo Supremo de las Fuerzas Armadas [military high court] could delay in producing a decision. The law also requires that all sentences of the military court be appealed before the

Federal Court of Appeals, thereby establishing the firm preeminence of the civilian courts (Law 20.049, Article 10).[5]

The long-silent courts stepped into their new role with enthusiasm on a few occasions, even taking the other branches of government by surprise. As federal prosecutor Luís Moreno Ocampo stated: "Really, in Argentina, the judiciary never was efficacious. . . . Suddenly we were effective with them, in a very complicated trial."[6] This sudden effectivity, in view of the common belief that the judiciary was subordinated to the executive branch, increased the conviction of many within the armed forces that the entire state mechanism was aimed against them.[7]

Human Rights Organizations

The civilian courts found their greatest allies in Argentina's famed human rights organizations. Throughout all the years during which the judiciary had been silenced, or forcefully subordinated to the purposes of the de facto government, several of the human rights organizations had been filling the gap, gathering information and collecting complaints often dangerous to openly recognize, much as the Vicariate of Solidarity did in Chile. The Madres de la Plaza de Mayo became the symbol of Argentina's human rights movement, with their regular Thursday marches outside of the presidential palace, the white handkerchiefs imprinted with names of disappeared sons and daughters tied around their heads, and the signs emblazoned with photographs of those about whose destinies they sought information. The Madres' use of the imagery of Christian motherhood made them particularly effective against the professedly Catholic military regime (Brysk 1994:48). The Madres de la Plaza de Mayo were, however, but one of several human rights groups, and the marches were just one of a variety of tactics taken by those groups.

The human rights community ranged from groups composed of relatives of the disappeared to religious organizations and explicitly political organizations, with an equal amount of variety in their methodologies (Brysk 1994; Leis 1989; Fruhling 1989; Osiel 1986; Sonderéguer 1985). The most extreme of those organizations tended to be the organizations of relatives, especially the Madres de la Plaza de Mayo and the smaller Familiares de Desaparecidos y Detenidos por Razones Políticas [Relatives of Those Disappeared and Detained for

Political Reasons]. These groups, along with the somewhat more moderate Abuelas de la Plaza de Mayo [Grandmothers of the Plaza de Mayo], concentrated on demanding the return of the missing people, with each emphasizing a slightly different focal group. The Familiares oriented most of their work around the causes of political prisoners, while the Abuelas directed their attentions toward returning the young children of the disappeared to surviving family members. Finally, the Madres had the broadest orientation of the three. Their hallmark demand was the "Appearance with Life" of all of the disappeared people. Although at earlier stages in the movement various other human rights organizations joined their voices with those of the Madres on this issue, it was the Madres who most persistently retained this stance, even long after it became clear that fulfilling that demand was impossible.[8] Similarly, the Madres also tended to be the most recalcitrant in insisting on the widespread prosecution of the military for violations of human rights.

Probably the most controversial position of the Madres and Familiares was the defense of the guerrilla groups by the more radical factions.[9] An article in the monthly publication of the Madres argues, in regard to the purported terrorists of the 1970s, that "the future will retrieve . . . the heroes and martyrs of the people, as we retrieve them. Because they were right."[10] Nor were the Madres alone in their vindication of the guerrillas. In an interview in the same publication, the Familiares were quoted as saying: "Familiares assumes the causes of their children's fight as their own, vindicates all the disappeared as fighters of the people, and understands that when in this country the situation for which these disappeared people fought occurs, that is, the defeat of imperialism and the sovereignty of the people, we will have achieved our objectives."[11] Thus, in a certain respect, the radical factions of the Madres and Familiares injured their own credibility by simultaneously portraying the disappeared as innocent victims of a cruel and unwarranted repression and as heroes fighting for a just cause.

For the most part, the other human rights organizations tended to be more moderate than the relatives' organizations. The Asamblea Permanente por los Derechos Humanos [Permanent Assembly for Human Rights], one of Argentina's earliest human rights organizations, was founded in reaction to the right-wing terrorism of the Triple A (Alianza Argentina Anticomunista) in the 1970s (Sonderéguer

1985:12). The Asamblea later evolved into a more generalized human rights advocate and, along with the closely related Centro de Estudios Legales y Sociales (CELS) [Center for Legal and Social Studies], began to focus largely on the formal, legal issues of human rights defense.

The remainder of the human rights organizations active during this period tended to have more international or religious orientations. For example, the Liga Argentina por los Derechos Humanos [Argentine League for Human Rights] was formed several decades before the Proceso de Reorganización Nacional, in connection with the Communist party. Servicio de Paz y Justicia (SERPAJ) [Peace and Justice Service], on the other hand, was formed as a regional Latin American organization with a Christian orientation, for the purpose of supporting the "poor, oppressed, and dominated in the search for justice, liberation and the surmounting of domination" (quoted in Sonderéguer 1985:12). Finally, the explicitly religious human rights organizations included Movimiento Ecuménico por los Derechos Humanos [Ecumenical Movement for Human Rights] and the smaller, less mentioned Movimiento Judio por los Derechos Humanos [Jewish Movement for Human Rights]. Of these organizations, SERPAJ was more frequently allied with the Madres, while the others tended to take more moderate stances (Fruhling 1989:13).

The variation among the purposes and political positions of the different organizations was accompanied by a corresponding variation among the roles that these groups filled. The Madres became the public face of the growing protests against human rights violations, both within Argentina and internationally. At the same time, however, other organizations were carrying out the quieter, more practical side of the battle. The Asamblea, for example, reportedly accumulated an archive of around seven thousand reports of purported crimes committed in the war against subversion (Leis 1988:4). CELS also accumulated a large archive of newspaper clippings and statements related to disappearances and human rights violations. CELS, however, also went beyond merely gathering information, concentrating as well on preparing and submitting lawsuits.

Alone, probably neither the human rights movement nor the judiciary would have exerted much influence on civil-military relations. The judiciary traditionally occupied a subordinate position to the executive branch, which, during the Alfonsín government, at various points indicated a preference for limiting the number and extent of trials of military officers. Even more significantly, the courts simply did not have the resources to independently pursue an extensive number of lawsuits regarding human rights issues. They had had neither the opportunity nor prior incentive to accumulate the necessary information and evidence. Organizations such as the Asamblea and CELS, however, did have both opportunity and incentive. Once legal groundwork was laid, permitting the initiation of human rights cases, these organizations filled in the gaps, using their vast archives and legal expertise to enhance the relevant capacity of the judiciary significantly beyond what might have been expected.

In sum, the executive branch maintained a predominant position in the process of creating the relationship between government and the military, but by no means did it enjoy complete control. The legislature remained fairly weak, but the judiciary actually found itself with new autonomy and influence. Finally, the human rights groups, with no official power, developed into an extremely powerful force, due to both their symbolic significance and their ability to fill a bureaucratic void created by the prior restrictions on the judicial system.

Outcome: Politics of Opposition

Despite important differences, all of the actors discussed above certainly shared one goal: to subject the military to civilian control. Furthermore, in this round of postauthoritarian rule, the government appeared to be in a relatively strong position to pursue this goal, in contrast to the more constrained governments of Frondizi, Illia, and, later, the combined experiments of Cámpora, Lastiri, Perón, and Martínez de Perón. Internationally, the 1983 transition to democracy came as part of a worldwide trend toward democratization. The apparent shift in U.S. foreign policy from promoting capitalism to emphasizing *democratic* capitalism was undoubtedly also advantageous. Finally, around the same time, the virtual collapse of communism diminished the likelihood of externally backed revolutionary movements, which in the past had frequently created support for military regimes.

Domestically, the new administration also profited from a favorable context. On the one hand, Alfonsín had won an absolute majority in an open election, a rare event in Argentine history. On the other hand, the military was relatively weak, much more so than those of Brazil, Chile, or Uruguay. The defeat in the Falklands/Malvinas war had torn the armed forces apart internally, forcing the transition and precluding them from imposing any restrictions on either the electoral process or the incoming government. Their one significant effort to do so, a hastily prepared self-amnesty law (Law 22.924, dictated on 22 September 1983) met a quick demise.

The context therefore favored a relatively aggressive approach toward subordinating the military. The degree to which the administration pursued this approach at the beginning of its term was reflected in a descriptive headline by an Argentine magazine: "The Military against the Wall."[12] When government leaders attempted to let the military slip away from "the wall," however, they found themselves obstructed by other political actors.

Designing the Future

The government's approach to tailoring the future of the armed forces emphasized diminishing the power and autonomy of the military, challenging the boundaries of the military caste, and erecting legal and organizational obstacles to domestic activity by the armed forces. In other words, all the major facets of the government's military policy—including material resources, military education, organization, and legal role definition—centered around the goal of reducing the threat from the military, rather than enhancing or readjusting their capacities to defend the country.

RESOURCES

All of the military's major material resources, including the budget, salaries, and number of conscripts, were quickly slashed under the Alfonsín government. In part, these reductions were undoubtedly necessary adjustments to a very difficult economic situation. In 1983, when Alfonsín inherited the Argentine economy, the national foreign debt had reached about $46 billion (Smith 1989:4). Inflation was essentially out of control (209 percent in 1982), and unemployment had climbed as well (Rock 1987:391).

Furthermore, despite the pretransition rhetoric that a democracy and economic success would go hand in hand, the Argentine economy continued to decline during the Alfonsín period. One major economic plan after another (Plan Austral in 1985 and then Plan Primavera in 1988) brought little more than short-term relief. By the beginning of 1987, inflation had again begun to rise, reaching an annual rate of 174.8 percent for the year (Smith 1989:23). The Plan Primavera permitted another momentary stabilization, but by the end of Alfonsín's government, inflation had again soared, this time easily passing the pretransition levels (Smith 1989:graph 1). In other words, the entire Argentine economy was in serious decline. Sections of the large middle class began sinking into relative poverty, and many Argentines found themselves forced to forgo their habitual daily steak. That the military was required to relinquish a few perquisites as well was not, therefore, incomprehensible.

The decision to reduce military resources, however, also formed part of the overall effort to diminish the weight of the armed forces and in this sense was clearly projected prior to the change in government. The electoral platform of the Unión Cívica Radical pledged to reduce military expenditures "drastically," adding that the military budget "in no case will exceed for the next period of government and in times of peace, as an average, 2% of the GNP" (UCR 1983:37). Although the reduction of the military budget was actually not this extreme, it was, nonetheless, quite significant. According to Thomas Sheetz, the proportion of the GDP allocated to the military diminished from a peak of between 4.7 percent in 1981 (shortly before the Falklands/Malvinas war) to 3.2 percent in 1984 (see table 3).[13] In many respects, this merely moved the military budget closer to normal levels, as indicated by the fact that between 1972 and 1975, the military's percentage of the GDP went no higher than 2.04 percent. Yet, the armed forces had not yet recovered from the Falklands/Malvinas war. According to Defense Minister Roque Carranza, by the middle of 1985, Argentina had still managed to replace only about 30 percent of the materials lost during the war."[14]

The decline in the overall military budget was accompanied by reductions in the size of the armed forces and by diminishing salaries. The number of soldiers drafted for the compulsory one year of military service shrank from 64,640 in 1983 to slightly under 25,000 in 1986 and 1987. The total increased slightly in the following two years, but remained well under half of what it had been previously (R. Fraga 1989:173).

For different reasons, the number of people training to become of-

Table 3
Military Expenditures in Argentina, 1972–1989

Year	Million $U.S.	% of Gross Domestic Product	Year	Million $U.S.	% of Gross Domestic Product
1972	965	1.85	1981	2700	4.72
1973	992	1.82	1982	2203	4.00
1974	991	1.67	1983	2499	4.39
1975	1278	2.04	1984	1980	3.23
1976	2293	3.79	1985	1681	2.84
1977	2483	4.01	1986	1760	2.90
1978	2699	4.73	1987	1899	3.72
1979	2814	4.67	1988	1832	3.36
1980	2561	4.20	1989	1461	2.72

Source: Data from Sheetz (1994):214.

ficers followed a similar decline, falling from 1,529 in 1983 to 781 in 1987 (173). In this case, the drop probably had more to do with the declining prestige of the armed forces than externally imposed constraints. A career in the military had ceased to be a very promising path for social mobility. Members of the military no longer seemed to be "living the good life," and the possibilities of achieving a position of political power, once undeniably part of the lure of the armed forces, began to appear less realistic. Budget constraints also interfered with the education of officers and noncommissioned officers, however, since the military schools were forced to reduce training periods in order to save funds.

The diminishing budget undoubtedly took its toll. Officers began to complain that they lacked bullets to practice shooting and fuel to fly their planes. Along with the NCOs, many lower- and middle-rank officers began to take second jobs to supplement declining salaries; by three o'clock any afternoon, army headquarters were deserted. With the combination of a decline in resources, extremely low morale, and increasing levels of internal factionalism, the military was far from being a prepared and capable force. On 23 January 1989, when Infantry Regiment number 3 of La Tablada was attacked by a group of about sixty guerrillas, the armed forces were in such disarray that the combined provincial police force, federal police force, and army delayed more than a day in repelling the attack. This was despite the fact that La Tablada is one of the more important Argentine military bases and that troops were called in to help from outside the Buenos Aires region. Military preparedness had sunk to a serious low.

SOCIALIZATION

The government also made a few attempts to resocialize the armed forces in accord with the needs of a democratic regime, a difficult goal to implement. On the one hand, there was a good deal of dissent about what should actually be done. Some talked about the democratization of the armed forces, in the sense of instituting democratic procedures and ideals internally. The argument was based on the observation that the principles of strict hierarchy and obedience that characterize military organizations are inherently authoritarian, thus leading to the conclusion that "democratizing" the armed forces would allow them to be more smoothly integrated into a democratic state. While this form of authoritarianism is natural to military organizations, a military that votes about what to do in combat would not likely last very long.

Enhancing ideological tolerance through education is also tricky, although less functionally determined. Even if textbooks could be controlled (and they could not), how a particular professor opted to interpret that text could not. As the appointment of professors remained under the complete control of the military, the content of courses was impervious to civilian efforts to intervene. Even those professors teaching nonmartial courses within the military schools were drawn from a select community, recruited for the most part from the conservative Catholic University.[15] Efforts to open the competition for these appointments were not very successful.

The most important reforms of military education that occurred during this period were initiated more from within the armed forces than from the Ministry of Defense, although these changes did correspond with the ministry's interest in more effectively integrating the military education system with the civil system. The project, which originated within the navy, promoted a system of exchange between the military schools and the civilian universities, allowing officers to study certain subjects in those universities (especially the Universidad Nacional de La Plata, la Universidad Tecnológica Nacional, and Universidad Católica de La Plata).[16] The plan was to facilitate the process of obtaining university degrees by military officers, thus enhancing opportunities in the civilian work arena. The air force and the army were somewhat slower to embark on such programs, although by the middle of 1989, these possibilities were increasingly being discussed. Doubts within the armed forces about whether such integration would risk "contaminating" the officers remained, however.

ORGANIZATION

The government also took a number of other measures designed to alter the future role of the military, including (1) organizational measures, such as restructuring the Ministry of Defense and formally eliminating the First Army Corps, and (2) legal role-defining measures, such as the Law for the Defense of Democracy and a new National Defense Law created to explicitly delineate the function of the armed forces.

The first of these reforms, the reform of the Ministry of Defense, sought to enhance the powers of the civilian-directed ministry (Law 23.023, República Argentina, *Anales de Legislación Argentina,* 1983: 4025–28). During the military regime, the Ministry of Defense had essentially served only administrative purposes, with all major decision making left in the hands of the military junta. Consequently, inheriting the Ministry of Defense initially gave civilians only limited control over military affairs. The new legislation thus transferred various powers from the heads of the three branches of the military (now called *jefes de estado mayor,* or "chiefs of staff," rather than "commanders") to the Ministry of Defense (Article 12). Among the areas now considered to be the domain of the Ministry of Defense were the military budget, defense production, research on issues related to defense, administration, logistics, and, above all, the formulation of national defense policy (modifications of Article 20 in Law 22.520, the previous ministries law, included in Article 1 of Law 23.023). At the same time, the military industries—previously under the control of the separate forces—also moved into the jurisdiction of the Ministry of Defense (Estévez 1990:85). The law thus significantly expanded the Defense Ministry's capacity to influence the armed forces.

The government also attempted to disband the First Army Corps, which had been based in Buenos Aires. The intent of the move was to shift the army away from the country's political center, thereby supposedly lessening the threat of military intervention. Nevertheless, the First Army Corps was really disbanded in name only. Control of the region shifted to the Second Army Corps in Rosario, but for the most part, the army suffered very little displacement. The Palermo headquarters continued to function, and nearby Campo de Mayo (located on the outskirts of the capital) remained Argentina's most important army base.

DEFINING ROLES

Finally, the Law for the Defense of Democracy (Law 23.077) and the National Defense Law (Law 23.554) attempted to legally limit the political role of the armed forces. The first attempt was the Law for the Defense of Democracy, proposed by the executive in December of 1983 and passed in August of 1984 (Sancinetti 1988:195–219). This law sought to increase the costs of any attempt to displace the constitutional regime, whether from the military or from the armed left (see chapter 7). The minimum penalty for leadership of a coup attempt (with no major consequences and in a nonwar context) increased from an earlier recommended sentence of eight to fifteen years in the 1951 Military Code of Justice to between eleven and twenty-five years of imprisonment. The law also shifted jurisdiction over cases of "illegal association" to the Federal Appeals, thereby discouraging renewed military investigations of "subversive" civilian groups.

In contrast, the main thrust of the National Defense Law (Law 23.554) was to legislate a separation of the areas of national defense and security, relegating the military to *external* defense. In contrast, matters of internal security were delegated to the police forces and border patrols (Gendarmería and Prefectura Naval), with details left to be elaborated in a future law. As Article 15 states, "Questions relative to the internal politics of the country shall under no circumstances constitute working hypotheses of military intelligence organizations" (República Argentina, *Anales,* 1988:1427). Yet despite the understandable concern of legislators with inhibiting any potential return to the military's domestic role in the 1970s, the separation of internal and external security functions was predicated on the assumption that Argentina would face no significant internal threat in the future. Unfortunately, in a region of the world long plagued with virulent and intransigent guerrilla movements, and in a context of declining economic conditions, this was perhaps unduly optimistic.

The law also creates a Consejo de Defensa Nacional [National Defense Council] to advise the president on matters of defense. The Consejo was to be composed primarily of the president, vice-president, and the National Cabinet, with the optional participation of the president and two representatives of each of the Congressional Defense Committees. Notably, the military chiefs of staff were only to be included upon the invitation of the Minister of Defense. Like the reform of the Ministry of Defense, this represented a deliberate effort to ban the military from any policy-forming roles, thus confining them exclusively to the position of armed bureaucrats.

The Defense Law is important for other reasons as well. Of all the different military policy measures that passed through the halls of Congress, this law probably showed the most significant participation by the opposition. The reform of the ministries and the budget passed through Congress, but, in these cases, Congress really only ratified what the administration had already decided (Druetta 1988: 33–35). The National Defense Law was, however, originally the initiative of the opposition Peronist party.[17] Members of the Peronist party began drafting the National Defense Law in 1983, under the assumption that they would win the presidency and would thus be in a position to enact the law. Confronted with a Radical presidency, the future of the initiative was far less certain, yet the authors opted to continue their efforts, and presented their project in May of 1984. Subsequently, the governing party presented its own national defense law, and a rare process of compromise and exchange was initiated between Argentina's two major political parties.[18] Over the following four years, more than a half-dozen National Defense bills were presented in Congress until, finally, in 1988, a law was passed incorporating measures that had been introduced by both the Peronists and the Radicals.

Nonetheless, the process of passing the National Defense Law in many respects further evidenced the limits of Congress. On the one hand, the seven proposed laws that were to accompany the National Defense Law (enumerated in Article 16), for the most part never moved much beyond the drawing board. Furthermore, the guidelines included in the law about the conditions under which the military should be utilized were not only nonbinding but also unworkable. Within a few months of the signing of the law, the military was fighting on the internal front, in the wake of the guerrilla attack at La Tablada. Nevertheless, the National Defense Law was a notable effort at redesigning the military's role.

Confronting the Past

The Alfonsín government's most dramatic initiatives concerned confronting the past more than constructing the future, however. It was not the budget cuts, nor the fortification of the Ministry of Defense, nor the National Defense Law that dominated national and international headlines. It was, instead, the phenomenon of bringing generals into the courtrooms. Never before had this occurred in South America; furthermore, the consequences stimulated such caution on the part of Uruguayans and Chileans subsequently considering such measures that such wide-reaching trials seemed unlikely to occur again.

The initiation of the human rights trials was among the government's earliest decisions. Within days of taking office, the new government ordered that the members of the first three juntas of the Proceso be tried for homicide, the "illegal deprivation of liberty," and the use of torture (Decree 158/83, Sancinetti 1988:175). The preamble to the law explicitly details the reasons for the trials and clearly reveals certain expectations and aspirations for their outcome. It stated that the first military junta and associated leaders of the armed forces "conceived and instrumented a plan of operations against the subversive and terrorist activity, based on glaringly illegal methods and procedures," and that "between the years 1976 and 1979, thousands of people were illegally deprived of their liberty, tortured, and killed as the result of the application of these procedures . . . , inspired by the totalitarian 'doctrine of national security'" (173). The trials, according to the preamble, would fundamentally restore a state of justice to Argentina.[19]

Almost simultaneously, a committee was formed to investigate the disappearances that occurred during the military regime (Decree 187/83, Sancinetti 1988:177–80). Although not granted judicial power, the Comisión Nacional Sobre la Desaparición de Personas

(CONADEP) [National Committee on the Disappearance of People] effectively supplemented the judiciary by facilitating the transfer of information and evidence from the human rights groups to the courts. The committee was only authorized to gather reports and evidence, and not to actually initiate cases, but given the weaknesses of the judiciary in this regard, this was sufficient. Other than the most radicalized members of the human rights community (such as the Madres), the human rights organizations willingly offered their aid and their archives to the CONADEP investigators. By the end of 1984, CONADEP had published their findings in a book entitled *Nunca Más* [Never Again]. At the same time, the committee had provided the courts with much of the material that they would need to prosecute military officers for human rights offenses.

LEGALIZING THE TRIALS

Initially, the process moved slowly. On the one hand, less than three months before relinquishing power, the outgoing military government enacted a law absolving themselves of responsibility for actions taken against presumed subversives (Asociación Americana de Juristas Law 22.924, 1988:22–23). On the other hand, even without the amnesty law, the system of military justice was such that almost all infractions committed by members of the military remained within the domain of military courts, where members of the military elite may well be unwilling to prosecute their colleagues. Legally, therefore, it was difficult for civilians to impose sanctions on members of the armed forces.

The Alfonsín administration moved quickly to eliminate these obstacles. Nine days after the trials had been ordered, Congress passed a law nullifying the military's amnesty law. The amnesty law was harshly criticized both for having attempted to "validate" the repression of the 1970s and for having unnecessarily extended the pardon to the military's internal enemies, the guerrilla leaders (Asociación Americana de Juristas 1988:181).

The reforms to the Military Code of Justice provided a contingency plan for the eventuality that the Consejo Supremo de las Fuerzas Armadas [military high court] might refuse to act, delay making a decision, or come to a decision that the government considered inappropriate (Law 23.049, *Leyes Sancionadas* 1984:1135–39). Along with requiring the military prosecutors to submit an appeal to the federal court of appeals, the law imposed a limit of six months for the military court to either reveal its judgments regarding the members of the military juntas or provide a full explanation to the federal courts as to why such a decision had not been reached. In the event of "unjustified delay or negligence," the federal courts would have the right to assume control over the cases (1138).

Nonetheless, the law also sought to shield some members of the military (Fontana 1987b:387). Thus, Article 11 indicates that military personnel who followed orders, acting without independent decision-making capacity, "barring evidence to the contrary," should be presumed to have "acted with unavoidable error respecting the legitimacy of the order received, except when consisting in committing atrocious or aberrant deeds" (Law 23.049, *Leyes Sancionadas* 1984: 1138). This measure has been interpreted as an effort to coopt lower-ranking officers in order to convert them into allies in the quest to convict their superiors; yet few were lured. Furthermore, the stipulation that individuals who had committed excesses could be tried blocked the courts from broadly applying the principle of "due obedience" (Acuña and Smulovitz 1993:5).

THE HUMAN RIGHTS TRIALS

The provisions for the transference of the trials to civilian courts proved to be indispensable, even though rather questionable legally.[20] The government's hope that the military hierarchy would respond to the challenge by issuing a critique and condemnation of their peers was clearly unrealistic. As their allotted six months came to a close, the Consejo Supremo still had not reached any kind of a verdict.

Finally, on 25 September 1984, the tribunal produced the required explanation for their failure to decide. In essence, the statement declared that (1) it would not be possible to obtain sufficient evidence within any foreseeable period to be able to reach a just decision, (2) that the individuals making the accusations were of dubious credibility anyway, since they were probably either members of the earlier guerrilla movements or relatives of those individuals, and (3) that the court remained unconvinced as to the illegal nature of the detentions under consideration, as those detained were regarded as dangerous criminals. Finally, the court proclaimed: "With reference to the responsibilities of the commanders in chief . . . according to the results of the present studies, the decrees, directives, orders of opera-tions, etc., that specified military action against the terrorist subver-sion are, in terms of content and form, unobjectionable and, conse-quently, [the commanders] could only be held responsible indirectly for the lack of sufficient control" (Asociación Americana de Juristas 1988:36). The officers concluded that they would be unable to reach a verdict within the required period.

The matter eventually passed to the civilian courts. Yet it was not until the following April that the trials began, with sentencing de-layed until December. The torpid appearance of the process ema-nated from its inherently complex nature. The nine members of the junta were being judged in terms of their liability for the totality of the countersubversive war—in all, several thousand individual cases. Each individual charge meant proving that the crime had been committed (difficult when the charge was murder and no body could be found) and then demonstrating that the defendant was responsi-ble for that crime. A thorough trial would therefore likely extend not months but years. Nevertheless, the trial did result in a guilty verdict for five of the nine defendants. General Videla and Admiral Massera, members of the first junta, were given life sentences, while Brigadier Agosti, General Viola, and Admiral Lambruschini were given lesser sentences. The charges in these cases included robbery, false im-prisonment, torture, and, in the cases of Videla and Massera, mur-der. Finally, Brigadier Graffigna, of the second junta, and all three members of the third junta, General Galtieri, Admiral Anaya, and Brigadier Lami Dozo, were absolved (Sancinetti 1988:46).

The apparent leniency of the sentencing again stimulated frustra-tion from many sectors of civil society, despite the difficulties of imposing any sentence at all. Yet the leniency was also deceptive. In-stead of imposing the harshest sentences possible on the junta mem-bers, thereby emphasizing their ultimate responsibility for the ex-cesses of the 1970s, the judges came to the conclusion that culpability was much more dispersed. Thus, in point 30 of the sentence itself, the judges ordered the Consejo Supremo de las Fuerzas Armadas to ex-tend the trials to the officers who had been commanders of the differ-ent zones and subzones during the countersubversive war, and to "all those who had operative responsibility in the actions" (San Martino de Dromi 1988, 2:559). The judiciary thereby thwarted the efforts of the executive branch of government to limit the breadth of the trials.

ESCALATION AND ATTEMPTED END TO THE TRIALS

The number of cases pending quickly expanded, as did their degree of penetration into lower levels of the military hierarchy. David Pion-Berlin writes, "In June of 1986, a Federal Court requested that the armed forces supreme council turn over some 300 additional cases (1700 charges) of junior officers—20 percent of whom were on active duty—to be tried on human rights offenses" (1990:29). According to Ernesto López, the total number of people awaiting trial around this time had reached approximately 1,700 (1988:61). Tensions within the armed forces rose concomitantly, and calls for amnesty resounded from various corners of the military community.

The government's first attempt to confront the situation entailed directly using the power of the executive to obstruct the landslide of human rights cases. Thus, in April of 1986, Minister of Defense Germán López directed an order to the Consejo Supremo to speed up the trials and to expand the application of the due obedience clause in the Military Code of Justice (San Martino de Dromi 1988, 2:560). The public uproar that followed the publication of this directive was so intense that López was forced to resign, and the earlier instructions were withdrawn.

Finally, in December of 1986, the legislature passed the Punto Final [End Point] law, according to which any human rights cases not yet under consideration would have to be initiated within sixty days of the date on which the law was published. Given that half of that period (the month of January) was a scheduled vacation for the courts, the Punto Final law seemed to hold substantial promise as an effort to end the tension-producing process of resolving the past.

Instead, the zealous courts suspended their vacations, dedicating all of their efforts toward the preparation of human rights cases.[21] As a consequence, more than 400 members of the military were added to the lists of those cited, which meant that trials could continue for quite some time (López 1988:66).[22] By early 1987, Rosendo Fraga reports that the number of military men being prosecuted for human rights violations had reached around 450 (1989:111). For the military, this went far beyond an acceptable level of sacrifice.

OBEDENCIA DEBIDA

With no end in sight to the human rights trials, the tensions long brewing within the middle and lower strata of the army exploded into a full-fledged military uprising in April of 1987, as is discussed in the following chapter. The government reacted to the uprising by soliciting an even more definitive reduction of the human rights trials. This time it was successful. Less than two months later, in early June, the administration had succeeded in convincing Congress to pass an Obedencia Debida [Due Obedience] law, which effectively reiterated and expanded the assumptions of the due obedience clause included in the reform of the Military Code of Justice (Law 23.521, República Argentina, *Boletín Oficial,* no. 26.155, 9 June 1987). The Obedencia Debida law declared that all members of the military who had been below the rank of colonel during the years of the countersubversive war could not be considered punishable for any crimes that were committed as part of their military duties. Instead, the law declares that those people would be assumed to have acted "in a state of coercion, subordinated under superior authority, and in compliance with orders, without the power or possibility of inspection, opposition or resistance to them in regard to their suitability and legitimacy" (1). The number of military personnel awaiting trial almost immediately shrank to less than a quarter of the prior total (R. Fraga 1989:120). Nonetheless, by this point, the damage to the relationship between the armed forces and the Alfonsín government was irreparable. The reduction of military tensions was, at best, only temporary.

Conclusion

The Alfonsín government's original plan to subordinate the armed forces by launching a widespread offensive, encouraging younger officers to disassociate themselves from the repression instigated by their superiors and balancing the administration's critiques of the military with equally virulent critiques of the armed left apparently failed. However profoundly divided the military may have been, they shared their belief in the necessity of the repression (see González Bombal 1991). By early 1987, and increasingly so thereafter, it became highly evident that if younger officers had disassociated themselves from the military leadership, it had not occurred as part of a process of transferring their allegiances to the civilian government. Furthermore, the military as a whole appeared unconvinced by the government's half-hearted efforts to include the guerrillas among the ranks of those responsible for the bloodshed of the 1970s. Thus, instead of perceiving the administration as an objective custodian of justice, the military increasingly came to perceive the government, and particularly Alfonsín, as the enemy of the armed forces.

How did this situation occur? As discussed above, Alfonsín's early discourse did not reveal such a predilection. His advocacy of human rights was unwavering, as was his dedication to a democratic system, but this did not seem to be accompanied by any generalized hostility toward the armed forces. Rather, the source of the growing rupture in the relations between the government and the military emanated from the cumulative impact of different political actors.

The disparate actions of the executive branch of government, the human rights groups, the judiciary, and even the legislature combined to create an approach to military policy that tended to be aggressive rather than cooperative. Of the policies discussed in this chapter, only in the area of education were efforts oriented toward solutions that could potentially benefit both the military and the civilians. Most other policies restricted or sanctioned the armed forces. Thus the budget cuts were unaccompanied by any positive, professional restructuring of the armed forces, the human rights trials quickly deteriorated into a generalized public condemnation of the military institution, and the National Defense Law managed to designate those areas where military action was prohibited, but failed to provide the armed forces with guidelines as to what hypotheses of conflict *should* direct their efforts. For the armed forces, the government's failure to reward them symbolically with praise and recognition cemented convictions that Alfonsín was hostile to them.

Finally, the few initiatives that were intended to placate the military, such as Punto Final and the Obedencia Debida laws, were reactions to pressure and mixed in their consequences. Again, these measures cannot be easily interpreted as indicating any concerted effort to define a positive role for the armed forces within a democratic state. Hence, the final result of the quest for control was not so much the institutional subordination of the armed forces as the alienation of the armed forces.

5

Emergence of Rebellion:
Origins of Factionalism

In April of 1987, more than three years after the Proceso de Reor-ganización Nacional, Argentina's military again exploded into the news. From their Escuela de Infantería [Infantry School] stronghold, the leaders of the rebellion proclaimed that they would no longer en-dure the existing state of affairs within the armed forces. To a weary and wary national audience, only one thing seemed clear: the rebels were a threat. The camouflage makeup that they donned appeared not as the intended symbol of battlefield professionalism but, in-stead, as a frightening representation of clandestine violence. The men with the weapons were hiding their faces. Many Argentine by-standers intuitively assumed that a coup was in the making, and their fledgling democracy was already collapsing.

Yet none of the four military uprisings that occurred between 1987 and 1990 metamorphasized into a coup d'état. Furthermore, most indications are that the leaders of the rebellions had no inten-tion of overthrowing the government, at least in the first three epi-sodes. Finally, the lack of such rebellions in the Brazilian, Chilean, and Uruguayan transitions indicates that such crises are by no means an inevitable part of postauthoritarian adjustment. Why, then, did the rebellions occur, and what did they mean?

The eruption of the Argentine armed forces in 1987 revealed three distinct components of rebellion: origin, form, and evolution. The advent of military reaction derived from multiple layers of formative conditions and events. Argentina had a long history of military in-volvement in politics, maintained and bolstered by various legal and material incentive structures (discussed in chapter 7). More recently, while in many respects the military regime of 1976–83 encouraged the rejection of military rule by both the armed forces and civilians, the repression of those years helped stimulate a strong backlash against the armed forces by sectors of civil society. Finally, the military policies of the Alfonsín government provided the catalyst for a military reaction, by exacerbating civil-military conflicts rather than ameliorating them.

A military reaction could be predicted from these historical layers, yet the form of that reaction could not. Instead, the composition of the uprisings reflected the more particular history of cumulating and deepening cleavages within the army. Those cleavages began with inherent bureaucratic tensions and divisions within the organization and were then deepened through a series of differing experiences. The challenges posed by the Alfonsín government provoked the ultimate fracture of the army along those lines, beginning in 1987.

Factions in the Intramilitary Crises

Factionalism is to some extent inherent to such complex organizations as modern militaries and by no means new to Argentina (see J. García 1978). Yet the particular lines dividing the armed forces vary. The cleavages that defined military factionalism in the mid-1980s fell partially along the lines of military specialization, professional role and wartime experience, and ideology (see table 4). By far the most prominent cleavage, however, was horizontal, between those officers who were colonels in 1987 and those below that rank. As discussed in chapter 3, the experiences of the countersubversive war, the Falklands/Malvinas war, and the military government of 1976–83 played a large role in separating the top leadership of the army from those officers at the intermediate levels. The high command's cooperation with the antagonistic policies of the civilian government also contributed to the disaffection of the lieutenant colonels with their leaders.

Yet the origins of the various intramilitary splits (including the horizontal cleavage) can be traced back much further. Some latent cleavages are relative constants, generated by either bureaucratic divisions or conflicts between bureaucratic and professional norms. Ideological rifts, while not necessarily inherent to the military institution, do have a long history in the Argentine armed forces. Finally, certain early experiences, particularly the period of initial training in Colegio Militar Nacional [Military Officers' School] also contributed to the split between the lieutenant colonels and their superiors.

Table 4
Army Cleavages during Alfonsín's Presidency, 1987–1989

Cleavages	Rebels	Legalists
Horizontal	Middle- and lower-ranking officers	High-ranking officers (generals and colonels)
Vertical (branch)	Infantry	Cavalry, artillery
Professional	Warriors	Managers
Ideological	Nationalists	Liberals
Political	Peronist	Neutral

On the one hand, the timing and content of the military education is at least in part responsible for the development of the different ideological and political propensities of the two generations. On the other hand, the shared experience of military training also contributed to the development of a particular cohort that, after years of shared ideas and experiences, eventually emerged as the core leadership of the initial Operación Dignidad [Operation Dignity] rebellions. Thus, at the inception of the rebel movement, bureaucratic and experiential cleavages were crucial in determining which actors entered which coalitions. As the movement progressed, some of the earlier cleavages faded in importance, to be replaced by new lines of dispute drawn by the rebellions themselves.

Bureaucracy and Professionalism

Military organizations are complex bureaucracies with a multiplicity of functional divisions. Those divisions affect not only the ways in which the military organizes work but also the ways in which it may fracture in the face of other kinds of challenges. Although on the surface the rebellions of the late 1980s certainly constituted a rejection of the Alfonsín government's military policies, they also reflected these underlying cleavages, and the experiences that over time had deepened them to the breaking point. Lines between the army, navy, and the air force, lines between the infantry, cavalry, and artillery, and, finally, lines between those in combat positions and those in managerial positions created the foundations for the evolving boundaries of factionalism. Which of those divisions became important and how they were actualized in the discourse and content of the later uprisings was the product of a series of circumstances and experiences.

The Faces of Professionalism: Warriors and Managers

One of the principal cleavages separating the rebels from the legalists surrounded the issue of professionalism. Each sector defined itself as the "professionals," with each interpreting the term quite differently. The rebels' notion of professionalism corresponded to the notion of the professional warrior, the expert in the arts of the battlefield distinctly separate from the civilian world (Waisbord 1991). Their leaders—first, Lieutenant Colonel Aldo Rico and, later, Colonel Mohammed Alí Seineldín—were both members of the Commandos, the army's elite fighting unit. They dressed for the uprisings in green camouflage uniforms, with black grease paint smeared across their faces. The image was clearly one of men who had trained for and experienced warfare. On the other hand, the legalists represented a very different form of professionalism. Their uniforms were the buttoned and pressed uniforms of the office. Their symbolic "home" was the Army Staff Building, rather than the battlefield. Professionalism, according to these sectors, meant restraint and discipline; certainly not the angry breaking of ranks instigated by the rebels.

Which of the two groups represented *professionalism,* and how could such different interpretations of the same concept exist within one institution? The answer to the second question perhaps reveals the answer to the first. The difficulty with defining and identifying professionalism within the military derives from the fact that the military institution encompasses both a profession and an organization (Janowitz 1961; Janowitz and Van Doorn 1971; Van Doorn 1965). The behavioral criteria inherent in each of these aspects are, furthermore, occasionally contradictory. This does not mean that bureaucratic norms are necessarily unprofessional, however. Rather, they may be quite professional, but professional for the *organization* instead of the *individual.* It is my contention that in the intramilitary conflicts between 1987 and 1989, the behavior of the rebels in many respects did correspond to professional norms, at the level of the individuals involved. On the other hand, the behavior of the legalists was appropriate to a professional organization.

According to Samuel Huntington, a profession is characterized by three essential traits: expertise, responsibility, and corporateness (1957:8). On the basis of this definition, Huntington argues that the military should be considered a profession. Military officers are experts in the "management of violence"; they are responsible to a specific client, usually the state; and they identify with a group sharing both their specialization and a set of ethical norms. Although Huntington recognizes alternatives, most interpretations of his work have concluded that military professionalism encourages apoliticism. By virtue of the functional specialization that supposedly occurs in the context of societal modernization (Durkheim 1933), the military expertise of the armed forces should theoretically mean their absence from the domain of political expertise.

Yet, the evidence from Latin America rather emphatically clashes with this eminently logical argument. In the 1960s and 1970s, Latin America's most highly developed countries, those with the most technologically advanced militaries, were also the countries that experienced the highest levels of military intervention (O'Donnell 1973, 1988; Stepan 1973; Collier 1979). Alfred Stepan explains this by an expanded definition of professional expertise (1973). Control of national defense was transformed into control of national security. Control of security includes not only explicitly military functions but political and economic functions as well.

Another reason that professionalism may not correspond with apoliticism derives from the differing implications of professionalism at the individual and bureaucratic level. This is perhaps evidenced less by the advent of bureaucratic authoritarianism, in which case military insubordination assumes the dimensions of military government, as by the recent episodes of military rebellion. In this case, the character of military insubordination arose at least partially from the conflict between individual professionalism and contrasting bureaucratic norms. The nature of military rebellion brings the armed forces into the political arena, despite the primarily institutional nature of their goals and general lack of civilian allies.

The relationship between these sets of norms has been explored most extensively in an article by Jacques Van Doorn, entitled "The Officer Corps: A Fusion of Profession and Organization," in which he argues that the primary difference between the professional and the bureaucrat is that the former "has a commitment to his vocation"

(1965:262), while the primary commitment of the latter is to the organization.

The loyalty of the military officer is divided, however. Loyalty is directed both toward the profession and toward the employing organization. In part, this derives from the nature of the military tasks. The military profession is to engage in violence on behalf of the client, the state. That violence is directed against other militaries, equally professional organizations, acting on behalf of their clients.

This bureaucratic component distinguishes the military from most other professions. First, the success of a military organization depends on tightly coordinated, highly disciplined action. This requires a very hierarchical form of decision making, far different from the more democratic patterns present in most professional organizations. Secondly, the nature of the commitment made by the military professional is an extreme one, in that it demands that he or she be prepared to kill and be killed in defense of his or her client. It requires an unusual level of loyalty to both the client and to the employing organization.[1] The result of this dual commitment to the profession and organization is that the different components of professionalism—rather than forming the basis for military unity, consensus, and relative apoliticism—can instead provoke internal dispute.

Professional and Organizational Norms in the Rebellions

In the Argentine military of the late 1980s, bureaucratic and individual professionalism were clearly at odds. Each of the features described by Huntington—expertise, responsibility, and corporateness—provoked conflicting notions of professionalism. Typically, one sector defended bureaucratic criteria, the criteria for a professional organization, while the other group defended individual professionalism.

The most explicit example of this is the debate that emerged over the meaning of the term *expertise,* the true heart of professionalism. As discussed above, the rebels defined themselves as the warriors, while the legalists' authority rested primarily on hierarchy and managerial expertise. The tension between these positions is certainly not novel. Morris Janowitz writes, "The history of the modern military institution can be described as a struggle between heroic leaders, who embody traditionalism and glory, and military 'managers,' who

are concerned with the scientific and rational conduct of war"
(1961:21).

A similar dualism has been noted in other kinds of organizations
as well as a response to the concomitant needs of organizations for
rationality and for innovation. The warrior-versus-manager conflict
also emanates from the conflict between professional and bureaucratic norms. The "warriors" (rebels) espoused values of the professional individual: skill in the use of violence and prestige based on the
demonstrated use of that expertise. On the other hand, the "managers" (legalists) advocate the values of the organization—hierarchy,
authority deriving from seniority, and, above all, following the rules.

The legalists' loyalty to hierarchical order and organizational procedure also permeated their interpretation of the professional criterion of "responsibility to a client." Yet, this appears to have placed
the legalists in the more classically "professionalist" position. The
client of the military institution is, conventionally, the state. In a
democratic system, the state is represented vis-à-vis the armed forces
by its highest elected officials, Congress and the president. In the context of the rebellions, the legalists defended the constituted order and
the rights of their client (the state) to impose certain demands on the
organization and its members.

In contrast, the rebels subjugated responsibility to the client to responsibility and loyalty to their corporate groups, or colleagues,
which they interpreted as loyalty to the institution. The external client was defined, furthermore, as the nation rather than the state. The
use of this definition of the military's role, which has been a recurrent
tendency in Argentina, provided the rebels with a more flexible
means of determining and legitimizing their actions. The interests of
a nation cannot be expressed by its constituents; they can only be as-
cribed by others. Thus, defining the client as the "nation" allows
members of the military to impose their beliefs and values on the si-
lent client, while technically maintaining professionalist behavior.

Finally, while loyalty to the corporate group was a commonality
between the two sectors, interpretations of how to express that loyalty again varied greatly. In this case, however, both perspectives
integrated professional and bureaucratic norms on their interpretations of the obligations of different hierarchical strata to the institution and the group. The expectations of the two sectors emanated
from a similar belief in the familial nature of intraforce relations. Ac-

cording to the rebels, their superiors had violated their obligations, thereby betraying the corporate group. Correspondingly, the organizational leadership (the generals) was expected to fulfill approximately the same role as parents: to provide guidance and discipline to their "family," the lower ranks, and to protect the organization and its members from the uncertainties and aggressions of the outside world. This adoption of the expectations and patterns of interactions inherent in family organizations thereby provides the armed forces with a creative way of integrating the frequently conflicting concerns with hierarchy and unity, thereby fusing certain professional and bureaucratic norms. At the same time, however, it also creates an additional set of expectations about the obligations of group members to one another. At the time of the uprisings, the rebels felt that their superiors had not done their "parental duty" in protecting lower-ranking officers. From their perspective, the generals' inadequate leadership—primarily manifested by their cooperation with the government's military policy—liberated the subordinate ranks from their obligation to obey.

The largely loyalist generals shared the rebels' vision of the military "family" and had fully incorporated the role of protector and caretaker. However, the military command had a distinctly different evaluation of the extant situation. They maintained that they had by no means failed to protect their subordinates, but had opted to use more gradual and less conspicuous channels than the rebels might have desired.[2] Like wayward children, the lower-ranking officers and NCOs had prematurely abandoned patience, refusing to trust their leaders' experience and loyalty.

Bureaucracy and the Rivalry between Arms

In contrast to the rivalry between managers and warriors, the rivalry between the different arms arises from inherently bureaucratic divisions. On the one hand, rivalries between the different services of the military and, within the army, between the different branches are essentially universal to military organizations, stemming from the natural competition for resources. On the other hand, these rivalries also have a foundation in the different functional roles of these branches, the backgrounds of those associated, and corresponding variations in the political attitudes of their memberships.

The Argentine army is divided into five branches, three primary and two secondary.[3] The secondary branches are communications and engineering, which, though of increasing functional importance given the highly technological nature of modern warfare, nonetheless have had less impact politically. The primary branches, which collectively form the bulk of the officer corps, are the infantry, cavalry, and artillery.

The roles of these branches have become far more complex than in the days of early modern warfare, when territory was the principal focus of war, and battles were fought using limited weapons in relatively restricted locations. However, the original functions still influence the political orientations of the army branches and the attitudes of their members. The infantry, for example, still has the primary task of occupying territory, thus requiring perhaps the highest degree of cooperation and camaraderie. The physical occupation of territory is also one of the most dangerous and probably least personally rewarding tasks of the army. Thus, for individuals with more privileged backgrounds and consequently more available options, the infantry is not commonly the branch of choice.[4]

In contrast, the cavalry historically has tended to recruit from more aristocratic sectors of society, due to their greater exposure to horses. For most purposes, horses have long since been replaced by tanks. Yet the symbol remains—cavalry officers are still expected to be equestrians, and participation in such sports as polo is both customary and encouraged. Along with biasing selection toward elites, the emphasis on horsemanship also facilitates interaction between these officers and civilians, particularly the aristocrats who can also be found on the polo fields. Thus, the cavalry has gained the reputation as the branch most in sympathy with these sectors.

Finally, the principal function of the artillery is to man the "big guns," such as cannons and other long-range weapons. In contrast to the infantry and the cavalry, the artillery is probably most aptly described as being composed of technicians. Thus, Janowitz writes that in the U.S. armed forces, "The aristocracy first gave way to the middle class in the artillery and the technical services, where specialized technical training was required. In the more honorific cavalry, with its natural link to feudal life, the upper social stratum concentrated its numbers in the face of military expansion" (1961:94–95).

Due to the numerical preponderance of the infantry and the relative prestige of the cavalry, the leadership of the army has emanated disproportionately from these two branches. Of twenty-one generals heading the army from 1959 until 1989 (commanders in chief and subsequently chiefs of staff), 10 were from the infantry, 6 from cavalry, only 2 from artillery, and 3 from engineering. None were from communications (see table 5). The majority of the political and ideological leaders of the army have also sprung from these sectors, with more nationalist and Peronist officers originating in the infantry and more liberal leaders (in the Argentine sense) emerging from the cavalry.

During the early rebellions, the branches manifested essentially these same propensities. The rebels, identified as nationalists, drew heavily from the ranks of the infantry, while the cavalry tended to remain allied with the more "liberal," and in this instance "legalist," sectors of the army. Members of the artillery played an inordinately important role, however, as two of Alfonsín's army chiefs of staff (Ricardo Gustavo Pianta and José Dante Caridi) were from this branch. Thus, the artillery also tended to be allied with the legalist position.

The Forgotten Heroes?

The coalitional propensities of different branches and specializations of the armed forces had more immediate antecedents, however, in the Falklands/Malvinas war. The relative prestige obtained by different branches and specializations, and the degree to which the different forces remained intact, affected both the likelihood that groups would rebel and the ability of different groups to lead.

According to Turner, "The air force came out of the war with the most glory, because its missiles were able to destroy several British ships, inflicting considerable loss of life. The navy, whose leaders had been the most bellicose before hostilities, prudently kept its ships near the Argentine mainland, out of reach of British nuclear submarines and Harrier aircraft, especially after the loss of the cruiser General Belgrano." On the other hand, "Most mistakes were made in the army campaign on the ground" (1983:60).

However, performance within the army was by no means uniform either. For example, in comparison to the other major arms, the cav-

Table 5
Army Commanders in Chief, 1958–1991

Dates	Name	Specialization
May 1958–July 1959	Hector Solanas Pacheco	N/A
July 1959–March 1961[a]	C. S. Toranzo Montero	Cavalry
March 1961–April 1961	Rosendo María Fraga	Infantry
April 1961–April 1962	Raúl Alejandro Poggi	Engineering
April 1962–Aug. 1962	Juan B. S. Loza	Infantry
Aug. 1962–Sept. 1962	Juan Carlos Lorio	Infantry
Sept. 1962–Nov. 1965	Juan Carlos Onganía	Cavalry
Nov. 1965–Dec. 1966	Pascual Angel Pistarini	Cavalry
Dec. 1966–Aug. 1968	Julio Rodolfo Alsogaray	Cavalry
Aug. 1968–May 1973	Alejandro A. Lanusse	Cavalry
May·1973–Dec. 1973	Jorge Raúl Carcagno	Infantry
Dec. 1973–May 1975	Leandro Enrique Anaya	Infantry
May 1975–Aug. 1975	Alberto Numa Laplane	Infantry
Aug. 1975–July 1978	Jorge Rafael Videla	Infantry
July 1978–Dec. 1979	Roberto Eduardo Viola	Infantry
Dec. 1979–June 1981	Leopoldo F. Galtieri	Engineering
June 1981–Dec. 1983	Cristino Nicolaides	Engineering
Dec. 1983–July 1984	Jorge Hugo Arguindegui	Artillery
July 1984–March 1985	Ricardo Gustavo Pianta	Artillery
March 1985–April 1987	Héctor Luis Rios Ereñú	Infantry
April 1987–Dec. 1988	José S. Dante Caridi	Artillery
Dec. 1988–July 1989	Francisco E. Gassino	Infantry
July 1989–March 1990	Isidro Cáceres	Cavalry
March 1990–Nov. 1991	Martín Bonnet	Engineering
Nov. 1991–	Martín Balza	Artillery

Source: Names and dates were facilitated to me by the Estado Mayor General del Ejército (Jefatura de Personel). Specializations were obtained from Ejército Argentino, *Boletín Publico del Ejército* and *Escalafón del Ejército Argentino;* Potash (1980); and Rouquie (1982b).

[a]For approximately one day in September 1959, the Army Commander in Chief was Pedro Francisco Castiñeiras. Toranzo Montero subsequently resumed his command.

alry played an extremely minimal role, probably due to both the characteristics of the terrain and the difficulties of transporting tanks. Only one cavalry squadron participated, although apparently with a high level of performance (Ejército Argentino, *Boletín Público del Ejército,* no. 4454, 30 March 1983). On the other hand, the infantry had an extremely heavy presence (nine infantry regiments were present), but was not particularly successful. In fact, because of the lack of sufficient backup and supplies, two regiments apparently surrendered without having ever fought (Comisión Rattenbach 1988:292). The artillery was also significant in the Malvinas war (five artillery groups) and, in contrast to the infantry, was considered to have performed quite heroically (Comisión Rattenbach 1988:202; Goyret 1984:22). Also considered particularly daring and competent within the army were the army pilots.

The unrivaled stars of the Falklands/Malvinas war, however, were the Commandos, the Argentine army's special forces. The Commandos are small, elite troops, largely composed of members of the infantry, although other branches of the army are also represented. All together, the two companies of Commandos (601 and 602) comprised only 111 men, including officers and NCOs. Of these, however, a full 19, or 17 percent, were decorated for their actions in the war. Of the 39 officers, an astounding 13, or 33 percent, were decorated (Ruíz Moreno 1986:447–50). With the Falklands/Malvinas war, the Commandos, already known by some for their early actions in Tucumán, fully came of age as a small but extremely important army elite.

The Commandos' prestige permitted them to play a particularly prominent role in the intramilitary conflicts of the late 1980s. Members of the Commandos were universally recognized as the prototypical warrior-professionals. Furthermore, their actions in the war with Great Britain were actions that *could* be openly recognized and lauded, rather than carrying the stigma that accompanied actions associated with the countersubversive war. At the same time, the military role of the Commandos enhanced the propensity of these individuals to rebel. The kinds of operations that Commandos are trained to carry out demand independent thought and decision making. The official requirements for becoming a Commando include the following description of Commando operations and the individual qualifications sought from potential candidates:

1. The management of the forces in the operational and tactical field needs to include the realization of operations that exploit the vulnerabilities of the enemy, in the depths of their territory or deployed in accordance with the combat setting, with the object of serving other military operations.

2. These operations require execution by relatively small groups, perfectly organized, instructed and equipped to operate in difficult situations.

3. For these circumstances, it is necessary that our army includes in the different organizations personnel who are specially qualified—intellectually, physically and spiritually—to advise, plan, direct and execute operations behind enemy lines, in support of a future or current operation. (Ejército Argentino, *Boletín Público del Ejército*, no. 3809, December 1971: Anexo 3).

Commandos must therefore be able to design their own plan of action during crisis situations. This emphasis on independent thought naturally transfers to other spheres of actions as well, increasing the Commandos' inclination to question the orders passed through the military hierarchy, despite the extreme emphasis on obedience in the armed forces. The unorthodox organizational norms of the Commandos augment this inclination, in that Commando units frequently ignore, or even invert, traditional hierarchies. Isidoro Ruíz Moreno notes that in the Commando training, officers often find themselves under the command of lower-ranking officers or NCOs who nonetheless have more experience as Commandos (1986:38). In sum, a variety of conditions facilitated the emergence of the Commandos as central to the rebel movement: they were highly unified internally, accustomed to forming their own conclusions, prone to rapid and decisive action, and able to command the respect of even less sympathetic colleagues.

The religious inclinations of the Commandos were also key to developing the content of the *carapintada* ideology. The "spiritual qualifications" referred to in the *Boletín Militar Público* are actualized as frequently doctrinaire Catholicism. Only declared Catholics are accepted as Commandos, and a former Commando reported having been compelled to pray the rosary on a daily basis. As this retired colonel explained, "What happens is that an institutional theme is combined with a theme of ideological fanaticism, of religious fanaticism that some of the instructors have instilled." Thus, the Commandos stood out not only as exceptional warriors within an already armed institution but as devout (sometimes extremist) Catholics within an already Catholic community.

Politics and Ideology

The political and ideological inclinations of the Argentine armed forces have perpetually intrigued concerned observers. Not surprisingly, in the rebellions of the late 1980s, these issues again surfaced. In some ways, the divisions along ideological and political lines replicated those of the past half century. Again, different factions of the military were identified as alternatively liberal or nationalist. Again, attitudes toward Peronism contributed to factional differences. However, perhaps one of the most intriguing aspects of the new military cleavages was the degree to which these oppositions and definitions had actually changed or, in some regards, even regressed to those of an earlier era. In particular, important strains of nationalism had evolved in such a way as to give a new tenor to the liberal-nationalist cleavage. The issues and divisions surrounding Peronism also appeared to have undergone a significant metamorphosis, or perhaps regression. In this respect, the army no longer resembled that of the 1950s and 1960s; instead, it appeared once again to have fallen into the patterns of the 1940s, the decade of Peronism's birth.

Nationalism and Liberalism; Peronism and Anti-Peronism

During the 1950s and 1960s, the military's ideological tendencies tended to have a rather complicated relationship with their political attitudes toward Peronism. Peronism emerged from the more nationalist sectors of the army, and shared the concern of those groups with promoting and protecting traditional Argentine values and reducing foreign influences. The liberals, on the other hand, tend to be identified with a more "internationalist" position—in earlier periods, relatively more pro-British; in later periods, more pro-American. Free market economic policies and a relatively small state also frequently attract their support. In regard to attitudes toward the political system, however, the liberals are a rather complex group. Rouquié writes that liberalism in the army "includes authentic democrats devoted to constitutional procedures, frequently conservatives . . . , and at times progressives. . . . It also includes extremists whose economic and social, rather than political, liberalism is accompanied by a Goldwater-like antistatism" (1982b: 351). Overall, military liberals usually do back political pluralism, but frequently only within certain bounds. Certain political groups (such as Peronists and communists) have historically met with little tolerance from this sector of the armed forces.

Compared to the liberals, the nationalist sectors have traditionally held the view that Argentine interests would best be protected by avoiding foreign domination (economic and otherwise) and by cultivating a strong and active state. Nationalists also tend to support relatively state-dominated education and cultural policies emphasizing, in particular, the tenets of the Catholic Church. Rouquie describes the nationalists as "marked by an authoritarian-corporativist ideology," adding that "this anti-liberal ideology has always been fortunate" (349). In comparison to liberalism, nationalism appears to have a more substantial development in Argentine writings. Authors such as Jordan B. Genta, Carlos Sacheri, and Juan Guevara are recognized as having had particular influence on nationalist thought.

Socially, liberals are significantly more likely to originate from the elites of Argentine society than are the nationalists. In respect to geographic origin, the liberals seem to be dominated by the Buenos Aires region, in contrast to the nationalists' frequently provincial roots. Of the three branches of the armed forces, the navy is usually identified as the most "liberal," due both to its higher level of exposure to other countries and cultures and to its initially British foundations. On the other hand, the army and the air force have, overall, a relatively nationalist orientation, although considerable variation exists between the different arms.

The most complicated branch, both politically and ideologically, is unequivocally the army. It is also the most important. Armies in all countries are designed for the control of territory. In Argentina, much of the territory historically contested is inside the country. Long and bloody battles were fought in Argentina to conquer land originally held by native populations. Part of the legacy of these battles is the multifarious regiments scattered throughout the country. This mode of organization, combined with the army's recurrent (although shifting) role in enforcing domestic security, heightens the army's concern with domestic politics.

The army has also endured some of the most intense internal rifts over Peronism, with all the virulence of a fight between brothers. After about 1956, however, no active pro-Peronist sectors manifested themselves within the army officer corps until around 1980. Those who might have been inclined to sympathize with Peronism were silenced; such sympathies were not to be tolerated.

During the Alfonsín period, this situation changed considerably. Rather than variation between degrees of anti-Peronism, the politics of army officers (when stated) appeared to vary between degrees of pro-Peronism and political neutrality. The rebels tended to sympathize with variants of Peronism, while the legalists were more inclined toward neutrality. The reasons for this rather dramatic change in political attitudes within the military were various. First, Perón himself had died in 1974. As a considerable degree of anti-Peronism involved opposition to Peronism's founder rather than concern with its substance, the absence of Perón diluted or extinguished much of the previous opposition to the Peronist movement. Secondly (as discussed in the previous chapter), the military policies of the other major political party, the Unión Cívica Radical, severely antagonized the armed forces during this period, thus leaving many in search of an alternative political ally. Finally, differences in training and experiences had stimulated generational changes within the military, which appear to have enhanced the younger sectors' receptivity to Peronism.

Colegio Militar and the Anti-Peronist Legacy

With few exceptions, the officers who supported the rebel movement within the army began their military education after the 1950s. In fact, the leaders of the first two rebellions all attended Colegio Militar Nacional [Military Officers' School] in the early 1960s, with most of them graduating in 1964. This has important implications both for what they experienced and what they did not experience. For many years after 1955, politics in Argentina were dominated by the polarization between supporters and opponents of Peronism. The military command was Peronism's most determined opposition, at least up until the present period. In fact, one of the primary goals of most military governments between 1955 and 1983 was to restructure political society, or at least the political system, in such a way as to assure that Peronism could not win.

However, the harshest "moment" of anti-Peronism within the military occurred during the military regime from 1955 to 1958. Memories of the personalism and corruption of Perón's government were still fresh, as were the perceived threats to the socioeconomic order. Perón's continued leadership of the movement also facilitated perceptions of Peronism as a concrete, confrontable enemy.

Consequently, the years between 1955 and 1958 were characterized by some rather brutal efforts to purge the armed forces of the remnants of Peronism. This endeavor was pursued particularly energetically within the army, as Peronism had penetrated the deepest within this force. Thus the majority of Peronist supporters among the officers who were either in training or on active duty at this time were eliminated. Most of the active-duty generals during the Alfonsín government belonged to this generation of officers (Pion-Berlin 1989a:11).

The leaders of the rebel movement, however, did not begin their military training until slightly after the Revolución Libertadora of 1955–58. In other words, they had not been in the military during either Perón's government or the subsequent internal purges. This meant that these officers already had the potential for developing a very different ideological and political position than their recent predecessors. For the younger officers, harboring a sympathy for Peronist-like nationalism or even embracing explicitly pro-Peronist sentiments was much less professionally dangerous than it might have been a few years earlier. Furthermore, with a more distant experience of Perón's initial presidency, these officers were significantly less likely to inherit the common antagonism toward Peronism.

The Leadership of Operation Dignity

The transformation of ideological and political predispositions within the army was only a part of the legacy of Colegio Militar. In addition, the experiences of Military School contributed to the creation of the primary leadership core of the *carapintada* rebellions— in particular, the lieutenant colonels. A list of 102 military officers graduating from Colegio Militar in 1964 (Promoción 94), included the following names: Aldo Rico, Ernesto Fernández Maguer, Santiago Roque Alonso, Ángel Daniel León, Luís Nicolás Polo, Hector

Claudio Álvarez de Igarzabal, and Enrique Carlos Venturino (Ejército Argentino, *Boletín Público del Ejército,* no. 3402, 17 July 1964: 604–8). All of these men emerged as early leaders of the *carapintada* movement. Interestingly, 5 of these 7 men (Fernández Maguer, Alonso, Polo, Álvarez de Igarzabal, and Rico) were in a group of 26 receiving a specialization in parachuting together a short time later (Ejército Argentino, *Boletín Público del Ejército,* no. 3447, 31 March 1965:263).

Hence it was no coincidence that these men emerged as a group in April of 1987. They had begun cooperating, sharing ideas and plans, at the earliest stages of their careers. A former superior of the *carapintadas* (and, subsequently, a professional victim of theirs) recounted the following history of the Rico group: "In Colegio Militar, a group of officers, confronting the advance of communism, of the danger that Marxism means for our traditional values, tries to fortify religious faith, belief, mysticism. And around this religious thought, they begin to establish practices, praying the rosary every night, reading books of men of the church. And already in that moment a community began forming. To this group belongs Polo, belongs Rico, belongs Alonso, Fernández Maguer, Venturino and the rest."[5]

Likewise, another member of the 1964 class, a friend and sympathizer of the *carapintadas,* described many of the shared military ideas of the group as having developed since the late 1960s in reaction to the international expansion of guerrilla warfare. A principal component of these ideas appears to be an emphasis on the cultural and psychological underpinnings of guerrilla warfare (Waisbord 1991:160). Somewhat later, the work of Antonio Gramsci was adopted as a framework for interpreting suspected "subversive" penetration of the national culture. Again, the beliefs of the 1964 cohort appear to have evolved together.

However, in the beginning, the cohort of 1964 probably constituted as much of a convenient "cap" for Operación Dignidad as its true instigators. The genesis of the movement actually emerged from a series of discussions among a group of captains, graduates of Colegio Militar in the early 1970s. Apparently, these captains contacted the lieutenant colonels (known to be sympathetic), proposing that they initiate some kind of organized, effective response to the trials. Since the group was unsuccessful in convincing any higher-ranking officer (a general was sought) to assume command of the effort, Rico and his peers became the rebel vanguard by default. As the movement acquired more strength, it did succeed in attracting some higher officers willing to openly assume *carapintada* goals, the most important of whom was Colonel Mohammed Alí Seineldín. Nonetheless, by this point, the Rico cohort had assumed an important and irrevocable public profile.

Conclusion

In sum, in many respects, the internal context of the Argentine army favored division in the mid-1980s. The latent cleavages that exist as permanent fault lines within the organization had been deepened by generational changes and exacerbated by a series of more recent experiences both during and subsequent to the military regime. Furthermore, an available leadership cluster existed, clearly an essential requisite for the success of any organized movement. Any who might have assumed an easy transition in Argentina clearly entertained unwarranted complacency.

6

Evolution of Military Rebellion

For more than three years following the April 1987 military uprising, army factionalism haunted the Argentine government. Yet, its form and implications evolved considerably. By December of 1990, the *carapintada* movement retained only remnants of the original cleavages that had contributed to its emergence. The essence of the movement remained, but the form had evolved. Bureaucratic lines of division had faded, while ideological and political content had matured. Correspondingly, the movement had come to be defined more by its content than its initial causes.

Phases of Rebellion

The military uprisings of April 1987 (Semana Santa) and January 1988 (Monte Caseros) dramatically demonstrated that important sectors of the military were unwilling to passively comply with the government's military policies. Such a reaction was not unexpected, particularly given Argentina's history. Yet, beyond merely confirming expectations, the military reaction enacted in the Operación Dignidad [Operation Dignity] rebellions, Semana Santa and Monte Caseros, exposed important details about military values and the nature of military rebellion.

As Alfred Stepan argues, militaries naturally react against the withdrawal of their prerogatives. In Argentina, every attempt to do so has met with some resistance (1988:115). However, as the rebellions revealed, the prerogative whose absence the military most lamented was neither budgetary advantages nor political power, but prestige. The trials for human rights offenses symbolized more than merely a reduction of the "autonomy of the military court system." From the perspective of the military, not only did the trials interfere with military procedure and control over internal matters, but, in essence, they reflected an official condemnation of the military institution, and condemnation on the one front where the armed forces believed they had succeeded. Rather than honoring the military heroes for defending the nation from a dangerous enemy, the trials portrayed them as criminals and the "enemy" as innocent victims.

Furthermore, from the perspective of many in the military, not only was the government trying them in the courts, but they were being tried in the media as well (see Rodríguez Zia 1987). The surge of artistic expressions of the terrors of the "dirty war" was interpreted by many military men as a deliberate attempt to tarnish their reputations. Thus, while budget reductions and the government's failure to provide a military mission were also important points of contention, it was the attacks on military prestige that provided the strongest motivation for the military's reaction.

Yet, military reaction composed only the first step in the *carapintadas'* transition from a provisional coalition to a fledgling institution. This evolution essentially paralleled the path of regime development described by Ken Jowitt in "Moscow Centre" (1987). According to Jowitt, the Soviet regime, as any regime, faced a series of "developmental tasks," each of which challenged its survival. The first of these is *transformation,* the initial conquest of political space. During the second stage, *consolidation,* leaders of the movement become more firmly established, defining their function and ideology and drawing firm lines between outsiders and insiders. Finally, Jowitt argues that once organizations or regimes have completed the first two tasks, they pass to a third stage: *inclusion.* With threats to the organization's identity largely eliminated, it must now expand its scope of influence, permitting previously excluded (but now non-threatening) sectors inside of its boundaries.

The particular character and context of the *carapintada* movement somewhat redefine the nature of these developmental stages. Thus, the first stage can perhaps be defined more precisely as *reaction,* rather than transformation. Although from the start the rebellions included an important leadership core with far-reaching ambitions, the overall character of the initial rebellions was transitory, a relatively spontaneous reaction against the perceived aggressions of the Alfonsín government. Despite aspiring to "transform" the military institution, the rebels' primary goal was merely to protect the institution from perceived outside aggression. Nonetheless, in the process of leading the military reaction, the rebels also inadvertently staked out their own political territory within the armed forces.

After the first couple of uprisings, the rebel movement passed into a *consolidation* phase, during which the rebels' ideas and goals became more carefully defined. Once it had become relatively clear what constituted a *carapintada*, the scope of the rebels' action began to expand. New groups and individuals were brought into the movement (including groups of allied civilians and noncommissioned officers); however, even more critical in this stage was the *diversification* of the movement. In the case of the *carapintadas*, the third phase (which culminated in the fourth rebellion) was characterized by the movement's division into two principal sectors: one that remained oriented primarily toward the military arena and one that had begun to focus on the political sphere. At this stage, the movement was compelled to expand its scope beyond its original boundaries (the army).

The Emergence of Rebellion: Operación Dignidad

During the first few years, the Alfonsín government enjoyed the fabled political honeymoon. The administration's drastic economic policies met with surprising (if temporary) success, and the equally drastic military policies confronted a target seemingly devoid of much capacity to resist. Gradually, however, small pockets of resistance had begun to emerge. The Consejo Supremo de las Fuerzas Armadas explicitly expressed its distrust of the government's methods in its communications concerning the trials of the commanders in chief of the armed forces. Furthermore, as charges began to be levied against members of the military further down the hierarchy, rumblings of discontent began to filter just as quickly up the line.

Concerned about the possible consequences of the building tension, Army Chief of Staff Hector Ríos Ereñú approached the Minister of Defense, Raúl Borrás, with the problem. He was assured that "President Alfonsín had promised that before handing over his command, those who had been convicted would be pardoned. . . . That is to say that I, the Chief of Staff, knew that the maximum that they would have to endure was six years. That during those six years, if things went well, only the military junta would be sanctioned, and a few Corp Commanders. That the majority would not have problems."[1] However, as discussed in chapter 4, Alfonsín did not have complete control over the trials he had initiated. Once the ball started rolling, stopping it became almost impossible. The only answer seemed to be to erect a wall that would bring the indictments to a sudden halt: the Law of Punto Final [End Point]. When this attempt failed, military rebellion became difficult to avoid.

Initiation of Operación Dignidad: The Semana Santa Rebellion

The first uprising began on 15 April 1987, in the province of Córdoba, with the refusal by Major Ernesto Barreiro to appear in court for the human rights trials.[2] By the following day, Thursday of Easter Week (Semana Santa), not only had the Córdoba regiment declared its support for Barreiro, but movement had begun in Campo de Mayo, just outside the capital. Within a short time, Lieutenant Colonel Aldo Rico had assumed control of the rebellion and, with his supporters, had occupied the Campo de Mayo Infantry School. Growing numbers of officers and NCOs converged on Campo de Mayo, dressed in combat uniforms, prepared for a battle that they (rightly) did not really expect to fight.

At the same time, angry civilians began flocking to Plaza de Mayo by the hundreds, responding with vigor to Alfonsín's plea that democrats make themselves heard. Proudly and dramatically, Argentine citizens declared their determination to preserve their newly acquired democracy. The military would not, they cried, return to power. *Nunca más* [Never again]. What had initially appeared to be a minor incident involving a mid-level officer had escalated to huge proportions.

By Easter Sunday, the Semana Santa uprising was ostensibly over. Campo de Mayo returned to normal, and Rico and Barreiro were placed under arrest. Yet both the internal balance within the army and the overall relationship between the military and the government had shifted significantly. The rebels had successfully challenged the generals, breaking the military's sacred rule of strict obedience. These were lieutenant colonels, majors, and, at the source, captains taking a stand against the political adaptation of their generals and, by implication, against the government itself.[3] To the generals, their principle offence was in violating institutional unity and rupturing the chain of command. For the government, however, the implications went further. Their position began to appear dangerously precarious, as it became increasingly evident that few within the army were willing to actively fight the rebels. With little to contain them, the rebels managed to obtain the vast majority of their demands.

The Semana Santa rebellion appeared, above all, as a protest against the military trials. Major Barreiro's refusal to present himself in court gave the leaders of the soon to be denominated Operación Dignidad [Operation Dignity] a concrete case, and thus an excuse to carry out the protest that they had been planning for some weeks. The demands, then, were fairly straightforward: an end to the military trials, the retirement of Army Chief of Staff Ríos Ereñú (or, even better, the removal of all the high command), an end to the "campaign of disparagement against the Armed Forces," and impunity for their actions.[4] As Lieutenant Colonel Aldo Rico, the leader of Operación Dignidad, declared, "The hopes that the present leadership of the force might put an end to the injustices and humiliations that weigh on the armed forces are considered to be extinguished" (quoted in López 1988:77). Feeling betrayed by their leaders, the middle ranks were taking things into their own hands.

Yet despite the undeniably political nature of the trial issue, the rebels' political demands went no further at this point. Repeatedly, the rebels emphasized that this was not a coup d'état, that they were not attempting to overthrow the constitutional order, and that the uprising represented an internal conflict. Their fight, they argued, was with their own military superiors, who had failed to adequately defend them from an antagonistic civilian government. In other words, the only policies of the government that were being criticized were those that directly affected the military itself. The shift within the post-Malvinas military toward a more limited professionalism had not yet been violated at this point (Norden 1990).

In large part due to the scarcity of troops willing to confront the rebels, the Semana Santa uprising was highly successful. By 20 April, less than a week after Barreiro had sought the protection of his comrades, General Ríos Ereñú had passed into retirement. With the appointment of General José Dante Caridi as the new army chief of staff, fourteen other generals were toppled.[5] Furthermore, within a month of the rebellion, the Obediencia Debida [Due Obedience] law was passed, exonerating all those below the rank of colonel from responsibility for their actions in the countersubversive war. In fact, perhaps the only respect in which the rebellion was not successful was in assuring Rico's impunity. However, for some, this remained a point of contention.

Provocation or Personalism? The Monte Caseros Rebellion

The Semana Santa uprising set the stage for three subsequent uprisings: January 1988 (Monte Caseros), December 1988 (Villa Martelli), and December 1990. The Monte Caseros uprising was, in many respects, a less successful chapter of Semana Santa. However, the focus of this incident centered somewhat more around the personal situation of Aldo Rico than around the shared interests of the institution. The uprising (believed by some to have been deliberately provoked) stemmed from a rather confused succession of decisions regarding Rico's state of arrest. Shortly after he was put under house arrest, the charges against Rico for the previous uprising were altered, thereby requiring that he be placed under preventative detention. With "loyalist" troops (primarily cavalry and artillery) already moving to detain him, Rico and his followers set up their forces in the Monte Caseros infantry regiment, demanding that the government comply with their earlier promises.

However, this time the situation was far less favorable for the *carapintadas*. The participants were much less organized and less cohesive than they had been during Semana Santa. Furthermore, as many in the army perceived the uprising as having its basis in personal interests (Rico's demand for exculpation), rather than institutional interests, they were far less willing to risk their lives and careers to support this second manifestation of Operación Dignidad. The end result, therefore, was a much lower level of success than in the previous uprising. On 17 January 1988, Rico and his men surrendered, without negotiation. No new demands were advanced, and rather than satisfying the rebels' primary outstanding demand (impunity), Monte Caseros led to the arrest of nearly 300 men, including 60 officers and 22 NCO's.[6]

Regardless, Semana Santa and Monte Caseros can be seen as part of the same stage in the development of the *carapintada* movement. Both were, above all, reactions to the policies of the civilian government. Furthermore, both uprisings were oriented toward protecting the military institution, or at least particular members. Despite their obvious hostility toward the government, the rebels carefully avoided references to any political affiliation or aspirations. Yet Operación Dignidad was controlled by the more pragmatic of the *carapintadas,* Aldo Rico's faction. While Rico and his allies did exhibit considerable political ambition, perhaps even more so than other members of the expanding *carapintada* coalition, their actions generally demonstrated a relatively realistic assessment of what could be achieved. As the political context and the leadership of the *carapintada* coalition shifted, pragmatism began to succumb to ideology and ambition.

Consolidation of the Rebel Movement

The Monte Caseros uprising proved to be no more than a temporary setback for the *carapintadas.* After an apparent lull in their activities, the *carapintadas* again erupted nearly a year later with a third large-scale rebellion, Villa Martelli. At this point, the *carapintada* movement began to develop beyond its initial, reactive phase. Rather than merely reacting to immediate circumstances, the leaders began to demonstrate concern for ensuring the future of the movement itself. This led to a phase of *consolidation* during which *carapintada* leaders began to establish a stable organizational basis for the movement. However, as the movement became more defined, it also became increasingly politicized and consequently less capable of relying on the support of the military institution.

The Villa Martelli Uprising

In the December 1988 rebellion, the trigger was far less clear than in Monte Caseros, and the opposition was therefore much less prepared to act. The show began with the reports by the media that fifty-four members of Albatros, an elite squadron of the Prefectura Naval (similar to the Coast Guard), had disappeared.[7] It was not known where they were headed or for what purpose. Media reports began to express increasing alarm, despite the usual marginality of the Prefectura in political questions. Simultaneous revolts in two army regiments increased the apprehension. Finally, the young Albatros officers reappeared in Villa Martelli, along with Rico's former superior and instructor, Colonel Mohamed Alí Seineldín, a man long considered to be a potential threat. Quickly, the rebellion spread to regiments throughout the country. Furthermore, while loyalist troops were summoned to suppress the uprising, very few seemed willing to actively oppose the rebels. Many tried to give the appearance of following orders, while actually obstructing efforts to reassert control. Thus, despite a few initial mishaps,[8] as well as three deaths and numerous injuries in conflicts between the police and civilian demonstrators, the rebels fully regained their pre–Monte Caseros standing.[9]

LEADERSHIP

Yet the character of the rebel movement had changed. With the shift from Rico's leadership to the leadership of Colonel Seineldín, the *carapintada* movement began to shift from institutionally oriented pragmatism toward more political and ideological directions. Initially subtle, the shift was accompanied more by an expansion of demands than by a real change in their content. Probably the most important indicator of the quality of the change, if not also its most important cause, was simply Seineldín.

Colonel Seineldín was more than merely the representative of a disgruntled army. He was a recognized leader. Seineldín had been stationed in Panama during the previous uprisings.[10] Yet after receiving the news that he was not to be promoted to general, in December of 1988, Seineldín heeded the calls of the many *carapintadas* who had been writing to him and returned to lead the third and most dramatic of the military uprisings in 1987 and 1988. Unquestionably, he was the right person to do so. Seineldín was perceived by many to be a charismatic leader. He was a devout Catholic (alternately called a fundamentalist or a fanatic by his opponents), frequently seen with a large crucifix adorning his chest. During the rebellion, one journalist observed Seineldín wearing an arm band fabricated of the Argentine flag with a cross in the center. When asked about it, Seineldín reportedly responded, "This? . . . It's the next Argentine flag."[11]

Seineldín was also seen as the prototypical commando. Isidoro Ruíz Moreno describes the colonel as "possessed of a patriotic and religious mystique" and an ability to infuse all of his subordinates with "the conscientiousness of filling obligations as an absolute priority, of total sacrifice, that finds its compensation in obedience to the orders received" (1986:36). Despite his realistically minimal participation in the Falklands/Malvinas war, the myth of Seineldín's indomitable bravery and unwavering ethics had long circulated among the lower and middle ranks of the military, propagated primarily by his many students.

At least in part because of Seineldín's charisma, the Villa Martelli uprising (called Operación Virgen de la Valle [Operation Virgin of the Valley] by the *carapintadas*) garnered a much higher level of support than had the previous rebellions. This time about a thousand men were involved, in contrast to the approximately 150 who had taken part in the Semana Santa rebellion (R. Fraga 1989:119). Furthermore, in addition to the army officers and NCOs who had participated in Semana Santa and the dozen or so members of the air force who had professed their support for the movement, Villa Martelli also counted on the aid of Albatros. With this growth in support, combined with an increase in planning and organization and the convenient absence of the president from the country, the rebels found themselves in a relatively favorable position to press their demands.

DEMANDS

Not surprisingly, the rebels' demands were an extension of those posed in the earlier rebellions, centering around the enhancement of military prestige and the impunity of the vast majority of the *carapintadas*. However, the situation was different this time. First, Seineldín had lent his own, more ideological slant to the movement. Secondly, despite the failure of the Monte Caseros rebellion, the elapsed time since the initiation of Operación Dignidad had given the *carapintadas* the opportunity to more effectively consolidate the movement. They had begun to entrench themselves in little pockets, such as ostensible research institutes, and were reputed to have established a virtual parallel army command. Finally, as Rosendo Fraga points out, the context of Villa Martelli had evolved from that of a year and a half earlier, in that while the trials were still an important rallying point, they had ceased to be a real issue (1989). By December of 1988, the number of military officers being prosecuted for human rights trials had been reduced from the pre–Semana Santa total of 450 to a mere 20. This meant that despite the similarities between the demands posed at this point and those posed previously, the implications were somewhat different. Rather than defending the military from a concrete, shared threat, the Villa Martelli uprising appeared aimed at securing a "place" in the political arena. In other words, the goals of this rebellion seemed to have more to do with increasing the prestige and status of the military institution and, in particular, the *carapintadas,* instead of merely protecting the army from punishment for what they consider to have been justifiable actions.

THE NONPACT OF VILLA MARTELLI

The precise form of the resolution of the conflict remains unclear, yet certain versions have emerged with such persistence as to seem, at a minimum, highly probable. The most definite point is that, in the context of Villa Martelli, a meeting took place between Colonel Seineldín, Army Chief of Staff General Caridi, General Isidro Cáceres (a cavalry officer who then held a high level of prestige among rebels and loyalists alike), and Colonel Jorge Toccalino, a member of Seineldín's team. During this meeting, an agreement was reached between Seineldín and Caridi, with Cáceres serving as a witness (guarantor, by some accounts) in regard to the terms for Seineldín's surrender.

What, then, were the terms? According to most reports, the agreement included the following terms: (1) the retirement of Caridi before the end of the year, (2) the assumption by Seineldín of all responsibility for the uprising and the trial for that offense to be held in the military courts, (3) the "revision of the trials" (elsewhere expressed as the expansion of the range of the Obedencia Debida law, an end to all human rights trials, and amnesty before the presidential elections), and, finally, (4) an increase in the military budget.[12] Yet, with no written, signed document for verification, the particular details of the "pact" were difficult to confirm and a continuing point of controversy. In June 1989, Seineldín declared that the pact was no longer in effect, due to the army command's failure to recognize it or comply with it, especially with respect to the "definitive solution to all the problems derived from the events of Semana Santa, Monte Caseros, [and] Villa Martelli."[13] General Cáceres countered by denying that this had been a part of the agreement, claiming instead that the *carapintadas* had not held to the agreement that Seineldín retire.

Despite the controversy over the substance of the pact, and the government's continued denial of its existence, several of the policies that were enacted clearly substantiated the terms that had originally been reported. As the headlines of one newspaper sarcastically announced, "There is no pact, but it is being fulfilled."[14] Military salaries were quickly increased, and by 20 December, General Caridi had offered his resignation.[15] Furthermore, the only officers who were arrested for the uprising were Colonel Seineldín, as agreed, and Major Abete, who had refused to surrender for several days after the end of the rebellion. On the other hand, amnesty, which realistically was a political impossibility for the Alfonsín government, was not pursued. In addition, while Caridi's replacement, General Gassino, eventually gained fairly widespread respect within the army, at the time he was not the *carapintadas'* leader of choice.

Politicization of the Rebel Movement

In addition to the concessions acquired from the government, the rebellion of Villa Martelli also had a significant internal effect within the *carapintada* forces of the army (alternately called the "national" or "parallel" army), setting off a new wave of political activity. Two events helped focus this activity: the January 1989 attack against a military regiment (La Tablada) and the upcoming presidential elections.

LAST REVOLUTIONARIES: THE 1989 GUERRILLA OFFENSIVE
In many respects, the guerrilla attack on La Tablada was a significant boon for the *carapintadas,* as well as for the military as a whole. In the early morning on 23 January 1989, around fifty leftist extremists invaded the regiment in what was alternately portrayed as an attempt to counter an expected military coup or as an effort to initiate a new revolutionary movement in Argentina. A little over a day later, the attack was over, with devastating consequences for the insurgents. Twenty-eight had been killed (in contrast to only eleven from the combined military and police forces), thirteen or fourteen were captured, and only a few had escaped (Amnesty International 1990:2; R. Fraga 1989:84).[16] Not only did the invasion itself clearly fail, but it managed to return the left as a whole in Argentina to a precarious, suspect position.

For the military, however, the attack on La Tablada had quite different consequences. Finally they felt able to graphically demonstrate the validity of the countersubversive war of the 1970s, along with the continuing threat from Marxism. The event also facilitated efforts by the government to pacify the armed forces, and particularly the *carapintadas*. The fact that the battle had dragged on for so many hours, despite the participation of the combined army (including various commandos), provincial police, and federal police, gave credence to the military's complaints about the deterioration of the armed forces, particularly due to declines in morale and budget. Military salaries had already been increased around the middle of December; however, within ten days of the Tablada battle, a 7 percent raise had been granted to the military for the month of January.[17]

At the same time, the attack also lent fodder to the *carapintadas'* claim that members of the government itself were subversives. According to many military officers, the Alfonsín government sought to destroy the military as part of an underlying plot to create a more favorable setting for a communist revolution. According to one officer, Gramsci's influence had taught the left that "revolution must be accomplished through ideas, ideology, the mass media" (quoted in Waisbord 1991:160; see also Carretto 1987:39–47). Consequently, with the presidential elections coming in May 1989, the *carapintadas* became increasingly determined to let their views be known and to ensure what they perceived as the only acceptable alternative for the contest—the defeat of the Radical candidate.

ALLIANCE BETWEEN REBELS AND PERONISM

Peronism thus became the rebels' new cause. In a predominantly two-party system, the Partido Justicialista (Peronism) posed the only realistic alternative to the Radicals, as well as neatly converging with many facets of the rebels' political perspective. Consequently, drawing on their warrior image, the *carapintadas* publicly offered themselves as the guarantors that Carlos Menem would not be illegitimately cheated out of the presidency.[18]

Aldo Rico revealed his sympathies for Peronism on various occasions, beginning with repeated quotes from Perón in a weekly newsletter entitled *Fortaleza,* which the Operación Dignidad leaders published from Magdalena prison in early 1988 (Chumbita 1990:86), and including appearances on such popular television programs as "Tiempo Nuevo" and "Hora Clave." Although expressing an innate distrust of political parties, Rico admitted having voted for Ítalo Luder in the 1983 presidential elections and lauded Peronism's nonrevolutionary mass appeal. "When I refer to *justicialismo,*" he explained, "what I understand is that, in its moment, it was a movement that had a solution for Argentine society. We must not forget that the Justicialist Movement is the only non-Marxist mass movement in the entire world" (Hernández 1989:77). In later contacts with the media, Rico elaborated his position toward Peronism, claiming that, while not a Peronist, he identified with such facets of early Peronist doctrine as its nationalist thrust and its emphasis on social justice (although both concepts are elaborated differently by Rico). Several years later, during the 1995 presidential campaign, Rico vividly illustrated his identification with Perón in a poster pitting Rico against the U.S. ambassador—a precise parallel to Peróns campaign against then Ambassador Braden nearly half a century before.

Seineldín's faction remained united with Rico during the pretransition campaign, although he tended to avoid openly political statements, at least to the media. Nonetheless, a publication circulated by Seineldín's allies among their supporters from 23 December 1988 until 12 July 1989 clearly demonstrates the changing emphasis of the rebel movement during this period. The one-page publication, entitled the "Hoja Avanzada 'Nuestra Señora de Luján'" ["Advanced Sheet 'Our Lady of Luján'"], expressed the editors' recommendations and aspirations for the professional development of the armed forces, their general ideological outlook, and their more specific reactions to political events and actors. By the third issue, Alfonsín had been explicitly identified as an enemy.[19] Shortly afterward, La Tablada became the center of attention, and the efforts of the "Hoja" were oriented toward demonstrating that the attack had been originated by Alfonsín and his associates.

However, as the elections came closer, the publication increasingly focused on this event and the ensuing administrative transition. The *carapintadas* denounced plots by the Radicals and the "liberal" sector of the military to conduct internal coups and proposed a series of tactics to deter such a plan.[20] Editors of the "Hoja" also reviewed alternative ways in which the Radicals might interfere with the election and assumption to office of the Peronist candidate, Carlos Menem. Finally, with the presidency in Menem's hands, publication of the "Hoja" was brought to a close. According to the editors, the inauguration of a president whose values paralleled their own expunged the need to continue their efforts.

The "Hoja" reveals the significant shift in the *carapintada* movement during the period between Villa Martelli and the presidential elections. From an emphasis on institutional, pragmatic goals, the movement had developed into a much more political and ideological quest. During the preelection period, the *carapintadas* saw their role as defending both the interests of the military institution and their own vision of the nation through their defense of the electoral process and their support of the Peronist candidate. This was, of course, in one sense a rather wise political investment. By supporting Menem, who was strongly favored to win the elections, the *carapintadas* were increasing the possibilities that Menem, during his presidency, would also support them. Again, the *carapintadas* would be disappointed.

Diversification of the Rebel Movement: Menem's Presidency

Under Menem's presidency, the *carapintada* movement entered a third phase: diversification and expansion. The diversification stage began with Menem's bitter divorce from the *carapintadas*. After expressing disillusionment with Menem's government on several points, the rebels began to go their own way, developing a newly independent political and military movement. Yet, during this period, these facets of the movement began to divide. After early efforts to maintain a united front, the Seineldín and Rico factions of the movement began to separate, each focusing on their own goals and tactics. Seineldín continued to focus on the military component of the movement, although increasingly expanding his efforts outside of the institution itself. Rico, on the other hand, gradually shifted into the political arena.

Menem's Military Policies

During the weeks that followed Menem's triumphant election and accelerated assumption of the presidency, the rebels' appreciation of Carlos Menem appeared to be fully reciprocated. The uprisings were treated as events of a crisis-ridden past, and the rebels themselves as respected allies. At the same time, Menem acted to assuage the wounded spirit of the armed forces, even while refraining from addressing the military's appalling material conditions. The Menem administration also worked to redefine the military's role, which by 1991 meant increasing involvement in international missions.

Menem especially sought to develop a harmonious relationship with Seineldín. On various occasions, representatives of the Peronist leader reportedly consulted with Seineldín, seeking the colonel's recommendations for future Ministry of Defense appointments, discussing possible positions for Seineldín himself, and negotiating trade-offs on personnel decisions within the army in order to diminish internal tensions. Dr. César Arias, one of Menem's representatives during the early negotiations, testified in the Seineldín trial proceedings that he met various times with Seineldín and his associates (particularly Colonel Toccalino and Colonel Díaz Loza) in order to discuss defense policy, the difficulties of the army, and "which men in the military sector were, in [Seineldín's] opinion, most capable" or most likely to find a solution to the army's problem.[21] According to Arias, the names mentioned by Seineldín were General Pablo Skalany and General Cáceres—the latter was later appointed to the position of Army Chief of Staff. In April of 1989, Seineldín also offered his recommendations for the Ministry of Defense, who Arias reports as having been Dr. Matera, Dr. Luder, and Dr. Romero (Poder Judicial de la Nación Argentina: Arias testimony, Díaz Loza testimony). A second witness recalled the names as having been Matera, Luder, and Arias (Poder Judicial: Toccalino testimony). According to a third source, the three names presented were Romero, Arias, and Luder (Simeoni and Allegri 1991:238). Regardless, Luder became the Minister of Defense, and Romero was assigned the second position in the ministry, secretary of defense.

Negotiations concerning matters within the army itself were probably even more critical, however, given the dual leadership within the army at this time.[22] Lieutenant Colonel Solari, a member of Menem's Defense Committee during his electoral campaign, acted as an intermediary between Menem and members of both the official and rebel armed forces. According to Solari's testimony at the Seineldín trial, when Menem offered Cáceres the position of chief of staff of the army (apparently following Seineldín's April recommendation), he accompanied the offer with the request that Cáceres work things out with Seineldín (Poder Judicial: Solari testimony). Solari reported that around this time, Cáceres and Seineldín met in the company of General Pablo Skalany and Lieutenant Colonel Solari to discuss how the unification of the army could be achieved. Seineldín reportedly offered his full support, including subordinating all his followers to Cáceres's command, but with the condition that Cáceres "comply with what we have pacted at this moment."

What kind of agreements did the two military leaders reach at this later juncture? According to the testimony of General Skalany, the most substantial negotiations occurred in July 1989 (before Menem became president), after tensions between Seineldín and Cáceres had already begun to escalate. At this time, Seineldín and Cáceres, in the presence of Skalany and Solari, elaborated a pact that included a list of eleven prominent rebel leaders who would voluntarily retire, including Seineldín and Rico, with fourteen others subject to sanctions. However, the remaining rebels were to be reincorporated into the armed forces, reinstated in their courses at the advanced military schools, when applicable, or offered employment within the state in some other capacity (Poder Judicial: Solari testimony, Skalany testimony).

Seineldín's personal future continued to be a matter of discussion. In the early months of Menem's presidency, rumors circulated in Buenos Aires about potential future positions of Seineldín—for example, his incorporation into the government or his reinstatement into active military duty at the head of a newly formed elite unit. According to Seineldín, it was Menem who was most concerned with providing the colonel with a special position. Seineldín later related, "Since he insisted, I proposed that he create a rapid deployment force of 200 or 300 men, and that when he needed it and gave the order, we would be prepared to fight against whomever it might be" (quoted in Chumbita 1990:271). At the trial, Arias testified that the creation of such a force had been under discussion (although he preferred a specifically counternarcotics detachment), but that Seineldín had not been promised leadership of the project (Poder Judicial: Arias testimony). However, Menem's frequent public praise of Seineldín gave credence to the latter's version of these discussions.

In October 1989, Menem offered an important demonstration of the sincerity of his professed goodwill toward the rebels. The president offered pardons to all of the participants of the rebellions, along with the vast majority of those implicated in the repression and the Falklands/Malvinas war (Decrees 1002/89, 1004/89, 1005/89, República Argentina, *Boletín Oficial,* 10 October 1989:4–8). More than a year (and a military uprising) later, subsequent pardons were extended to the remaining junta members and such controversial cases as General Ramón Camps, General Suárez Mason, and Mario Firminich.

DISILLUSIONMENT

Nonetheless, many of the *carapintadas'* expectations were not fulfilled. On almost every issue previously negotiated, the rebels faced some degree of disappointment. For example, Seineldín's recommendations were apparently followed in filling the top posts of the Ministry of Defense, but the subsequent results of those appointments did not prove significantly beneficial for the rebels. As Seineldín explained: "We put in a patriarch like Dr. Luder. He calmed things a bit. But the man who should have solved the problem was Dr. Humberto Romero. He was our man, but bit by bit he turned" (quoted in Barral 1991:68). Furthermore, Menem began to habitually bypass the Ministry of Defense in order to communicate directly with the military chiefs of staff. This not only reversed the prior administration's efforts to strengthen this office and provoked the resignation of the first defense minister, Ítalo Luder, but it also minimized the impact of the rebels' personnel recommendations.

The greatest disappointment to the rebels, however, proved to be Army Chief of Staff Cáceres. During the Alfonsín government, Cáceres was one of the few generals respected by the *carapintadas*. His position as "witness" or "guarantor" of the agreements between then Chief of Staff Dante Caridi and Seineldín was a consequence of his reputation as a loyalist with nationalist leanings. Few others could have elicited the trust of both Caridi and the *carapintada* leadership.

From the *carapintada* side, Cáceres lost that trust even before his appointment as chief of staff. The source of the conflict was the highly debated "pact" of Villa Martelli. After various instances in which the rebels protested that the terms of the agreement were being ignored, on 16 June 1989, Seineldín finally declared the pact to be void. The last straw was a document obtained by Seineldín (supposedly formulated by members of the army command) that harshly criticized the *carapintadas* ("Grupo Sectario Consolidado [Consolidated Sectarian Group]") and proposed various methods to weaken this group, including "administrative reconsideration of some individual situations" and impeding the *carapintadas* contacts with political leaders (Simeoni and Allegri 1991:236). The document exacerbated frustrations that had been brewing since March, at which time the army command had targeted various rebels with disciplinary sanctions (Chumbita 1990:159).

Once Cáceres was appointed army chief of staff, his treatment of the *carapintada* issue was mixed. Shortly after taking command, the general publicly expressed his intention to pursue reconciliation within the army, following Menem's wishes. In this context, some of the generals most adamantly opposed to the *carapintadas* were retired, and some of the rebels were returned to active duty (Chumbita 1990:244). According to a high ranking officer: "When General Cáceres took charge, many people were reincorporated, many people were given posts, and many people continued in their careers without problems. There were other people that did not, that remained in the same situation. But . . . there is a greater number of people who returned to the army and were incorporated without problems than those who had to leave the army."[23] At the same time, however, the army command displayed little patience with officers and NCOs who continued to be actively involved with the rebel movement. The confidential official stance of the army was that the *carapintadas* posed a threat to institutional unity and stability and should be treated as dangerous ideological opponents, essentially on the same level as the extreme left.[24] Acting on this redefinition in October 1989, Cáceres (with Menem's collaboration) discharged Rico and four other rebel officers from the army, thereby rescinding their military status (Chumbita 1990:247). Twenty other officers, including Seineldín, were forced into mandatory retirement—significantly more than the Seineldín-Cáceres agreement had anticipated. Cáceres's successor, General Martin Bonnet, continued to pressure the rebels throughout 1990, "severely sanctioning all those troops who demonstrated, in some manner, their adhesion to the *carapintadas*" (Simeoni and Allegri 1991:270). The army command thereby significantly undermined the rebels' pardons. The pardons only spared the rebels from the civilian courts; they did not grant them impunity.

Menem thus gradually siphoned away the influence of the *carapintadas*. Nonetheless, many of the conditions that originally provoked military dissatisfaction remained. The financial conditions of the armed forces, including both the budget and salaries, continued to deteriorate. Media reports cited Ministry of Defense estimates that from the end of the military government until May of 1990, real

Table 6

Hierarchical Balance in the Argentine Army, 1983–1990

Year	Officers	NCOS	Soldiers	Ratio of Soldiers to NCOS
1983	6,154	24,805	64,640	2.6:1
1984	5,891	23,536	62,902	2.7:1
1985	5,804	24,182	35,527	1.5:1
1986	5,857	23,575	24,930	1:1
1987	5,900	22,583	24,921	1:1.1
1988	5,895	22,510	28,343	1:1.3
1989	5,878	22,494	29,169	1:1.2
1990[a]	6,000	24,000	16,000	1:1.5

Source: R. Fraga 1991:155, "La incorporación de conscriptos al Ejército."

[a]Numbers from 1990 are estimates.

salaries had diminished 75 percent for noncommissioned officers and 211 percent for officers.[25] In 1988 and 1989, it was common to see military officers leaving their stations to work a second job; two years later, military units were shortening the number of days in the work week in order to cut costs.[26]

The shortage of soldiers had also been further aggravated since the change in government. The ratio of NCOs to soldiers in the army went from approximately 2 to 5 in 1983 to 1 to 1 in 1985 and down to 3 to 2 in 1990 (see table 6). The implication for day-to-day life within the army was that NCOs were forced to perform the kinds of duties usually delegated to soldiers during their year of serving the draft. Rather than commanding troops, NCOs were sweeping floors and carrying papers—before, of course, moving on to their second jobs. Frustration among these ranks was thus particularly acute.

Nonetheless, Menem managed to avoid the hostility generated by the Alfonsín government through his deliberate use of positive gestures. As a senior officer explained in September 1991: "The president has made gestures, let us say, of affection toward the armed forces. . . . Even though the situation is much worse than it was during Alfonsín. That is, in politics, man is a consumer of material resources. But he is also a consumer of symbolic resources, much more so. As a provider of psychological resources, Alfonsín was very negative and Menem is positive."[27] When asked to elaborate, he referred to a number of Menem's public acts, from visiting military units to promoting military parades on Argentina's national holiday. The parades on 9 July were widely perceived as part of a deliberate effort to foster better relations with the armed forces.[28] The pardons were, of course, another significant point.

These efforts, combined with a continuous stream of discourse expressing sympathy for the armed forces, succeeded in displacing much of the potential anger toward the Menem government. As General Laíño so aptly pointed out, symbolism counts more than money in determining military reactions. The budget cuts created distress throughout the armed forces, but only within a few sectors did that distress create a more pointed hostility. Most seemed to trust that the government would do its best to act in the military's best interest.

The *carapintadas,* however, were left increasingly frustrated by the situation. Not only had the favored status that they had expected not come to fruition, but Menem's government had also taken an unexpected direction overall. Rather than pursuing the nationalist policies traditional to Peronism, Menem opted for a neoliberal political and economic plan (Armijo 1994; G. Munck 1994). Álvaro Alsogaray and other members of the politically conservative and economically liberal Unión del Centro Democrático party (UCeDe) [Union of the Democratic Center] were given top positions in the government, as Menem launched an extensive plan for the privatization and opening of the country. Concomitantly, Menem's quest to make Argentina the most loyal ally of the United States transformed U.S. Ambassador Terence Todman into one of the most powerful individuals in the country. These policies obliterated much of the sympathy the *carapintadas* had felt for Menem. The nationalist sectors continued to favor Peronism, but Menem himself ceased to be considered an authentic Peronist.

From the Barracks to the Barrios: Separation and Segmentation

The government's ambiguous treatment of the *carapintadas* and the generally less pressing context helped postpone a consolidated reaction. Yet neither Rico nor Seineldín appeared to have any intention of relinquishing their newfound public influence. Rico's elimination from the force and Seineldín's retirement contributed to their need to find new means to pursue their goals, however.

During the first months of Menem's presidency, *carapintada* appearances continued to center around military issues. For example, in a notorious demonstration following the discharges and mandatory retirements applied at the end of October 1989, some five hundred *carapintadas* appeared in a public park in Buenos Aires for a joint "exercise" session.[29] The Palermo jogging session carried an obvious message for the army command—the rebels were still strong and not likely to remain passive. Despite the cleverly nonconfrontational character of the episode, those participants who could be identified received disciplinary sanctions from the military. The event also contributed to hardening the army leadership's position toward the rebels.

A less innocuous episode involved Seineldín's clandestine training of around two hundred civilians as an unofficial "Dignity Battalion," based on the identically named troops Seineldín had trained in Panama. A civilian leader of the Dignity Battalion was quoted as saying: "In the world, we admire Khaddafy and Noriega. The principal enemy is not Russia, because Marxism is dying. The principal enemy, not counting Zionism, is the United States and England."[30] The participants claimed that the purpose of the Dignity Battalion was to be prepared for an eventual replay of the Falklands/Malvinas war, rather than to threaten the government. After their actions were reported in November, little more was heard of Seineldín's unofficial troops.

Gradually, the scope of the rebels' aspirations expanded. Both the Rico and Seineldín sectors of the *carapintada* movement appeared to be attempting to develop a new civil-military populist movement. Toward the beginning of 1990, Seineldín and Rico began reaching out to the Argentine community for support, especially to the poorer and more marginalized sectors. They continued to make their presence known, making excursions to poorer neighborhoods in various parts of the country and, in the case of Rico, frequent media appearances as well.[31]

The Political Debut of Aldo Rico

Rico, in conjunction with his close associates, eventually began to develop an explicitly political project. In part, his ability and proclivity to do so derived from his military discharge. As he no longer legally held military rank, he ceased both to enjoy the privileges of his rank and to be subject to the commitments and constraints that membership in the armed forces (either on active duty or in retirement) entails. His possibilities for successfully directing an intramilitary movement had thus been significantly reduced. Yet so had the likelihood that he might confront disciplinary actions for behavior deemed, in one way or another, inappropriate by the military hierarchy.

Shifting into politics, therefore, became a natural outlet for Rico's sector of the *carapintada* movement. The media appearances and forays throughout the country soon began to develop into a more directed and organized enterprise. In March 1990, Rico announced the formation of a new political party, Movimiento de Renovación Nacional [Movement for National Renovation]. About a month later (24 April), at a conference at the Naval Noncommissioned Officers Club, the former lieutenant colonel called on Argentines to join with his political project.[32] A pamphlet distributed on this occasion announced: "We summon Argentine men and women, with love for the Fatherland, volition to serve, confidence in themselves and hope for the possibility for a better future, and all the organizations with which they associate, to contribute with their intelligence and courage to the reflection, debate, formulation, development, and concretion of a National Political Project" (Movimiento por la Dignidad 1990:33). The objectives the political *carapintadas* sought included "restoring the full operation of the spirit of the national constitution and a truly representative and federal republican regime"; "recuperating for our nation cultural and political autonomy"; and completing the process of "national independence" (33). Military and defense concerns also figure prominently; however, by this point, the Rico group had reached the conclusion that those goals could only be achieved in the context of more extensive political reforms.

The first open political campaign of the *carapintadas* involved a proposed constitutional reform in Buenos Aires. The reform would have radically revised the provincial constitution, permitting reelection of the governor and expanding certain powers of the governor, among other things.[33] Rico's group opposed the project primarily on the basis that such an extensive number of reforms should take place through a constitutional convention, rather than through a plebiscite.[34] In the August 1990 plebiscite, the reform was defeated, with 68 percent opposed.[35] The plebiscite succeeded, however, in changing Rico's image in Buenos Aires, bringing him a wave of new supporters and much needed positive publicity.

In October 1990, Rico's party merged with the already existing Partido de la Independencia to become Movimiento de la Dignidad e Independencia (later rechristened MODIN), with Aldo Rico as president and gubernatorial candidate for the September 1991 Buenos Aires elections. The party also presented candidates for national and provincial congressional competitions in Buenos Aires, Tucumán, Salta, San Luis, Córdoba, Entre Rios, and Santa Fe.[36] The party succeeded in placing three deputies in the national Congress. Finally, in October 1993, the former lieutenant colonel himself was elected to the National House of Deputies. Rico's transformation from military rebel to politician was essentially complete.

The Caudillo Politics of Colonel Seineldín

Compared to Rico's goals and actions, Seineldín's were much more ambiguous. The retired colonel claimed that his excursions in early 1990 were not meant to be political, but to "give hope." "I work for God and only seek to take the fatherland forward."[37] Yet the content of his discourse on these occasions lent some doubt to that assertion. Seineldín presented himself, in essence, as a new and more religious Perón. For example, in one conference, Seineldín asserted: "Man needs the family, the school, the unions [and] the Church, because he is basically weak and the enemy attacks those points. Because of this, a national project is necessary. [This] appeared in 1943, but it was lost."[38] Seineldín seemed to be offering a new such national project.

As 1990 wore on, Seineldín's activities intensified. "At the end of September, active duty officers began to receive a sort of flier signed by Seineldín," referring to "difficult times" and encouraging recipients to choose to defend "the permanent values that we swore to guard" (Simeoni and Allegri 1991:262). In October, Seineldín turned his attention to the upcoming round of promotions within the army. In a letter co-written with some of his close associates and addressed to the "Commander in Chief" (Menem), Seineldín complained strongly about the discriminatory treatment his followers had been receiving by the army command and warned of "vindicatory incidents" (264). According to the *Latin American Weekly Report* (8 November 1990:4), the publication of the letter "came at the peak of a two-week agitation campaign, mostly through the media, to create a climate favorable to the staging of a 'new 17 October' (the date in 1945 when a mass mobilization secured

then-Colonel Juan Domingo Perón's release from arrest)." Colonel Seineldín was placed under arrest, and discussions of a possible discharge
from the military ensued.

During the same period (somewhere around September 1990), Seineldín and some of his close associates produced a video for circulation
among their supporters. The video includes a series of short lectures on
the Argentine political situation by members of the group. One of the
most interesting segments is the first, in which the speaker discusses
three possible political states. The first of these states is "normal" politics, in which religious values dominate decision making. The second is
referred to as "game" politics and sounds much like democratic government. Finally, the third phase is referred to as the "cure." In this stage, a
"witness," or charismatic leader, plays a critical role, serving as a moral
and religious guide in reestablishing "normal" politics, generally
through the use of violence. The speaker points to Jesus as history's
most important witness (Operación Virgen de la Valle 1990). Taken in
the context of the conference, Seineldín would appear to be the proposed "witness" for contemporary Argentina.

Seineldín's discussion focuses on Argentine history and national security. Included in his analysis is a complex hypothesis about a British
plot to assert control over South America (expanding their presence
from the Falklands/Malvinas Islands), apparently in conjunction with
the United States. Correspondingly, he suggests that U.S. counternarcotics efforts in Latin America are actually part of an effort to maintain a
military presence that could defend the overall project for economic
domination. Needless to say, Seineldín held little sympathy for
Menem's United States–oriented political and economic strategies.

Collapse of Seineldín's Rebels: Operación Virgen de Luján

The most crucial difference between the two rebel leaders was that Seineldín did not choose to pursue his aims through the democratic process. Rather, the colonel continued to emphasize military goals and military means. During the post–Villa Martelli period, the *carapintadas*
were already rumored to have developed a complete parallel army
within the army, with an independent staff and hierarchy. Certain references in the Seineldinista "Hoja Avanzada 'Nuestra Señora de Luján'"
support those rumors. For example, in the event of crisis, followers
were instructed to report to their superior in the "National Element"

within the army in order to ascertain their orders. The leadership of the "National" army would determine whether or not the official orders should be followed.[39]

On 3 December 1990, the Seineldinistas mobilized their followers for what appears to have been the last major *carapintada* uprising. At about three-thirty in the morning, some fifty followers of Colonel Seineldín entrenched themselves in army headquarters (Edificio Libertador), just around the corner from the government house in Buenos Aires. Almost simultaneously, rebels occupied the Patricios infantry regiment in nearby Palermo, the TAMSE tank factory in Boulogne, and a quartermaster battalion in El Palomar, and sequestered a cavalry regiment in the province of Entre Rios.[40] Insurgents from Albatros, the elite Prefectura Naval [Coast Guard] unit active during the Villa Martelli, moved to occupy Prefectura headquarters. Over six hundred men are estimated to have participated.[41]

After a few signs of early success, the rebels' good fortune quickly diminished. The December Third rebellion, named "Operación Virgen de Luján," broke the unwritten rule of military uprisings in Argentina— no bloodshed among comrades. During the first hours of the operation, the commander of the occupied Patricios regiment approached the rebels' Palermo headquarters in conjunction with the loyalist Granaderos regiment (the regiment charged with protecting the government house). Two loyalist officers, Lieutenant Colonel Pita and Major Pedernera, and a noncommissioned officer were killed in the process.

The unanticipated violence dramatically turned the tide against the rebels. Many who might have felt sympathy for the uprising, or who at least might have avoided actively confronting the rebels (as in the other incidents), suddenly became willing to fight. Others, initially involved in the plan, anticipated that the uprising had become a losing enterprise and chose the expedient route of avoiding involvement in a probable defeat. Most dramatically, Captain Gustavo Breide Obeid, responsible for the occupation of Edificio Libertador, was left awaiting replacement by a superior officer (rumored to be a colonel who shortly thereafter became incorporated into Rico's political staff) who was to take command of that facet of the operation (Simeoni and Allegri 1991:308). The officer never appeared.

Loyalist forces organized quickly this time to retake the occupied units. The Escuela Superior de Guerra [Superior War School] and Escuela Superior Técnica [Superior Technical School]—the principal academies for advanced officer training—contributed officers from the combined branches of the army, infantry, cavalry, and artillery. The third infantry regiment of La Tablada (previously considered to be dominated by *carapintada* sympathizers) was sent to take over the Patricios regiment and apparent rebel headquarters—an effort that succeeded only after intense combat. Members of a commandos company also played a surprising role, integrating part of the force sent to recover the TAMSE factory. Finally, the loyalist command sent cadets from the Colegio Militar [military officer's school] to regain the Quartermaster Battalion. As the rebels were unwilling to fire against the young cadets (which, they claimed, the loyalists probably anticipated), this aim was achieved rapidly and without blood. By around nine o'clock the same evening, the rebels had surrendered.

The collapse of the fourth *carapintada* uprising induced considerable relief on the part of the government and the Argentine public. Yet the event also left numerous questions. Why had the uprising occurred? What were its goals? Why did this uprising collapse? Finally, where did this leave the rebel movement? Was this rebellion really the end, or just one more round in a continuing series of confrontations?

CONTEXT

The December third uprising occurred in the context of increasing tension between Seineldín and his followers, on the one side, and the government and military command, on the other, exemplified by Seineldín's letter to Menem. Seineldín's resulting incarceration and expected discharge exacerbated dissent among his followers.

Along these lines, there is some evidence that the movement Seineldín controlled had in some ways come to control him. Since returning to Argentina for the Villa Martelli uprising, Seineldín had actively mobilized the noncommissioned officers. The particularly stringent economic conditions faced by these sectors facilitated this endeavor, as did the predominantly nationalist orientation of the NCOs, a function of their frequently less advantaged and provincial backgrounds. In other words, the NCOs were clearly available to back a leader who could articulate their interests. Seineldín, in one respect, and Rico, in another, effectively addressed that gap.

Yet in the process of integrating Seineldín's movement, the noncommissioned rebel officers also began to organize independently. According to Simeoni and Allegri, at the beginning of 1990, a group denominated Suboficiales del Ejército Nacional (SENA) [Noncommissioned Officers of the National Army] was formed in alliance with Seineldín (1991:257). As early as January, members of the group began agitating for a new protest; at Seineldín's urging, they agreed to wait. Gradually they became less patient, however. A junior officer recruited by Operación Virgen de Luján organizers reported that the officers had explained to him that, "as the NCOs had increasingly more pressure and received less answers to their worries and problems, before the NCOs had a revolution on their own or a general insubordination, they preferred to put themselves at the head of the movement and try to keep it within an established order" (Poder Judicial: Martella testimony). The "bottom-up" character inherent to the *carapintada* uprisings since its inception appeared to have moved to an extreme.

Nonetheless, the particular timing of the rebellion seems unlikely to have been random. Clearly the impending annual personnel decisions factored in the rebels' decision. Another likely contributor was the imminent visit by U.S. President George Bush, which had elicited numerous protests from *carapintadas* resentful of Menem's exaggeratedly pro-American policies.

DEMANDS AND INTENTIONS

As in past rebellions, the rebels emphasized that the uprising was not a coup and demanded both the elimination of the army command and the restoration of the army's status and capabilities. However, there were some important new elements distinct from the earlier uprisings. No longer was replacing the army chief of staff considered sufficient; now the insurgents wanted a complete purge, with Seineldín assuming the command. In addition, economic deterrents to institutional morale appeared to have replaced such earlier irritants as negative media coverage and prosecution for human rights violations. In the early hours of the episode, Major Abete announced: "This is a continuation of Monte Caseros because we cannot permit that a member of the military is a taxi-driver or a newspaper vendor. We should be defending the fatherland 24 hours. This is not a coup d'état; we respect the Constitution but we do not recognize the generals. The legitimate commander of the army is Colonel Mohammed Alí Seineldín.[42]

However, this time the assertions that the rebels were not trying to overthrow the government sounded somewhat less convincing than previously. To begin with, the rebels' stated objectives had a significantly greater political content. Demands included asserting Argentina's political neutrality and "proclaiming that the Argentine army will not be the praetorian guard against its people or defend interests foreign to the Nation."[43] The recent history and discourse of the Seineldinistas also lent some doubt to the argument. In an article based largely on interviews with Rico allies (particularly Lieutenant Colonel Enrique Venturino), Diego Pérez Andrade asserts that "Seineldín's theoretical-political plan always ended with taking power" (1990:5). Nonetheless, the rebels were clearly cognizant that direct intervention remained unpopular within the armed forces.

COMPOSITION OF THE COALITION

One of the greatest differences between Operación Virgen de Luján and the previous uprisings concerned the coalition that was involved. The rebel group active in December 1990 retained few of the bureaucratic characteristics of Semana Santa. This time members of the cavalry composed a critical proportion of the rebel coalition. In a similar reversal, members of the infantry and the commandos were among the leading loyalist forces. The composition of the rebel coalition also shifted in respect to rank. In the earlier rebellions, junior and mid-level officers (above all, those between the rank of captain and lieutenant colonel) were the heart of the *carapintadas*. In this case, noncommissioned officers were central. The ratio of NCOs to officers participating in the uprising was on the order of 14 to 1, in contrast to a normal ratio within the military of approximately 4 to 1.[44]

This distortion of the standard military order was also apparent in the decentralized nature of the rebel command during the operation. Seineldín may have been the recognized leader, but he was also absent from the entire event due to his imprisonment. Control, therefore, appeared to be shared between Colonels Baraldini, Romero Mundani, and Vega, Lieutenant Colonel Tévere, Major Abete, and Captain Breide Obeid, with the lower-ranking officers (Breide and Abete) probably representing the true leadership.

In sum, the composition of the 1990 insurgent coalition represented a personal network of Seineldín's political allies. Both the organization of the uprising and the form and makeup of participation were based on relative power and prestige within Seineldín's organization. Standard intramilitary cleavages and criteria carried only minimal influence.

RESULTS

The uprising ended disastrously for the rebels. By the time it was over, approximately 14 people had been killed, including 6 loyalists, 3 rebels, and 5 civilians, and around 55 more were injured.[45] This time, instead of having the luxury of imposing their demands, the rebels were taken prisoner. The military prosecutor almost immediately demanded capital punishment for five of the officers presumed to have held primary responsibility—Seineldín, Baraldini, Tévere, Abete, and Mercado.[46] The sentence reached by the Consejo Supremo de las Fuerzas Armadas was considerably less harsh, but nonetheless demonstrated that the era of impunity had definitively passed. Of the fifteen leaders tried in the first round (hundreds more participants were tried in subsequent lawsuits), seven were given life sentences, and six others were sentenced to between twelve and twenty years of imprisonment. These sentences were later modified by the Federal Court of Appeals, which, in September 1991, announced its decision of life imprisonment for Seineldín, and sentences ranging from two to twenty years for the other leaders.[47] Nonetheless, the final terms continued to be debated, with the prosecution itself (reportedly at the government's urging) submitting an appeal in respect to some of the decisions.

Why did Operación Virgen de Luján fail so definitively? As usual, the answer stems from a combination of factors, including the external and internal contexts and circumstantial events that occurred during the uprising itself. To begin with, the relationship between the armed forces and the government was considerably different during this period than during Alfonsín's presidency. Despite the crises in finances and morale, members of the armed forces tended to see Menem's attitude as being more benign.

At the same time, opposition toward the *carapintadas* had grown, both because of the policy shifts by the government and the army command and because of the gradual consolidation of this new internal cleavage. General Anibal Laiño (who at the time was the colonel responsible for reclaiming Edificio Libertador) explained that in the army during this period, "two sectors became polarized, enemies to the death, that were the *carapintadas* on the one side, and the others who are called the *cortacabezas* [head-choppers], who were those who wanted to eliminate all of the *carapintadas* and not leave any."[48] It thus had become increasingly difficult for the rebels to portray themselves as the representatives of *military* interests rather than *carapintada* interests. The rebels' reiterated complaints about their treatment within the forces, and the again promotion- and retirement-related timing of the incident undoubtedly augmented suspicions that the rebels' efforts were not necessarily for the benefit of the institution. The government effectively capitalized on this new situation by staunchly refusing to negotiate or grant concessions to the rebels.

The rebels, furthermore, were themselves divided. Rico's faction had already opted for the electoral path and thus, for the most part, abstained. In public statements, Rico carefully expressed his sympathies for the motivations of the rebellion and his continued respect for Seineldín, but he emphasized that in choosing to project himself in politics he was relinquishing military methods. "Since February of 1989, I separated myself totally from the military theme and adopted a political attitude. That is to say, not because the military theme or defense theme does not interest me, but because it seemed limited and not very ambitious to me. There are not partial solutions, this is what we are saying . . . no military, business, or union claim is going to change the political situation of the country" (Poder Judicial: Rico testimony). Rico also claimed that he and Seineldín had definitively parted ways in February 1989, and that he and the colonel had not even seen each other since that moment (Rico testimony).

Finally, the uprising transpired in such a way as to alienate many potential allies as well as disrupt the rebels' plans. The early deaths of the two loyalist officers, Pita and Pedernera, certainly harmed the operation, as did the absence of anticipated leading participants. The rebellion ended up depending on atomized leadership, without the aid of the active-duty superior officers who might have had more authority.

END OF THE REBEL MOVEMENT?

From all appearances, Operación Virgen de Luján destroyed Seineldín's leadership within the military. Seineldín and his associates were later referred to as "mistaken" or "misguided" by some of the very individuals who had previously expressed their profound admiration for the colonel—including Aldo Rico. Furthermore, Seineldín accepted this defeat. When asked if he would be likely to initiate other uprisings, Seineldín responded, "No. This team has ended. We are finished. If it is necessary to find another path, the men who are inside the army will do it. I have already given everything; I have no more to give. I lost. Now, others will have to risk themselves. Myself, never again" (quoted in Barral 1991:68). Recognized by all as a man of his word, Seineldín had announced his retirement from military insurgency.

Conclusions

The *carapintada* movement in Argentina passed through three phases between April 1987 and December 1990: emergence (or reaction), consolidation, and diversification. During the first phase, the *carapintadas* emerged as the defenders of the military institution, based on a relatively apolitical, professional orientation. The second phase brought increased politicization and definition to the movement, along with an important alliance with the orthodox Peronists. As this continued, the *carapintadas* developed into an independent civil-military movement, with separate military and political factions. The military faction, unable to compete in an increasingly unsupportive intramilitary environment, finally collapsed in December 1990. On the other hand, the political sector of the movement achieved a successful transformation from military rebellion to civilian politics.

In addition to reflecting the changing demands placed on the movement at different phases of its development, the shifts from one phase to another were also related to the changing leadership and composition of the coalition and to the context. Thus, the movement underwent a major shift from Rico's pragmatic leadership to Seineldín's more ideological leadership. The incongruously personalistic nature of the coalition during the last uprising, which undoubtedly arose as a consequence of the new organization's greater level of consolidation, contributed further to perceptions of Seineldín's maneuver as "something new" and no longer coherent with the military mode of operation. The lack of a conventional military command structure also severely debilitated the rebels during the uprising, thus hastening their collapse.

Thus, in certain respects, the very process of development followed by the rebel movement led to its demise. Consolidating the movement necessitated defining its objectives and ideas more explicitly. Yet the more those ideas were defined, the easier it became to identify the boundaries of the *carapintada* movement, and the more difficult it was for them to present themselves as representative of the entire military. Organizational development also entailed generating a leadership based on shared goals, rather than the bureaucratic proximity that initially proved more relevant in determining the lines of factionalism. However, this kind of leadership is relatively less effective within the context of such a strongly hierarchical bureaucratic institution as the military. Nonetheless, in a more pluralist context, such as a political party system, these coalitions are far *more* effective. This helps explain why Seineldín's efforts failed and Rico's succeeded.

Regardless of the inherent obstacles to building military opposition movements, Argentine history seems filled with military protests that succeeded—obtaining their demands, or even obtaining the government. Yet most of these, I would suggest, did not develop *publicly* as movements, or did not do so prior to reaching power. Thus, military governments have frequently been characterized by complex coalitions of nationalists and liberals in which the battle to define the regime continues well after its initiation. The *carapintadas,* therefore, were probably most severely crippled by a context that did not allow them (or, in the case of many, inspire them) to openly and promptly pursue military intervention. The intermediate path as a military pressure group proved unworkable.

7

Foundations of Chronic Interventionism in Argentina

To the casual observer, military coups and rebellions appear to be discreet events. Coups explode on the political horizon with a drama that contrasts starkly with the usual subtleties and intricacies of political change. Yet the drama is deceptive. Military coups come from a complex series of conditions and organizational maneuvers. In Argentina, they are also part and product of a pattern of chronic interventionism, unique among the more advanced countries of South America. Argentina's military interventionism stems from both a civilian predilection to seek military allies (Rouquie 1982a) and the military's tendency to respond. To understand the latter, one must consider such characteristics as: (1) the myth of the military's responsibility for the nation; (2) traditionally low costs for intervention; and (3) the politicized character of military promotions.

Causes of Prolonged Interventionism

In a classic book on Argentine politics and society, José Luis de Imaz wrote: "In Argentina, the armed forces are not a pressure group. Pressure groups are sporadic, and their action is directed toward passing ends. . . . In Argentina, the armed forces are a power factor. . . . The objectives of power factors are permanent, as are their manifest and latent functions and the interests that they personify" (1977:59). Why did the Argentine military become a "power factor"? Control of weapons creates the *capacity* for such a role, but this is true of any modern military. It does not explain why the Argentine armed forces have been especially inclined to assume this role.

The military's predilection toward political involvement in Argentina has both ideological and "rational" causes. Ideology, by which I mean shared systems of beliefs, determines what military officers are likely to consider as important, and how they perceive their professional role.[1] On the other hand, the "rational" component of decision making refers to actors' assessments of the relative costs and benefits of particular strategies. These two dimensions of decision making are by no means incompatible. Ideologies, or belief systems in general, help delineate which goals decision makers consider worth pursuing, and which strategies they consider legitimate. At a more concrete level, these beliefs also influence the formulation of laws and regulations that help determine some of the costs actors might incur.

Mythical History of the Argentine Military

The myths about the relationship between the Argentine military and the nation help form a standard by which members of the military evaluate events and circumstances and directly influence decision making within the armed forces.

Despite the extensive history of factionalism in the Argentine military, exemplified by the outbreaks of 1962–63 and 1987–90, there is much to unify the military. Members of the armed forces share a function, a history, and a particular position within the society and within the state. Some of those commonalities contribute to the overall esprit de corps and camaraderie of the military. Others enhance the military's propensity to assume political roles. In particular, popular conceptions about the relationship between the military and the nation have stimulated members of the Argentine armed forces to assume a much broader role than that which traditionally defines modern militaries.

Birth of the Nation-State

Argentina, like the rest of the countries in the Americas, originated as a European colony. Its birth as a sovereign state occurred, again as elsewhere, through revolutionary warfare under the leadership of José de San Martín. Yet the popular image of the revolution of the United States is very different than that of Argentina. In U.S. folklore, the New England colonists stand out as the revolutionary heroes— ordinary townspeople picking up arms to free themselves from a distant ruler. The revolutionary army makes its appearance on the pages of the history books, but its mystique fades before the likes of Paul Revere. In contrast, the Argentine army preserves a much different myth. In this conceptualization, it is the army that came first—it is the army that liberated Argentina from colonial rule, and the army that created the nation. As an Argentine general commented: "On the army crest, it says that the army was born with the country. I believe that it is not exactly so, but that the army existed before the country. It existed before the Argentine state. . . . Argentina is the 'daughter of the sword' at the service of a great political [design]— national emancipation and national organization and, following peace and order, a life of democracy. This is the tradition of our army."[2]

The military's founding role in Argentina is a popular theme in military discourse, emerging frequently in military journals. In one article, an officer detailed the army's founding role as having essentially three phases (Teissere 1953:33−34). The first phase was the formation of the Buenos Aires militias, organized to ward off the British during 1806−07 (see Rock 1987:71−74). The second phase was the revolution of 1810. Although this independence movement was actually regional, freeing various southern territories of South America from the Spanish, the leader of the movement, José de San Martín, was originally Argentine. Thus the symbolism of independence, and of San Martín, became relatively more important in Argentina (Diamint 1990). Finally, during the third phase, the military assumed the task of achieving real control of the formally delineated territory of the newly constituted, primarily immigrant Argentine Republic. Without the shiny packaging, this essentially meant killing and displacing the vast majority of Argentina's native inhabitants. In sum, Teissere describes military actions as having been responsible for all relevant steps in the formation of the nation-state. The people of Argentina (*el pueblo*) are depicted as the spirit behind the process but not as central to the events as the organized army.

Guardian of the Nation

From facilitating the "birth" of the nation, the military moved to guarding its interests. Yet it has rarely accepted the interpretations of intermediaries regarding what those interests may be. Neither the government nor the Constitution are consistently accepted as the "voice" of the nation. For example, Lieutenant Colonel Florentino Díaz Loza argued:"The people are the custodians of their republican institutions and, furthermore, the only ones who should determine their destiny. Because of this, the army cannot have as its transcendental mission keeping watch over the maintenance of the National Constitution, because this neither is, nor by any means, can be permanent or immutable" (1973:19–20). Díaz Loza's position certainly does not represent the totality of the armed forces, as evidenced by the frequent use of the constitutional violations as a justification for military intervention. However, it does point to a sentiment that is rather prevalent: the feeling that the military has the right to decide. It may decide on issues of constitutionality, or it may decide what is in the interests of the nation. But in either case, it sees itself as invested with *discretion*. The armed forces thus have historically placed themselves somewhat above the nation and the state.

Correspondingly, the armed forces have traditionally seen themselves as the nation's conscience. According to an army document, "The mission of the army is to safeguard the superior interests of the Nation. . . . The army constitutes one of the most elevated moral reserves of the spiritual life of the country."[3] An article in a military journal elaborates this sentiment:"it is in the barracks where the character is forged and the virtues refined that structure the personality of the citizens. In the barracks the basic elements are elaborated that constitute the intimate essence of the moral values of the people, and in the barracks, these values are disciplined, that they may be transformed into an active social power, based on a solid, conscious nationalist concept, propellent of the progress of the nation" (Teissere 1953:35). The article thus portrays the military as producing not only Argentina's statehood but also its values and morals. This myth provides members of the armed forces with a driving justification for the military's interventionist role as guardian of the nation.

National Security Doctrine

The 1960s witnessed an expansion of the military role throughout Latin America, significantly enhancing Argentina's already active interventionist military myths. Largely in reaction to the Cold War and, more directly, the Cuban revolution, Latin American militaries began to explicitly expand their roles to encompass different facets of security. Latin American militaries increasingly defined their roles as including national security, which implies preventing both military threats and other threats to national autonomy, rather than merely national defense. As Fitch explains, "According to the national security thesis, the military has a professional responsibility for all issues which affect national security—the economy, external ideological influences, foreign relations, political leadership—instead of purely external defense" (1986:19). The perceived need to prevent or abort revolutionary movements dominated military strategy. Since economic and ideological factors are critical to the early development of revolutionary movements, promoting economic development and guarding against the development of revolutionary ideologies was considered an essential part of a strategy of preventing revolutionary warfare.

The national security doctrine has received extensive attention from observers of Latin American politics, many of whom have employed it as the principal explanation for authoritarianism and repression in the 1960s and 1970s (López 1987). As doctrines of national security do promote a higher level of interventionism along with a stronger propensity to combat ideologies, rather than solely military action, such arguments are fairly convincing. However, certain misinterpretations have tended to dominate these discussions, including (1) the degree to which the United States defined and successfully promulgated the national security doctrine, (2) the uniformity of conceptualizations of national security in different cases, and (3) the degree to which emphases on national security were actually new.

Analysts of Latin American politics have frequently portrayed the national security doctrine as a blatant example of a U.S. attempt to utilize Latin American countries for its purposes. According to these interpretations, the United States disseminated the national security doctrine to Latin American countries in order to combat the U.S. enemy, international communism. As with most popular arguments, important elements are true. The United States did train Latin American militaries in counterinsurgency tactics and did promote anti-communist notions of national security (Stepan 1973:50; Rouquie 1987:248; Child 1985). Furthermore, the national security orientation did contain an internationalized vision of the nature of military threats. The fact that Latin American guerrilla movements were frequently regional or dependent on external support lent credibility to this vision (Alexander and Kucinski 1985).

However, Latin American militaries had an important role in designing their own national security doctrines. Particularly in Brazil, military strategy in this epoch clearly did not merely mimic doctrines developed in the United States. Stepan writes that "By the late 1950s and early 1960s, the ESG [Escola Superior de Guerra] had developed its key ideological tenet: the close interrelationship between national security and national development" (1973:54). Elsewhere as well, Latin American militaries undertook their own studies of how to combat revolution and, in general, how to enhance the security of their own countries.

United States–centered analyses of the national security doctrine also tend to create a mistakenly monolithic vision of the doctrine. While there was a relatively generalized trend in the region toward emphasis on national security as opposed to merely national defense, in other respects, the versions of the national security doctrine differed significantly from country to country (Pion-Berlin 1989b). For example, the emphasis on the economy, with the consequent military inclination toward promoting economic development, was an important element in the strategies of the Brazilian military. Thus, during the years of military rule (1964–85), the Brazilian state became heavily involved in development projects (Evans 1979). In Argentina, however, the national security doctrine placed more stress on ideological factors. The military involved itself in economic promotion only minimally in this case and instead focused more attention and concern on culture and education.

These differences illuminate the degree to which the national security doctrine reflected earlier trends rather than emerging as a new invention of the 1960s. The vision of a completely subordinated military, dedicated only to the defense of the nation-state and acting consistently at the command of an elected government, is rather foreign to the reality of many Latin American countries. Military intervention certainly did not begin with the bureaucratic-authoritarian regimes of the 1960s and 1970s, nor were all earlier cases of intervention propagated by military caudillos. Rather, many of these cases reflected the fact that the Latin American militaries' perceptions of their role were already quite a bit broader than in the north. In Argentina, the myths of the military's role in the founding of the nation and its subsequent role as guardian have long been mainstays of military ideology. The Teissere article quoted above, which discussed the phases in the military's founding of the nation-state and the role of the military in developing the values and morals of the nation, was published in 1953, before the national security doctrine became defined (which occurred around the beginning of the 1960s). In sum, while the national security doctrine did contribute to the propensity toward interventionism in Latin America, it built upon a base that— at least in Argentina—had existed long before.

Costs of Interventionism

Another factor contributing to chronic interventionism in Argentina has been the limited costs generally endured by those participating in interventionist actions. Legal reprisals have been limited, and those sanctions that have been imposed have frequently lasted only briefly, due to the lack of continuity in the overall political system.

Until relatively recently, jurisdiction over insurrectionary actions taken by members of the military resided primarily in their own courts. The Código de Justicia Militar [Military Code of Justice] defined what actions were punishable and how, and military officers decided whether offenders should be sentenced and what that sentence should be. From the perspective of the military, however, coup attempts are not necessarily the most horrendous of all possible violations. Infractions against the military hierarchy or wartime violations of discipline appear to be viewed as significantly more serious.

In the 1951 Código de Justicia Militar, military rebellion is defined as follows: "Members of the armed forces commit rebellion who promote, aid, or sustain any armed movement to alter the constitutional order or impede or hinder the exercise of government in any of its powers" (Law 14.029, República Argentina, *Anales*, 1951:86). If rebellion were to occur in the context of a war, then the penalties were quite severe—leaders could face the death sentence, and other participating officers could be sentenced to life imprisonment. However, if the rebellion or coup attempt occurred under normal conditions, then the leaders confronted a sentence of only eight to fifteen years of prison, and the sentence for other officers was placed at three to eight years. Furthermore, the sentence was even shorter if the officers surrendered voluntarily before the attempt led to confrontation.

All participants would still be dismissed from the armed forces, but officers other than the leaders faced only a maximum of one year in prison.

This contrasts sharply with the penalties incurred by violations of discipline or attempts against the military hierarchy. For example, a member of the military who attacked a superior either in front of the troops or in front of the enemy was, according to the Código de Justicia Militar, subject to either the death penalty or life imprisonment. This was the case even if the victim was entirely unharmed and the assailant used no weapon. Additionally, any act of disrespect toward a superior could mean imprisonment or, in time of war, execution.

The strongest parallel with rebellion, however, is probably the case of *mutiny,* defined as aggression against the military command. In the case of mutiny, in which four or more members of the military "collectively adopt a hostile or tumultuous attitude toward the command," the sentence for leaders was set at a minimum of five to twenty-five years imprisonment (Law 14.029. República Argentina, *Anales,* 1951:89). The maximum in this case was a full ten years *more* than that incurred by attempts against the constitutional regime. If the attempted mutiny were to (1) result in loss of blood, (2) occur in the presence of the enemy, or (3) endanger the existence of a military force, then the sentence was, again, life imprisonment or death. The relative severity of these latter regulations, when contrasted to the moderation of the penalties for attempts against the constitutional regime, would appear to encourage members of the military to vent their dissatisfaction against the regime rather than their own leaders.

These laws remained largely unchanged until 1984. At this point, the newly elected Alfonsín government passed the "Law for the Defense of Democracy." A primary aim of this law was to increase the punishment for attempts against the constitutional regime. At the same time, it sought to eliminate the distinction between threats from the military and threats from guerrilla insurgents, subjecting both groups to the same set of laws, following the "two demons" approach of shared blame. Thus, the law begins by changing the term *rebellion* (which remains in use in the 1984 version of the Military Code of Justice) to "attempts against the constitutional order and the democratic way of life" in order that either source of instability would be covered (Law 23.077, *Leyes Sancionadas,* 1984:3839).

The actual changes in the sanctions were relatively minimal, however. A sentence of five to fifteen years of prison is recommended for "those who lift up arms to change the Constitution, depose any public power of the national government, . . . or impede . . . the free exercise of their Constitutional powers" with no other complicating circumstances (3839). If such actions are undertaken by a member of the military, the minimum sentence is increased by a third. In essence, this establishes approximately the same eight- to fifteen-year sentence as recommmended in the 1951 Código de Justicia Militar for rebellion.

However, a few revisions and additions were included in the new law that did increase the penalties for potentially destabilizing activities. First, the condition was added that if the previous actions (lifting up arms to change the Constitution) were to occur with the intention of "permanently changing the democratic system . . . , eliminating the division of powers, abrogating fundamental human rights or suppressing or damaging, even temporarily, the economic independence of the Nation," then the recommended sentence would be set at eight to twenty-five years (3838). Again, for a military offender, the minimum increases by a third. Thus, the minimum penalty for leadership of a coup attempt (with no major consequences and in a nonwar context) was increased from the earlier recommended sentence of eight to fifteen years to approximately eleven to twenty-five years of imprisonment.

Secondly, the Law for the Defense of Democracy also recommended a sentence of five to ten years for taking part in an "illegal association" intending to threaten the constitutional regime (3840). In these instances, the Law for the Defense of Democracy claims exclusive jurisdiction for the Federal Court of Appeals—by implication prohibiting the military from even considering any of these cases. By giving control of these cases to the civilian courts, the law's authors attempted to avoid the military's renewed involvement in investigating "subversive" civilian groups, a practice that precipitated many of the disappearances of the late 1970s.

Finally, the new law also included cooperation by public officials as a punishable offence. Any member of the executive, legislative, or judicial branches of the state who remains in office after the government has been overthrown, assumes public functions after irregular constitutional changes have been induced, or otherwise cooperates with the usurpers becomes subject to one to eight years of prison. For those who succumb to the temptation of accepting any of the top positions in the new government, the recommended sentence is doubled. Thus, the new law explicitly recognizes the combined civil-military character of military intervention and the possibility that threats to the constitutional regime could emanate from multiple directions. By expanding the scope of the law to include these other actors, along with augmenting the penalties for direct efforts to overthrow the government, the authors of the Law for the Defense of Democracy apparently hoped to dissuade future discontented individuals from choosing these kinds of strategies.

Unfortunately, however, the penalties recommended for attempted coups or rebellions by the various laws are not necessarily an accurate indicator of the kinds of penalties that are actually imposed. Frequently, those in a formal position to impose severe sanctions do not have the real power to do so. Civilian governments have habitually opted to tread lightly, particularly if the opposing group appeared to have significant strength. As discussed in chapter 2, Arturo Frondizi habitually conceded to military rebels, usually not even trying to defeat them, let alone applying sanctions.

More recently, in the rebellions of 1987–90, the relationship between the strength of rebellious or mutinous movements and the penalties applied was quite clear. Of four military uprisings between 1987 and 1990, two resulted in large numbers of arrests, and two resulted in only minimal arrests. The numbers did not correspond to the absolute number of participants but, rather, represented an inversion of the rebellions' relative strength. Not surprisingly, the uprisings in which the rebels commanded a fair amount of support and relatively little opposition, and in which they succeeded in obtaining a significant amount of their demands, resulted in minimal punishment. Apparently, neither the government nor the government-allied military hierarchy was in a position to be able to impose these penalties.[4] On the other hand, the less successful uprisings were followed by numerous arrests and, in the final case, relatively severe sentences.

Another problem with the use of the legal system as a deterrent to military interventionism stems from the lack of continuity in the political system. Not surprisingly, the repeated shifts from civilian to military regimes and back, referred to by Marcelo Diamond as "the Argentine pendulum" (1983), have created significant inconsistencies in the application of the law. This is amplified by the considerable strength of the presidency. Presidents have significant powers to decree laws (obviously more so during military regimes), along with relatively frequently used powers to grant pardons. Historically, Hector Cámpora's pardon of 1973 stands out as one of the most important examples of the use of the presidential pardon in Argentina. The consequences of this decision included not only the revival of certain guerrilla organizations but the military's increased distrust of legal processes. Carlos Menem (elected president in 1989) also made notorious use of the presidential pardon. All military officers convicted of human rights abuses or participation in military uprisings during the previous government (Alfonsín) were set free and pardoned. By the end of 1991, the only officers still imprisoned for insurrectional activities were those who participated in the uprising of December 1990 during Menem's presidency. Hence, the combination of relatively mild legal penalties for attempts against the constitutional system and the high probability that members of the military would escape those penalties anyway has kept the overall costs of interventionist behavior historically rather low.

The Politics of Career Advancement

Another issue potentially encouraging the Argentine military's interventionism is the impact of political participation on officers' careers. Of course, careers may be severely hurt or even terminated if an officer participates in a failed uprising or coup attempt. However, officers may also stand to gain from such participation. Certainly if a coup attempt succeeds, members of a winning coup coalition share the spoils of power. Officers loyal to the coup leaders may find themselves placed in prestigious and financially rewarding positions, either within the military or within the government. In Argentina's military government of 1976–83, the extensive colonization of the political system by the military resulted in numerous officers landing in rather profitable positions (Ricci and Fitch 1990). Furthermore, those officers placed in government posts had the added advantage of receiving double salaries, adding the new salaries to their continuing military income.

At the moment of a military coup attempt, such considerations may be critical. Yet the history of the Argentine military has been filled with less drastic moments of crisis during which officers need to decide the direction and degree of their political loyalties. Formally, officers are not encouraged to have political affiliations. According to the Military Personnel Law, military personnel are permitted "neither acceptance nor discharge of elective public functions and no participation, direct or indirect, in the activities of political parties" (Ejército Argentino, *Boletín Público del Ejército*, no. 3783, 30 June 1971:Supplement 1:6). Officers may vote, but they cannot run for office or take any more active role in politics. The Military Code of Justice states that "the member of the military who, while in active service, openly participates in political activities not authorized by the laws or regulations, or who, in public meetings or through the press, makes commentaries of a political party or electoral character, will be reprimanded with disciplinary sanctions or dismissal" (Código de Justicia Militar, Article 700:257). In other words, open, active participation in civilian politics is proscribed for members of the military, thereby limiting officers' options for expressing their views within the confines of a democratic political system.

These limitations on democratic political participation by members of the military emanate as much (or more) from military conceptions of their role as from any civilian-imposed constraints. As the midwife and, subsequently, guardian of the nation, the military purports to remain above politics. By retaining this position, the armed forces have hoped to remain unsullied by what is perceived as the corrupting influence of politics. Military officers are thus expected to avoid the supposed bickering and trivialities of political competition, guiding their decisions by a larger, ostensibly identifiable concept of national interest.

However, the exclusion of the armed forces from certain political privileges, combined with this underlying vision of the military's relationship to the nation, has not succeeded in eliminating politics from the military. On the contrary, this practice appears to lead to the internalization and distortion of political competition. The national interest is not so objectively identifiable as many would wish. Instead, different groups and individuals have historically adhered to quite distinct interpretations of what has constituted the national interest and how the military should act to defend it. Without standardized means of resolving these debates, political games are played

through intramilitary feuds and clashes, and through military uprisings and military coups, rather than through elections.

While many of these clashes arise out of particular circumstances,
others emanate from longstanding cleavages within the armed forces
(see chapter 5). Ideologically, the tension between liberalism and nationalism has been central. Organizationally, nationalist and liberal
inclinations have dominated different services and branches. For example, the navy tends to be perceived as the most liberal service,
while the army and air force are more nationalist. Within the army,
the infantry is considered to be the most nationalist branch, and the
cavalry is seen as the most liberal.

Belonging to a particular military service and branch certainly
does not guarantee that an individual has the generalized political
and ideological orientations conventionally attributed to that group.
Yet the organizational and ideological overlap does have some implications. The different branches of the army do represent clusters of
shared ideas. Granted, members of the army cannot choose to move
from one branch to another, nor do leaders present openly political
"platforms." Yet the branches do compete for power within the organization, whether that power is inherently political or merely bureaucratic.

Furthermore, there does appear to be a relationship between the
politics of the president and the military branch of the army chief of
staff. A list of the army leadership from 1958 until 1989 reveals a
clear dominance by the infantry during the Peronist period of civilian
government from 1973 to 1976, which apparently emanates from the
shared nationalist inclinations of the Peronists and the infantry (see
table 5). In contrast, during the military government from 1966 to
1973, which was in part a reaction against Peronism, the cavalry controlled the army. On the other hand, in the military government from
1976 to 1983, infantry control gave way to control by engineering,
one of the army's two smaller branches. Such a shift seems to fit well
with the technocratic tendency of bureaucratic-authoritarian regimes discussed by Guillermo O'Donnell (1973).

The apparent relationship between the ideologies imputed to
army chiefs of staff (loosely indicated by the military branch) and the
politics of the distinct presidents is not necessarily a surprising one.[5]
Since 1930, Argentine presidents have consistently governed in a
context of instability. Whether military or civilian, all have faced the

threat of being overthrown by some organized opposition group. Thus, appointing an army chief of staff whose political beliefs seem likely to be compatible with those of the president would seem to be a necessary preventive measure, particularly given the degree of power held by those individuals and the danger to the government should the army chief of staff become uncooperative or antagonistic.

Yet such a practice may contribute to continued military politicization and the cycle of interventionism. Various Argentine army officers suggested to me in interviews that while promotions up through the level of colonel are based primarily on merit, promotions to brigadier general or general of division have a more subjective, or "political," basis. This perception stems from the complicated system deciding the criteria that determine promotions. According to an informant, up through the rank of major, promotions are decided on such objective criteria as the officer's position in his courses, days of sick leave, and (if applicable) days of arrest. For promotions to the rank of lieutenant colonel or colonel, those factors are still taken into account, but their impact is reduced to around half, and the remainder of the score is conferred according to the assessment of the promotion board. Finally, for the rank of general, the entire score is based on subjective criteria. Given the virtual impossibility of identifying and classifying the political beliefs and personal networks of most officers, the assumption that the high-ranking promotions involve political values would be rather difficult to test. However, by using the military branch as a substitute for these other factors, it is possible to gather at least a general impression of whether that may be true.

Before comparing the composition of the groups promoted to different ranks in different years, one must ask how much difference exists overall in the weight of the five army branches at the different ranks. As table 7 indicates, members of the infantry constitute well over a third of the graduates of Colegio Militar Nacional (CMN) [Military Officers' School] and promotions to colonel and brigadier general. In terms of the overall composition of the officer corp, as indicated by graduations from CMN, the cavalry and the artillery are the next largest branches, with 18 percent and 19 percent, respectively. Communications and engineering then follow with 11 percent and 14 percent.

Table 7

Promotions by Branch in the Argentine Army, 1958–1988

	Inf.		*Cav.*		*Art.*		*Com.*		*Eng.*		*Total*
Colegio Militar[a]	1727	38%	809	18%	853	19%	490	11%	623	14%	4502
Colonel[b]	704	38%	343	19%	456	25%	149	8%	185	10%	1837
Brigadier General	129	34%	93	25%	84	22%	22	6%	48	13%	376
General of Division	32	30%	38	36%	22	21%	4	4%	9	9%	105

Source: The data for this table were compiled from a combination of the *Boletín Público del Ejército* (1958–88), the *Boletín Reservado del Ejército,* and the *Escalafón del Ejército Argentino.* In cases when I was not able to obtain the specializations of officers from formal sources (1958–66 for promotions to colonel, brigadier general, and general of division), I relied on the help of a retired Argentine colonel.

[a]Colegio Militar refers to graduates of Military Officers' School from 1960 to 1988. Colonel, brigadier general, and general of division refer to officers promoted to these ranks from 1958 to 1988.

[b]In January 1992, the rank of major colonel was added to the military hierarchy, between colonel and brigadier general.

However, there is a shift in the weight of the different branches at the higher levels of the army. Most conspicuous is the disproportionate representation of the cavalry. Promotions of members of the cavalry jump from 19 percent at the rank of colonel to 25 percent at the rank of brigadier general and 36 percent at the rank of general of division. This rise is paralleled by a drop in the size of infantry representation at the higher ranks, eventually leading to the complete elimination of the infantry's advantage over the cavalry.

What might cause these differences? One possibility is that the numbers represent a general trend in the composition of the army, which cannot be adequately discerned using this limited time frame. It takes a minimum of eighteen to twenty-five years before graduates of CMN have the possibility of being promoted to colonel, and a minimum of four years more before they might be promoted to brigadier general (Ejército Argentino, Boletín Público del Ejército, no.3783, 6 July 1971: Supplement 3). Hence those officers promoted to brigadier general in 1958 probably graduated from Colegio Militar Nacional close to thirty years earlier, in the late 1920s. (See figures 1–3 for a breakdown of CMN graduates by infantry, calvary, and artillery.) It may be, therefore, that during that period there was a trend toward a decreasing infantry and an increasing cavalry, which only appeared at the higher ranks a few decades later. However, figures 4–12 would actually seem to demonstrate the opposite trend, with a growing infantry and decreasing cavalry.

Another possibility is that the different balance at the higher ranks of the army stems from the relative prestige of the branches. In many respects, the cavalry is the army's most prestigious branch. Members of the cavalry are viewed as the aristocrats of the service, while the infantry tends to be perceived as the army's proletariat. Thus, the infantry's strength at the higher levels of the army seems to derive primarily from sheer numbers. The power of numbers might not be sufficient to compete with the power of prestige, however.

The final possible explanation for the differing composition of rank promotions to be considered here is the most relevant to the military's chronic interventionism. According to this hypothesis, promotions at higher levels of the army are quite political in nature. Thus, once again using army branches as substitutes, one might expect promotions to the higher levels of the service, particularly to brigadier general and general of division, to favor the specialization of the army chief of staff.

Figures 1–12 indicate that while the evidence is not as conclusive as might be hoped, some relationship does seem to exist. The figures indicate the percentages from the major branches of the army—infantry, cavalry, and artillery—represented in the groups graduating from CMN and promoted to each of the highest ranks of the army from 1958 until 1988. The letters along the bottom of the graphs indicate the branch of the army commander in chief—infantry, cavalry, artillery, engineering, and communications—at the time of promotions each year (around early December). Not surprisingly, there appears to be practically no relationship between the chief of staff's specialization and the balance between the branches in either the Colegio Militar graduating classes (figures 1–3) or in the promotions to colonel (figures 4–6). At the level of promotions to brigadier

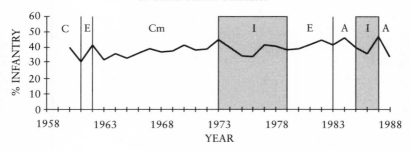

Figure 1. Infantry Officers as a Percentage
of Officer School Graduates

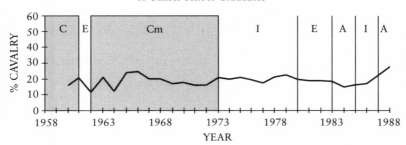

Figure 2. Cavalry Officers as a Percentage
of Officer School Graduates

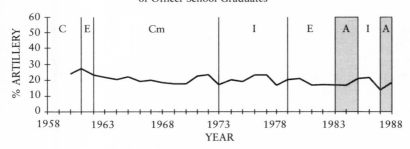

Figure 3. Artillery Officers as a Percentage
of Officer School Graduates

I=Infantry C=Cavalry A=Artillery E=Engineers Cm=Communications
Shaded boxes indicate when chief of staff is of same
branch as those in figures

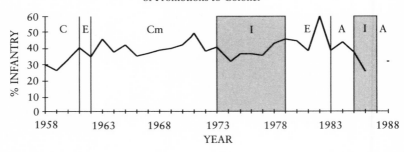

Figure 4. Infantry Officers as a Percentage
of Promotions to Colonel

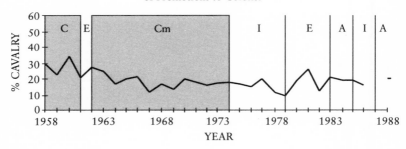

Figure 5. Cavalry Officers as a Percentage
of Promotions to Colonel

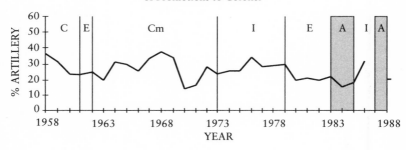

Figure 6. Artillery Officers as a Percentage
of Promotions to Colonel

I=Infantry C=Cavalry A=Artillery E=Engineers Cm=Communications
Shaded boxes indicate when chief of staff is of same
branch as those in figures

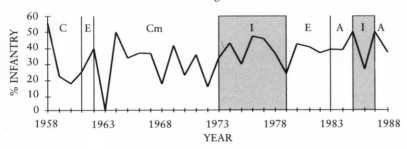

Figure 7. Infantry Officers as a Percentage
of Promotions to Brigadier General

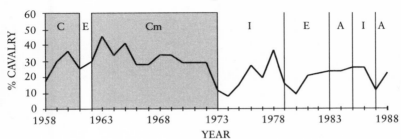

Figure 8. Cavalry Officers as a Percentage
of Promotions to Brigadier General

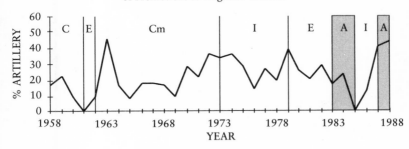

Figure 9. Artillery Officers as a Percentage
of Promotions to Brigadier General

I=Infantry C=Cavalry A=Artillery E=Engineers Cm=Communications
Shaded boxes indicate when chief of staff is of same
branch as those in figures

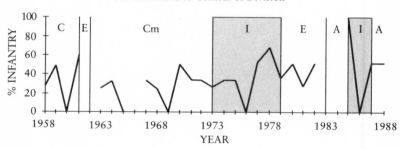

Figure 10. Infantry Officers as a Percentage
of Promotions to General of Division

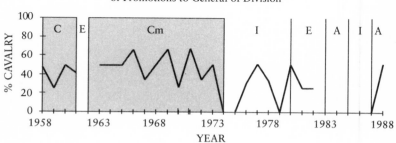

Figure 11. Cavalry Officers as a Percentage
of Promotions to General of Division

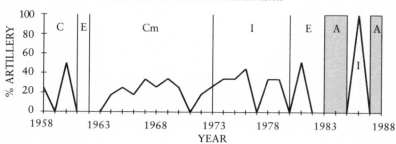

Figure 12. Artillery Officers as a Percentage
of Promotions to General of Division

I=Infantry C=Cavalry A=Artillery E=Engineers Cm=Communications
Shaded boxes indicate when chief of staff is of same
branch as those in figures

general, figures 7–9 indicate that the specialization of the chief of staff may have some relationship, particularly if the patterns in these figures are compared to figures 4–6. Finally, a significantly stronger relationship does seem to exist between the specialization of the commander in chief and promotions to general of division (figures 10–12).

Although the varying success of the artillery does not fit the pattern very well, the shifts in representation from the infantry and the cavalry largely parallel shifts in the branch of the army chief of staff. When the army is under the command of infantry chiefs of staff, the infantry receives a higher proportion of the promotions, while the proportion of promotions granted to the cavalry increases under cavalry chiefs of staff. Thus, the data indicate that at the higher ranks, members of each branch of the army generally seem to favor their own.

The explanation for this may simply lie in the greater personal ties between members of the same branch. Years of training together and practicing together, combined with the traditional rivalries between the different branches, undoubtedly create strong loyalties among those from the same branch. Yet the results discussed above may also reflect a tendency toward shared political beliefs within each branch. If promotions *are* affected by political sympathies, what might this imply about the probable impact of the overall environment of political instability on career advancement, and what kinds of adaptations might result?

In a situation in which one's political beliefs affect eventual professional success, gauging the political climate and carefully choosing how to communicate political beliefs, along with choosing what beliefs to communicate, become central choices. The risk-averse actor probably plays it safe, following the rules and remaining as publicly apolitical as possible. Those who do otherwise face the possibility of strong repercussions from their military subordinates. For example, toward the end of the last military government in 1981, a group of thirty-three officers was forced to retire from the army due to their suspected sympathies for the Peronist left. At the same time, however, taking such political risks can propel an officer to the top.

Admittedly, the relationship between the subjectivity of promotions and the politicization of the army is based largely on speculation. However, what is less arguable is that whether or not promotions are based on "political" criteria, the common perception by officers that this occurs can have some important repercussions. Consequently, during every December, the month in which the high command compiles the lists of promotions, uncertainty and tension pervade. Not coincidentally, both the third and fourth *carapintada* uprisings occurred in early December. Colonel Seineldín led the first of these immediately after having been denied a promotion to general. Although this was not the articulated reason for the uprising, and certainly was not the only reason, it undoubtedly played an important role in provoking Seineldín's participation. Supporters of Seineldín claimed that the decision not to promote Seineldín was political in nature and essentially unrelated to his military credentials. Along the same lines, the military uprising of 1990 occurred at least partially as a reaction to perceived injustices suffered by Seineldín's supporters during that round of promotions.[6]

Conclusion: Confronting the Foundations of Interventionism

The existence of underlying patterns that encourage pervasive interventionism places the problem of subordinating the military in a new light. The challenge to democratic consolidators is neither so simple as avoiding direct provocation of the armed forces, nor is it necessarily as complex as restructuring the entire socioeconomic and political systems. Instead, democratizing civilian leaders confront a series of ideological traditions, patterns of interaction between the armed forces and civilian governments, and formal incentive structures that help encourage the continuation of these patterns of interventionism.

How might such patterns be altered? Each of the factors discussed in this chapter suggest some possibilities. The first factor, the myth of the special relationship between the military and the nation, is probably the most difficult to change from outside of the institution. A civilian trying to restructure military thought would probably be dismissed as not fully understanding and might also be suspected of having "antinational" reasons for wanting to impose change. Change can, however, occur for internal reasons. For example, the failures of the government of 1976–83, especially the lack of economic success and the Falklands/Malvinas debacle, seem to have contributed to the redefinition of military roles. If members of the military still believe they have a special responsibility for the nation, they are perhaps less likely to believe they have the capacity to resolve all of its problems.

The second factor discussed in this chapter was the limited legal costs of interventionist behavior. Formally, altering costs is fairly straightforward: the legislature merely needs to impose stricter sanctions for interventionist behavior and penalize actions against the constitutional regime more strongly than disciplinary lapses. However, it is considerably more difficult to change the *application* of legal sanctions. One possible solution would be to eliminate the presidential pardon, thereby prohibiting future discontinuities. Yet this method would also eliminate a significant executive prerogative and could excessively restrict the flexibility of the president. In certain circumstances, such concessions may be unavoidable to temporarily patch up incipient rips in the political fabric. Nonetheless, presidents hoping to ensure the continuity of the democratic system should certainly avoid, or at least limit, the use of this prerogative.

The final factor discussed concerned the politicizing effect of the system of promotions. The implication of this discussion is that leaders should make a very deliberate effort to utilize only professional criteria for promotions at the top of the military hierarchy. The temptation to appoint political allies, while certainly understandable, in the long run may undermine efforts to stabilize the system.

Members of the Argentine armed forces are not armed lunatics, fanatically seeking all and any methods to increase their power. Nor, however, are they saints. Like any of society's actors, their decisions are formed by a combination of their own beliefs and ideologies, the overall structure of costs and benefits, and the pressures of the immediate context. In the Argentine case, these conditions have tended to impede the development of a stable constitutional regime. Instead, they have facilitated the frequent seduction of Argentina's soldiers into deleterious interventionist roles.

8

Shadows of Military Rule: Legacies of Bureaucratic Authoritarianism in South America

The 1980s brought a new era of democratic government to South America. By 1990, the military regimes of the 1960s and 1970s had all but vanished. In Argentina, Brazil, Chile, and Uruguay, the militaries previously responsible for the era of bureaucratic authoritarianism relinquished their political command, retreating to the sidelines. Yet the stability of the new order continued to be questioned. Not only in Argentina, but in all of these countries, policymakers faced the question of how to reverse recently established or long entrenched patterns of military interventionism. What are the legacies these military regimes left, and how do they affect the new democracies?

Democratic Consolidation and the Legacies of Military Government

In the late 1960s and 1970s, military regimes flourished throughout South America. The challenge to scholars was to explain these phenomena, particularly as the pattern did not fit the expected trend toward modernization and democratization. Various explanations were posed for the emergence of these military regimes; however, one of the most popular analyses was undoubtedly Guillermo O'Donnell's (1973) *Modernization and Bureaucratic Authoritarianism* (see also Linz and Stepan 1978).

The explanation O'Donnell offers for the emergence of bureaucratic-authoritarian regimes (a form of military rule in which the military institution dominates) is based on a combination of economic cycles and perceived levels of political threat. Bureaucratic-authoritarian regimes thus sought to reform the economy and control the political threat from the popular sector (generally through repression). The relative success with which regimes met these goals, and through what means, left important legacies for the democracies that followed. Argentina's rebellions may have been unique, but many of the problems of postauthoritarian rule are shared among these countries.

Democratic Consolidation

The most important question about the legacies of military rule is whether those legacies are likely to hinder or facilitate democratic consolidation. By the term *democratic consolidation,* I refer to the institutionalization of a system of procedural democracy (a system containing both the formal mechanisms and requisite conditions for electoral decision making) in a context characterized by the absence of significant threats to this system (see S. Valenzuela 1992). In other words, in a consolidated democracy, uncertainty remains *within* the system rather than *surrounding* the system (see Przeworski 1986; O'Donnell and Schmitter 1986). For this to occur, the military must cease functioning as a political alternative.

What determines whether or not a newly established democratic regime becomes consolidated? I would argue that the process of democratic consolidation includes three dimensions that influence the degree to which this process is successful. The first dimension relates exclusively to the political system and concerns the rules surrounding political competition, the party system, and the establishment of such requisite conditions as free speech and a free press. These criteria affect not only the degree to which the system is *democratic* but the degree to which it is likely to be *stable*. Most cases of democratic collapse result at least in part from dysfunctions in the political system (see, for example, Linz and Stepan 1978; Scully 1992). In both Chile and Brazil, the electoral system was stable only as long as certain groups were not mobilized. When more progressive political parties began mobilizing peasants and urban marginals, the ability of elites to retain their economic and political bases of power was threatened, and the uncertainties of the democratic system began to exceed what those sectors could consider acceptable. Thus, socialism in Chile and populism in Brazil both terminated in military rule. Similarly, a popular explanation for Argentina's chronic instability has been the lack of a peasantry and the consequent electoral weakness of rural elites. In order to achieve a stable democratic system, the interests of all important sectors of society would need to be represented.

The second facet of democratic consolidation has to do with the armed forces. Overall, do the armed forces seem willing to accept a subordinate, apolitical role within the state, or do they seem to retain a predisposition to intervene in politics? This question is particularly important when military intervention has been recurrent, as in Argentina. However, given that in all of these cases the military has displaced civilian governments, future instances of intervention are certainly a possibility.

Finally, the third dimension concerns the relationship between the armed forces and civil society. The likely actions of the military derive not only from unilateral conceptions about its role but also from the interactions between the military and other actors. In other words, the armed forces do not act in a vacuum. Part of what determines whether the military becomes integrated into a democratic state is whether the government and civil society are willing to have that happen. If relations between the military and civil society remain largely antagonistic, then integrating the armed forces will be rather complicated. The armed forces are likely to be perceived as outside of the state, as a persistent threat to both the political system and the people. In this situation, sectors of the armed forces may well be placed in a situation in which they feel compelled to defend their interests against civil society or the government.

Given our focus on military behavior, the present discussion is limited to the latter two dimensions of democratic consolidation, namely the internal conditions of the armed forces and the relations between the armed forces and civil society.

Legacies of the Military Regimes

Any effort to classify military regimes according to just a few variables entails some extreme simplification. Economic and political policies change over time, as does the leadership. Frequently, leadership changes through internal coups, rather than regularized internal procedures, leading to even further discontinuity. When one takes this into account, there are three components of military regimes that seem to have a particularly strong influence on the subsequent process of democratic consolidation: success as government (measured primarily through economic performance), organization, and the relationship between the military and civil society during the period of military rule.

The degree to which the military "succeeds" in running government seems likely to have a strong effect on how both members of the armed forces and civilians think about military intervention in the future. If the military is relatively successful, the view that the armed forces are more capable than civilians will be maintained. On the other hand, if the military obviously fails, such prior assumptions are likely to be questioned. In this case, the military would be more likely to accept a more apolitical, specialized role. At the same time, the receptivity of civilians to military intervention is also affected by prior experiences with military government. Military coups consistently depend on the support, or at least acquiescence, of important sectors of society. Coups have frequently been preceded by a barrage of public statements by prominent civilians, essentially goading the military to take action. If, however, evidence suggests that military governments are no more effective than civilian governments (and perhaps even less so), then civilians will probably withdraw from their coup-provoking role. In sum, an unsuccessful military government diminishes the probability that governing the country will continue to be considered a legitimate role for the armed forces.

Even bureaucratic-authoritarian regimes are not, however, equally "military." Some place few officers in the government palace, while others transfer the vast majority of public offices to the military domain. These variations undoubtedly influence how the successes or failures of military governments are interpreted. The relationship discussed above between the relative success of the military government and subsequent propensities toward military intervention is likely to be strongest when military participation is high. On the other hand, when a military government includes large numbers of civilians at high levels, the military receives neither all the credit nor all the blame.

The final factor to be considered concerns the relationship between the military and civil society during military government. The most critical component of this relationship is the level of repression. Higher levels of repression during military government are likely to stimulate stronger reactions from civil society.[1] Those who have relatives who have "disappeared" are not likely to accept the military's withdrawal from power as sufficient. In addition, they demand justice or retribution, considered by some as essential to reinforce a democratic society (Malamud-Goti 1990, 1991). They insist that those who ran and carried out the repression move into courtrooms and jails, not just back to the barracks. Consequently, in these situations the potential for conflict between the armed forces and civil society is quite high. Whether or not the military maintains an interventionist perspective of its role, sectors of the military will almost inevitably react to efforts to chastise the armed forces for their earlier actions.

Taking into consideration the above factors, one can predict to some degree the kinds of difficulties that postauthoritarian regimes are likely to encounter (see table 8). A military government that utilizes only moderate repression and is generally unsuccessful seems to leave the most promising inheritance for the postauthoritarian regime. The military's capacity to govern has been discredited, thereby lessening the propensity to intervene; and conflict between the military and civil society is likely to be limited, thus avoiding defensive political actions by the armed forces. As is discussed below, of the four cases considered in this chapter, Uruguay seems to be the closest to this position. On the other hand, the top left quadrant of table 8 represents the most precarious situation. The level of repression under military government was high, thus providing the potential for high levels of conflict between civilians and the military; and the military government was generally successful, permitting the retention of interventionist role beliefs. Chile seems to be in this position, although, as is discussed below, the danger of the Chilean situation is somewhat ameliorated by other factors.

The other two quadrants represent intermediate cases. The bottom left quadrant represents a situation in which the military was relatively successful in governing the country, and repression was kept to a moderate level. In this situation, interventionist role beliefs have not been modified, hence permitting patterns of military intervention to continue. However, the lack of a high level of repression at least prevents an immediate clash between the military and civilians. In this situation (exemplified by Brazil), the stability of the democratic regime will depend on the capacity of the civilian government to effectively govern the country while simultaneously working to diminish the long-term threat from the armed forces.

Finally, the top right quadrant represents a situation in which the

Table 8
Democratic Consolidation and Legacies of Military Rule

Repression	Success of Military Government	Failure of Military Government
High	Interventionism is maintained, potentially high civil-military conflict. Most precarious situation for democratic consolidation—possibility for either autonomous or interventionist military. (Chile)	Lowered interventionism, high civil-military conflict. Military reaction likely, which, although not inherently interventionist, could lead toward a coup through a series of events. (Argentina)
Low	Interventionism is maintained, low civil-military conflict. Threat of intervention remains, but with successful civilian government, threat will not be immediate. (Brazil)	Lowered interventionism, low civil-military conflict. High potential for democratic consolidation. (Uruguay)

military government failed but utilized a high level of repression. In this case, the military's overall propensity to intervene is reduced, but the level of immediate conflict between the military and civil society is likely to be quite high. In this situation, the danger is that these early clashes will induce a domino effect, provoking an initially defensive reaction by the military that could develop toward more directly interventionist behavior. Argentina falls within this category.

Legacies of Military Rule in Argentina

Recapping briefly, Argentina's military government of 1976–83 was characterized by failure as a government, a high level of participation by members of the military in the government, and a high level of repression. These factors appear to have had a very direct influence on the experiences of the civilian government elected in 1983. Raúl Alfonsín's government of 1983–89 encountered a series of difficulties in dealing with the armed forces in particular, confronting three military uprisings between April 1987 and December 1988. Yet, in June of 1989, Alfonsín succeeded in passing the presidential sash to Carlos

Menem. After a final military insurrection in December 1990, the armed forces ceased posing a major threat to the democratic government.

There are two obvious indicators of the military's failure as a government in the case of Argentina's military regime of 1976–83. The first is the economy, the most obvious indicator of success or failure in any of these regimes. The second is the Falklands/Malvinas war of 1982. This war demonstrated not only the military's desperation to legitimize their rule but also their diminished capacity to perform militarily.

Given the military's domination of political decision making during this period, it was also difficult to shift the blame for these failures. Thus, these combined failures led to the revision of the interventionist national security doctrine and a reversion to an interest in a more technologically defined professionalism. For civilians, the regime effectively destroyed any lingering doubts about the desirability of military government.

Nonetheless, while the military's record on economic affairs and foreign relations favored democratic consolidation, the legacy of human rights violations posed some problems. The harsh repression of the 1970s created an extremely hostile relationship between the military and significant sectors of the civilian population. In the post-authoritarian period, those affected either directly or indirectly by the state-directed violence of the 1970s were unlikely to simply let matters pass. Nor did they. Alfonsín's government embarked on an extensive campaign to reduce the overall power of the armed forces and to let it be known that repression would not be tolerated in Argentina.

Consequently, despite the depoliticizing effects of failed military rule, sectors of the military were eventually provoked to react. The military uprisings from 1987 to 1990 originally emanated from this series of events, although (as chapter 6 discusses) they quickly developed a dynamic of their own.

The Uruguayan Case

Uruguay's military came to power in 1973, after a long history of stable two-party democracy. As in neighboring Argentina, the years prior to the coup were plagued by guerrilla violence (considered more successful than in Argentina) and economic decline. Given Uruguay's substantially more democratic history, however, overt military rule was a more questioned solution. Thus, the military government initially preserved the facade of constitutional rule, retaining civilian president Juan María Bordaberry as a figurehead. By the middle of 1976, the facade had ended.

Military government in Uruguay (1973–85) was in many respects similar to that in Argentina, but it was more moderate on each dimension.[2] In terms of overall performance, Uruguay's military regime largely replicated Argentina's failure, although the Uruguayan armed forces at least escaped the added stigma of losing a war. The Uruguayan economy clearly suffered during the years of military rule (see table 9). Early gains in the national GDP were quickly replaced by a gradual, seemingly irreversible decline. At the same time, the foreign debt quadrupled, and unemployment consistently increased. As Ronaldo Munck writes, "In 1982, a deeper conjunctural economic crisis overtook the economy, which led to a sharp rise in the fiscal deficit and in unemployment" (R. Munck 1989:161). Clearly, the military government left the Uruguayan economy in much worse shape than it had found it.

The Uruguayan military was also extensively involved in governing the country, which augmented the degree of its perceived responsibility for the economic crisis. Congress was closed, to be replaced by a forty-six–member Consejo de la Nación [Council of the Nation], drawing nearly half of its members from the armed forces (Weinstein 1988:50). Most political power was concentrated in the military junta, composed of members of each of the three services. In sum, while civilians were included at some levels of the government, the military character of the regime was irrefutable.

Assessing the intensity of repression during Uruguay's military regime is somewhat more complicated. On the surface, Uruguay appears to have suffered significantly less than its western neighbor. Estimates of the number of disappearances rarely surpass two or three hundred, most of whom perished over the border in Argentina.[3] However, the use of torture in Uruguay was probably more extensive than anywhere in South America. According to Ronaldo Munck, "it is estimated that one in 500 citizens passed through prison, and that one in 50 of these was tortured" (1989:71). As an Uruguayan once

Table 9
Economic Indicators of Military Government in Uruguay, 1973–1985

Year	Gross Domestic Product (Million $U.S. 1980, Deflated)	Total External Debt (Million $U.S.)	Unemployment (%)
1973	4,942	416	8.9
1974	5,097	715	8.1
1975	5,340	228	—
1976	5,500	282	12.8
1977	5,676	452	11.8
1978	5,927	615	10.2
1979	6,305	807	8.4
1980	6,661	954	7.3
1981	6,713	1,150	6.6
1982	6,068	1,296	11.7
1983	5,667	1,414	15.4
1984	5,570	1,470	13.9
1985	5,664	1,816	13.0

Source: GDP from Wilkie and Contreras (1992):1368; Debt from Wilkie and Contreras (1992):1360; Unemployment in 1975–79 from Wilkie and Perkal (1984):269; Unemployment in 1980–85 from Wilkie and Contreras (1992):378.

said to me, the difference was that in Uruguay they had doctors to keep the victims alive.

The legacies of the repression in the postauthoritarian military period were thus significant but perhaps less traumatic than in Argentina. Not only did the civilian government avoid a similar campaign against human rights abuses, but in December of 1986, Congress actually passed a law declaring that no action would be taken to prosecute members of the armed forces for violations of human rights during the earlier period. The law was, of course, not accepted with complete equanimity by all members of civil society. An extensive campaign was launched to conduct a referendum repealing the law. On 16 April 1989, the referendum was held—55 percent of those voting elected to uphold the amnesty law (Rial 1990:31). The issue of repression in Uruguay thus passed definitively into the past.

The absence of this immediate cause of conflict does not, however, assure a lack of future military intervention. On the contrary, militaries have supplanted civilian regimes numerous times in the history of Latin America and without the legacy of repression. Conflict over the issue of repression exacerbates tensions between the armed forces and civil society, but the absence of this issue does not guarantee that the armed forces will abstain from politics. Thus, perhaps the more pertinent question is whether the Uruguayan armed forces have reassessed the expediency of military intervention.

The economic failures of the Uruguayan military would lead one to expect some kind of internal reevaluation. In the case of Uruguay, this may be facilitated by the historical neutrality of the armed forces. Before 1973, Uruguay prided itself on a long-term, smoothly functioning two-party democracy. Some indications exist that the military may, at this point, welcome a return to such a system. According to Ronaldo Munck, "There was . . . a genuinely constitutional streak in the military of Uruguay, and now the armed forces did seem to want to return to a more 'non-political' role, acting as a last resort should the constitutional regime lose control of the situation" (1989:172). Hence, although the legacies of Uruguay's military regime did create some tensions in the postauthoritarian period, on the whole these legacies appear to have facilitated the consolidation of democracy in Uruguay.

The Brazilian Case

Brazil's authoritarian period left somewhat less auspicious legacies for the new democracy. Brazil has had a long history of governments that in one way or another combine elements of democracy and authoritarianism (see Skidmore 1988). The military regime of 1964–85 was no exception. The military controlled politics, but it did not eliminate them. Congress for much of this period continued to function, although its actual decision-making power was severely constrained. A political party system of sorts was also permitted, although the military rather drastically redesigned it, creating an official government party and an official opposition party.

In terms of the immediate legacies of the bureaucratic-authoritarian period, the mixed character of the Brazilian regime may be positive, as the military could not claim sole responsibility for the relative economic success of that period. Brazil's military regime did, however, give considerable emphasis to economic development, placing the state in a partnership with foreign and domestic capital to advance industrialization (Evans 1979). Economic development constituted a central concern of the Brazilian national security doctrine, with domestic insurgency posing little challenge. Nonetheless, economic policies met with mixed results.

Like all of these countries, Brazil suffered from a dramatically expanding foreign debt during this period (see table 10). However, in the Brazilian case, certain profits were gained from this borrowed capital. The Brazilian GDP continued to climb, gradually but consistently, throughout the military regime. Brazil was touted as South America's NIC, or "newly industrialized country," destined to join the ranks of the advanced industrial countries of Western Europe. Although such an outcome never quite materialized, the Brazilian government was clearly more successful than the governments of Argentina and Uruguay.

The legacies of the Brazilian regime thus seemed to encourage a continuing role for the armed forces. The success of the military government suggested that the armed forces would retain the belief that certain conditions may dictate military rule and that military government can be a workable option.

Brazil, however, did enjoy one advantage in the game of democratic consolidation. Repression under the military government was kept relatively low.[4] Only around 125 people were reported to have disappeared between 1964 and the 1985 transition (Dassin 1986: 205). Given the size of Brazil's population (more than four times that of Argentina, the country with the next largest population in South America), the number of individuals directly affected by the repression was quite moderate. This, combined with the extremely gradual nature of the Brazilian transition, prevented any significant backlash against the Brazilian armed forces.

The particular context of the Brazilian transition made the successful consolidation of democracy in Brazil especially dependent on the performance of the new civilian government. With a good excuse, the military could renew their interventionist role relatively easily. The inability of the government either to cope with the coun-

Table 10

Economic Indicators of Military Government in Brazil, 1973–1985

Year	Gross Domestic Product (Million $U.S. 1980, Deflated)	Total External Debt, Nominal (Million $U.S.)	Unemployment (%)
1973	151,323	12,940	—
1974	163,903	19,420	—
1975	172,152	23,750	—
1976	189,738	29,050	2.8
1977	198,933	41,410	—
1978	208,834	53,750	4.3
1979	222,964	60,560	—
1980	243,500	70,957	—
1981	232,793	80,640	4.3
1982	234,291	92,812	—
1983	226,562	98,095	4.9
1984	238,608	105,015	4.3
1985	257,702	105,026	3.4

Sources: GDP from Wilkie and Contreras (1992):1368; Debt from Wilkie and Contreras (1992):1360; Unemployment in 1975–79 from Wilkie and Perkal (1984):269; Unemployment in 1980–85 from Wilkie and Contreras (1992):378. (Military government began in 1964.)

try's economic problems or to confront the country's skyrocketing crime rates could create a situation in which the armed forces would feel it necessary to take a more activist role.

In this respect, the early years of Brazilian democracy were mixed. The first freely elected president, Fernando Collor de Mello, led a government that was both ineffective and notably corrupt. Collor de Mello resigned in December 1992 as the Senate began planning his impeachment. Inflation during this period soared to an estimated 1200 percent annually,[5] and street crime continued at epidemic proportions. By mid-1993, open calls for military intervention began to resonate in Brazil.[6] Despite this, Wendy Hunter (forthcoming) observes that the civilian government has made incursions into military terrain, including shrinking the budget and increasing civilian control over areas such as intelligence and nuclear policy.

The Chilean Case

Of the four cases considered in this chapter, Chile conforms the least to the model. Based on the factors I have underlined, Chile would appear to offer the least auspicious prognosis for democratic consolidation, at least from the side of the military. The legacies of military rule do not seem to favor the development of a subordinate military—the military government was relatively successful, and repression was high (see Arriagada Herrera 1988; Valenzuela and Valenzuela 1986). Nonetheless, these variables have been mediated by other factors that, at least in the short term, appear to have lessened their detrimental impact.

Chile's military regime arose as a backlash against Salvador Allende's elected socialist government. With modest support (only around 36.2 percent) and ambitious goals, Allende had little hope of a smooth presidency (Sigmund 1977:107). Nevertheless, Chile's multiparty democracy had as much history of stability as that of Uruguay, and the military, although fairly autonomous (Aguero 1989), showed little inclination to intervene. This ended in 1973, with a harsh military regime that outlived by far the others in the region, lasting until 1990.

Overall, Chile tends to be seen as Latin America's most successful case of institutionalized military rule. Economic performance during the military regime was perhaps less impressive in Chile than in Brazil, but it was certainly better than in Argentina and Uruguay (see table 11). According to Genaro Arriagada Herrera, "In 1977, Chile enjoyed a spectacular growth rate of 9.9 percent, the highest in several decades. This notable growth continued in 1978 and 1979, when production increased 8.2 percent and 8.3 percent respectively" (1988:27). After this point, the economy began to slow down somewhat, while the foreign debt grew to forbidding proportions. Nonetheless, the GDP did remain at respectable levels, and the overall performance of the regime was positive enough that military president General Pinochet managed to retain substantial popular support until the end of his rule. In a 1988 plebiscite, fully 43 percent of Chilean voters supported Pinochet's continuation. It was not enough to prevent the transition, but it did leave Pinochet with considerable power (Drake and Jaksic 1991:13).

However, the extent to which the successes of the military regime

Table 11

Economic Indicators of Military Government in Chile, 1973–1989

Year	Gross Domestic Product (Million $U.S. 1980, Deflated)	Total External Debt (Million $U.S.)	Unemployment (%)
1973	20,559	3,275	4.8
1974	20,900	4,522	8.3
1975	18,315	4,762	15.0
1976	18,983	4,849	17.1
1977	20,674	5,884	13.9
1978	22,268	7,374	13.7
1979	24,013	9,361	13.4
1980	25,799	12,081	10.4
1981	27,309	15,664	11.3
1982	23,880	17,315	19.6
1983	23,574	17,928	14.6
1984	24,904	19,737	13.9
1985	25,459	20,384	12.1
1986	26,921	21,144	8.8
1987	28,458	21,502	7.9
1988	30,578	19,578	6.3
1989	33,568	18,241	5.3

Sources: GDP from Wilkie and Contreras (1992):1368; Debt from Wilkie and Contreras (1992):1360; Unemployment in 1975–79 from Wilkie and Perkal (1984):269; Unemployment in 1980–85 from Wilkie and Contreras (1992):378. (Military government continued until 1990.)

reflected the skill of the armed forces, or would subsequently bolster military interventionism, is another question. The 1973 military regime interrupted a long tradition of competitive rule in Chile—a tradition that had earned Chile a reputation as a paragon of democracy. Furthermore, in Chile, occupation of the political system by the military institution was in some respects limited. Military officers may have held political posts (generally dominating the cabinet), but overall control became quite personalized. Power in Chile rested in the hands of Augusto Pinochet, not in the military institution. Pinochet instituted a variety of highly effective mechanisms to ensure his control both over the armed forces and throughout the country (Arriagada Herrera 1986, 1988). Consequently, both credit and blame for the results of the military regime also remained largely centralized around Pinochet. Thus, although the armed forces may not have had a strong reason to reverse incipient inclinations toward prolonged interventionism, those inclinations may have remained relatively transient.

The legacies of Chile's repression may also prove to be less consequential than might have initially been expected. Chile's repression was unquestionably harsh. According to reports, more than 2,000 people were killed by the military regime, in contrast to only about 132 who were killed by guerrilla groups.[7] Taking into account population size, this places Chile at about the same level as Argentina. However, civil-military conflict on this issue was delayed for some time after the transition. In part, this was due to the continued strength of the armed forces. The success of the Chilean military regime left its leaders in a position such that they were able to retain close control over the 1990 transition to constitutional rule. Pinochet remained scheduled to continue as commander in chief of the army until 1997. Furthermore, the military assured itself of the continued representation of its interests throughout the political system, including the Supreme Court, the administration, and Congress. According to Samuel Valenzuela, "by offering financial incentives it [the military government] induced older judges to retire and thereby appointed about half of the members of a Supreme Court with expanded powers; it named all but 16 of the nation's 325 mayors; and it legally prohibited the new democratic government from appointing all but the top officials at all levels of the state administration, effectively granting tenure to all civil servants" (1992:66). At the same time, electoral laws were instituted that would allow Chile's political right to dominate Congress.

The peacefulness of Chile's transition was also facilitated by the particular structure of the human rights movement and its circumstances under the civilian regime. Chile's human rights movement became relatively more integrated than that of neighboring Argentina, with the majority of its diverse organizations tied together under the auspices of the Catholic Church. This arrangement would, theoretically, permit these organizations to act in a fairly unified manner. Yet the Catholic Church also had close ties to the civilian government of the transition, with the first two presidencies in the hands of the church-oriented Christian Democrats. This situation thus appears to have reduced pressures for the government to take a strong position toward the armed forces and perhaps gave the government more capacity to control (or stifle) the human rights movement.

The civilian government of Patricio Aylwin therefore tread extremely lightly with respect to the human rights issue, as well as leaving the internal structure of the armed forces largely untouched. A human rights report was compiled in 1991, but the government did not immediately pursue prosecutions. Only in 1993 did human rights trials really begin to menace the armed forces, with around five hundred officers cited by the middle of the year.[8] The trials were largely symbolic, given the protection offered by Chile's amnesty law. Nonetheless, they provoked considerable anxiety within the military and helped motivate military demonstrations of force rather reminiscent of the period preceding the *carapintada* rebellions.

The government also avoided challenging Pinochet's constitution and the military's related political prerogatives. It was not until Eduardo Frei assumed the presidency in 1994 that the government began to challenge the Pinochet regime's presence throughout the political system.[9]

In sum, the Aylwin government's relative caution and moderation in dealing with the armed forces prevented overt civil-military conflict until democracy was on somewhat more solid ground. However, this approach allowed the military to preserve a level of autonomy incompatible with a subordinated role and incompatible with democratic consolidation. Thus, in Chile, what appears to have been a smooth transition is probably more accurately described as an incomplete transition.

Conclusion: Limiting Factors

The process of democratic transition and consolidation continued for some time in Argentina, Chile, Uruguay, and Brazil. In the discussion above, I have attempted to pinpoint some of the conditions that seem to most strongly condition the process of democratic consolidation—in some cases facilitating it, in others severely crippling it.

Economic performance, as mediated by the degree of military control over the military regime, is used to predict the likelihood that the military's prior propensity toward intervention will be modified. On the other hand, the level of repression during the military regime is considered as an important determinant of civil-military conflict during the postauthoritarian period.

Yet this analysis must be interpreted with caution. Clearly, the variables considered here are only a few of those that ultimately determine the outcomes of these experiments with constitutional rule. Chilean democracy is not doomed to failure, nor is Uruguayan democracy guaranteed success. One of the more important factors that has not been considered in this chapter is one least subject to prediction—leadership. In Argentina, Alfonsín's overwhelming concern with human rights issues—his early initiation of prosecutions against military officers and his inability to control the overly dedicated courts—undoubtedly facilitated and encouraged the extension of those prosecutions and the ensuant military uprisings. The restraint of Uruguayan and Chilean leaders has probably been equally important in limiting the degree of confrontation.

Another issue concerns political capacity at the systemic level and, related to this, the more extended historical trajectory of the armed forces in each country. Based on the variables considered in this chapter, Chile's situation appears quite bleak. Yet Chile's armed forces have not internalized interventionist roles in the same way the Argentines did. Up until 1973, Chile's political system was quite functional, as was that of Uruguay. Thus, establishing a working democratic system may be somewhat easier in these cases, with history working against a permanent political "space" for military intervention. Finally, a successful military coup requires not only political space but also political allies. Military intervention is almost always a combined effort of members of the military and sectors of civil society. If the experience of military government was so negative that interventionist sectors of the armed forces are unable to find civilian allies, then it will be difficult to organize a coup coalition, however motivated the military might be. In other words, the legacies of military rule affect the process of democratic consolidation from various angles—from within the military, from the relationship between the military and civil society, and from the political system itself.

9

Context, Coalitions, and Political Outcomes

By the mid-1990s, Argentina no longer stood out as South America's paragon of military interventionism. Relations between the military and the government became increasingly cooperative, particularly as Argentina began radically expanding its role in United Nations peacekeeping around 1992. In fact, other postauthoritarian countries began to appear more problematic: the delayed issue of human rights in Chile began to produce unavoidable tension, and in Brazil, the military maintained an important presence in a wide range of policy areas.

In Argentina, however, the crisis appeared to have passed, and the military's rebel movement no longer seemed to threaten the Argentine constitutional order. The process of consolidation and diversification of the movement had helped defeat its military project; force ceased to be a viable method for pursuing the rebels' aims. Yet that defeat was also a consequence of the larger context and its interaction with the aforementioned developmental process experienced by the rebel movement.

This chapter explores the relationships between the internal processes of organizational development and such contextual factors as the legacies of military rule and the policies of the civilian government. I begin with an analysis of coalition formation in military rebellions to determine when those coalitions are successful and when they fail. I then consider how both developmental and external factors contribute to those outcomes. Finally, the chapter concludes with a discussion of the relative balance between decision making and contextual causality in producing political outcomes. More specifically, to what degree are democratic consolidation and its reverse, constitutional collapse, predictable from the context? Is democratic consolidation the product of wise choices or favorable circumstances?

Goals, Coalitions, and Outcomes

Despite important commonalities, the *carapintada* rebellions from 1987 to 1990 varied considerably, particularly in regard to their level of success. This varying success can be explained largely by changing perceptions of the rebels' goals. When the rebels' apparent concerns were shared by a large proportion of the military institution, the uprisings were successful. When their concerns appeared to be more narrow or to go beyond the scope of the institution (for example, reflecting the political aims of those involved), the uprisings were much less successful. In sum, the rebels achieved the most success with discourse that appealed to the largest proportion possible of the relevant public—in this case, the army.

"Minimal Winning Coalitions"

The argument that the breadth of the appeal determines the breadth of support is intuitively reasonable; nonetheless, it in some respects conflicts with much existing coalition theory. According to certain standard interpretations of coalition behavior, coalition participants must limit the size of their coalitions in order to maximize their success. Thus, William Riker's theory of "minimal winning coalitions" suggests that leaders will try to limit the size of their coalitions to the bare minimum necessary to win in order to limit the number who share in the spoils of a win. Using an admittedly restrictive set of assumptions, Riker argues: "In social situations similar to n-person, zero-sum games with side-payments, participants create coalitions just as large as they believe will ensure winning and no larger" (1962:32–33) Riker uses this argument to contest Anthony Downs's (1957) assumption that political parties seek to maximize support.

Yet both arguments are partially right. Their differences stem from a lack of differentiation between the leaders of movements (or core coalition members) and their supporters. The leadership core will be inclined to limit the inner circles to those absolutely necessary, while simultaneously trying to maximize their external support. To take the example of political parties, active politicians do not share all of the perquisites of political office with the voters who brought them to that position. Members of the general voting population gain only indirectly by having in office someone presumed to represent their political ideas. Similarly, leaders of military coups can place only a select few in cabinet positions; followers are likely to be favored professionally, but not in the same way as central coalition members. The same kinds of dynamics occur within military uprisings that seek control of the military institution. If rebel leaders manage to obtain that control, or at least strengthen their hand within the institution, the leadership will undoubtedly pocket the majority of the gains—commiserate with their greater proportion of the risk. Yet achieving those advances requires convincing a much larger support group that they, too, have something to gain.

Thus, contrary to Riker's argument, while leaders may benefit by minimizing the size of the inner coalition, the ultimate success of different tactics depends on maximizing the size of the relevant supporting coalition. The broader their goals, the broader the supporting coalition must be. Hence, in order to carry out a coup d'état, a tactic whose target arena is the nation-state, conspirators must be able to count on the support or acquiescence of important sectors both within the military and within civil society. As Luttwack writes, successful coup conspirators must:

> state the aim of the coup in terms of a political attitude rather than in terms of policies or personalities, because the latter are necessarily more specific and therefore liable to specific opposition. The attitude which we will project will have to be calculated carefully: it should reflect the preoccupations of the target country, implying a solution to the problems which are felt to exist, and in *form* it must reflect the general political beliefs of the majority of its people. (1968:85)

By extension, coalition leaders with somewhat more limited goals and the military institution as the target arena must direct their discourse to reach the largest proportion possible of that institution.

Appeals of the Carapintada *Rebellions*

Consequently, in Argentina's four military uprisings between 1987 and 1990, the rebels had the greatest success in those uprisings in which they directed their appeals to the broadest possible military constituency. The appeals that achieved this kind of popularity were primarily *professional*—claims and demands oriented around the interests of the institution as a whole. In contrast, appeals that members of the army perceived as based on personal or suborganizational interests (relating to an organization within the greater institution) gained less of a following. Finally, political and ideological claims have the potential to reach a broad audience (within and outside of the organization), but naturally they can do so only if the ideas espoused converge with the dominant ideas in the target arena. In the wake of the Proceso, the armed forces appeared more interested in withdrawing from politics than delving back in.

The first of the four uprisings, Semana Santa, was most clearly organized around institutional interests (see table 12). The rebels recruited support by emphasizing the threats to the institution as a whole that the upper echelons had, in their perspective, refused to combat. By framing their discourse in this manner and emphasizing professional values, the rebels managed to achieve considerable backing. Monte Caseros, on the other hand, was much less successful, demonstrating that the support that can be obtained for a movement perceived as based on personal interests is highly limited. A small circle of close associates might still be brought in, but it is much more difficult to appeal to the bulk of the forces.

With the third rebellion, Villa Martelli, the *carapintadas* recuperated their pre–Monte Caseros position. In this instance, institutional claims became meshed with a strong dose of nationalist ideology. Yet Seineldín and his coalition partners presented their ideology in such a way that it appeared relevant to large sectors of the military institution, rather than being directed by the political ambitions of a few. Because of this, the *carapintadas* were again able to garner substantial support and achieve some important concessions. Nonetheless, much of the reason this formula could work was probably largely due to Seineldín's particularly charismatic character.

In general, political and ideological claims tended to be suspect in the postauthoritarian period. The traumas of the military government of 1976–83 had pushed the armed forces toward a more traditional, apolitical form of professionalism. Thus, as the *carapintadas* began taking an increasingly overt political stance in the post–Villa Martelli period, they also began losing much of their internal support. Pursuing their demands through military rebellion became an increasingly less viable outcome, as the final uprising (Operación Virgen de Luján—commonly referred to as simply "December 3rd") dramatically illustrated. By this time, the *carapintadas* had established identifiable and specific organizations, representing the particular interests of the two, now separate, rebel factions. The uprising

Table 12

Military Uprisings of the Argentine *Carapintadas*, 1987–1990

	Leader	*Dominant Interests*	*Coalition Members*	*Outcome*
Stage 1: Reaction to the Military Policies of the Alfonsín Government				
Semana Santa, April 1987	Lieutenant Colonel Aldo Rico	Institutional (Army)	1964 officers cohort: allies throughout the ranks of lieutenant colonel and below	Successful: only 2 arrests, Due Obedience Law, and retirement of army chief of staff
Monte Caseros, January 1988	Lieutenant Colonel Aldo Rico	Personal	1964 cohort, plus a few staunch supporters	Unsuccessful: resulted in some 300 arrests
Stage 2: Consolidation and Politicization of the *Carapintada* Movement				
Villa Martelli, December 1988	Colonel Mohammed Alí Seineldín	Institutional/ Ideological	Much support below lieutenant colonel except those alienated by prior rebellions	Successful: only 2 arrests and retirement of army chief of staff José Dante Caridi
Stage 3: Diversification of the *Carapintada* Movement (Menem Government)				
Operación Virgen de Luján, December 1990	Colonel Mohammed Alí Seineldín's associates	Ideological/ Suborganizational	Members of Seineldín sector, numerous NCOs, few officers	Unsuccessful: over 600 arrests; many convicted; several deaths

(and possibly intended coup) thus clearly appeared to be an action of the *carapintadas,* rather than of the military. Again, however, less predictable circumstances also helped determine the direction of events. In particular, the early deaths of legalist officers proved critical in congealing antagonism toward the rebels.

Organizational Development and Coalition Formation

As the discussion above has implied, the varying success of the *carapintada* rebellions was closely linked to the process of organizational development. The *carapintadas'* drive for consolidation as a movement eventually conflicted with the more inclusionary requisites of a successful military uprising. As the *carapintada* movement developed organizationally, the rebels defined themselves into a corner, losing their ability to present their ideas in ambiguous generalities that would offend minimal numbers of their colleagues. Thus, while the growing political and ideological definition of the *carapintada* movement established a more permanent foundation for the movement, it eventually diminished its ability to generate support within the military institution. By the final uprising, the institutionalization of the *carapintada* movement had become largely incompatible with the achievement of widespread support within the organization. They had defined themselves beyond the professional interests that serve as common ground within the armed forces.

Organizational Development and External Context

Notwithstanding the impact of developmental processes, it would probably be a mistake to infer from this case that the organizational development of rebel movements inevitably leads to their demise, or to suggest that this internal dynamic is exclusively responsible for variations in their success. Instead, a number of contextual factors contributed significantly to the fate of the rebels.

On the one hand, the rebels' quest for expanded power was undoubtedly constricted by the strong distrust during this period of potentially interventionist, or "political," ideas or behaviors. Disillusionment with military government had thrust the armed forces toward a more apolitical, classical interpretation of professionalism. Thus, although the myths regarding the privileged relationship be-.

tween the armed forces and the nation continued to prevail, the military's traditional "guardian" or "oversight" role of earlier periods had been somewhat moderated.

At the same time, the policies that developed under the Alfonsín government helped the rebels overcome this obstacle by unifying members of the armed forces in the face of a perceived external onslaught. Of particular importance were those policies that challenged the military's prestige, rather than their material benefits. The sense of threat the armed forces had felt during the guerrilla years found its parallel during the Alfonsín period as military officers' pride and status (rather than physical security) was slashed. Using the model most readily available to them, members of the armed forces accused the government of leftist, revolutionary aspirations—purportedly revealed by aggression toward the military—and important sectors came together to challenge the policies of the government and the military command. The less abrasive military politics of Menem's government weakened that temporary bond, however, despite the military's decreasing security as a state institution.

Nonetheless, the developmental processes of military movements also appear to have an independent impact on their eventual outcome. Of most importance is the issue of *timing*; in particular, the relationship between stages of development and particular strategies. In Kenneth Jowitt's analysis (1987), successful organizations or movements are presumed to pass from the "developmental task" of transformation to that of consolidation only after they have conquered their functional territory. As the present study demonstrates, movements that begin refining their organizational definition before this point become vulnerable. In contrast, rebels or coup conspirators are probably much more successful in cases in which they do not acquire much of a public face or known organizational structure before solidifying their position of power. For example, Perón's success was undoubtedly facilitated by the fact that consolidation, and his own personal rise to power, were postponed until after the coalition had achieved control of the government.

In Pursuit of Democratic Consolidation

The collapse of the *carapintadas* thus would appear to have been a mixture of context and strategy—both the strategies of the rebels and the strategies of the government. The rebels' initially generalized discourse facilitated their ascent, while their subsequent inability to avoid polluting their public image with more personalized and specifically political goals disabled them. At the same time, the policy "choices" of the civilian administrations (which, as discussed in chapter 4, emerge from the interaction between the strategies of different actors, rather than the specific decisions of any individual) also affected the trajectory of the rebel movement.

Yet while such choices are critical, frequently the context so constrains decision making that other choices seem unlikely. In Chile, the military's relatively successful economic strategies and continued political support virtually prohibited Patricio Aylwin's postauthoritarian government from mounting any immediate challenge. The choices of the Alfonsín government were also severely limited, although in a very different way. Alfonsín's administration inherited the prior regime's economic crises, along with the crises of adjustment inherent in any major transition. Given this context, in conjunction with the legacy of intense repression of the early 1970s and the military's prevailing state of collapse, the government found itself in a situation that imposed few obstacles to harsh military policies and, in fact, strongly encouraged such a position. An immediate amnesty for the military, such as that in Uruguay, was not initially an option in Argentina. In fact, when Menem did pardon the armed forces in 1990, the act stimulated extensive public outrage. At the moment that Alfonsín assumed the presidency, without the subsequent years of crisis, ignoring the military's past would have been politically impossible. Furthermore, tempering the massive symbolic critiques (such as the trials) with material benefits was not particularly feasible economically—and probably inadequate anyway.

The emergence of rebellion was also strongly conditioned by events and circumstances prior to the transition. Long entrenched patterns of interventionism, encouraged by military ideology, the legal system, and the system of promotions, undoubtedly contributed to officers' and noncommissioned officers' decisions to pursue an active strategy of opposition. At the same time, bureaucratic and experiential cleavages helped determine which groups would associate themselves with either the rebel or legalist sectors.

By the end of 1990, Argentina's *carapintada* rebellions appeared to have ended. Seineldín had been defeated, and Rico had opted to pursue his political goals in the electoral arena. Four year later, Seineldín remained in jail, and Rico began planning for the 1995 presidential elections.

Yet the *carapintada* rebellions had left their mark. The uprisings subtantially delayed the consolidation of democracy by repoliticizing the armed forces and impeding the institutional incorporation of the armed forces. Again, the military—at least these sectors—appeared as an active opposition to the government, rather than as a tool of the government within the state. The rebellions could only exacerbate the government's distrust of the armed forces, thus amplifying the voices that claimed that weakening the military was the only possibility for controlling it. The armed forces remained weak and impoverished throughout the Alfonsín and Menem governments.

As Argentina began preparations for the third postauthoritarian round of presidential elections, the success of democratization still appeared mixed. On the one hand, Menem appeared to have debilitated the democratic system through his liberal use of decrees to confront the economic crisis. On the other hand, he appeared—at least temporarily—to have succeeded. Menem achieved a level of economic stability that had eluded most of his recent predecessors. He had also established a much more positive relationship with the armed forces, despite continuing budget difficulties. Much of this resulted from Menem's symbolic support for the armed forces (praise, visiting barracks, etc.), and his more active redefinition of the military role. In particular, the expanded use of the armed forces in peacekeeping involved them in a mission that was both integrally connected to the government's policy agenda and professionally and institutionally of interest to the armed forces. At last, the military knew not only what it should *not* do, but also what it should.

Finally, Argentina's 1994 Constitution seemed to hold much promise for a country that had long struggled with political instability. Notable reforms included shortening the presidential term (an important antecdote to political impatience) and reducing the powers of the presidency. The Constitution also allowed for reelection, which permitted Menem the hope of another term. Argentina's military perhaps still had a while to go before intervention would cease to be considered as an option, but the political "space" for this option appeared to be shrinking.

What are the lessons from Argentina for other new democracies? Clearly, the specific conditions within any country will vary. Nonetheless, the Argentine experience has much to teach later democratizers. First, if a military is to become a reliable state institution, the government must be careful to treat the armed forces as such—as a valued part of the state, rather than a threatening opponent. The symbolism of Alfonsín's criticism of the armed forces and misplaced attempt to divide repressors from innocents did considerable harm to his relations with the military, certainly more than his budget policies. Reversing the symbolism helped Menem fortify his relationship with the armed forces.

Secondly, if militaries are to consider themselves as an integral part of the state, then the government must provide them with a positive role, rather than merely prohibiting them from engaging in certain activities. That role should coincide both with the government's overall political and foreign policy goals and with military professionalism. Providing militaries with nondefense missions has frequently brought the armed forces too close to politics; providing them with no missions generates frustration.

Third, while the appearance of military groups on electoral ballots may stimulate some concern, allowing this option may have considerable benefits. During a transitional period, democratic participation by dissenting sectors of the military may have an overall stabilizing effect. A legitimate means of expressing dissent creates an important outlet for those sectors—in Albert Hirschman's terms, a "voice" that precludes their need to "exit" (1970). Notably, after having chosen the political path, Rico and his associates appeared to distance themselves from the still rebellious Seineldín faction.

Finally, leniency toward insurrection (rebellions or coup attempts) is a mistake. Establishing a tradition of stability requires that rebels face legal consequences, without easy recourse to political pardon. With both the Frondizi and Alfonsín governments, leniency appeared only to increase the likelihood of further insurrection. Furthermore, the Argentine story clearly demonstrates that rebellions are unlikely to be isolated events; and the nature of organizations means that goals have a tendency to expand, rather than contract. With the leaders of the last rebellion still in jail, the lesson that rebellions have costs may at last be taking hold. Argentina's pattern of military intervention may have finally been broken.

Notes

1. Democracy and the Armed Forces

1. This category excludes members of the military who assume power through constitutional means (e.g., Dwight Eisenhower in the United States).

2. The Chilean military government of 1973 to 1989 is a clear exception to this. In this case, the government did pursue economic orthodoxy, with significant success.

3. In Venezuela, much effort was made to "democratize" the values of the armed forces. The officers most targeted by these teachings became the leaders of the 1992 coup attempts, partially because of their empathy and identification with Venezuela's suffering poor.

4. Huntington's argument has an important parallel in deterrence theory, which suggests that the best way to avoid war is to construct a military arsenal sufficiently powerful that no potential enemy would dare to challenge it.

2. Political Roles of the Military

1. Saenz Peña belonged to the Partido Autonomista Nacional, the elite party that controlled Argentine politics during this period.

2. The air force did not come into existence until 1944.

3. The GOU has been alternately interpreted as "Grupo de Oficiales Unidos" and "Grupo Obra de Unificación."

4. Translations from Spanish to English are the author's.

5. Perón was promoted to general a week before assuming the presidency.

6. In 1951, General Benjamín Menéndez led a coup attempt against Perón.

7. The actual "game" was in some ways more complicated than O'Donnell's model, partly due to the lack of unity within the armed forces.

8. Arturo Frondizi, written response to questionnaire, May 1989.

9. Rouquie claims that there were a total of twenty-eight executions, including General Juan José Valle, the leader of the rebellion (1982b:137).

10. Admiral Rojas's own account conflicts with this depiction. Rojas claims that the navy in general favored minimizing the tenure of the military government (interview, Buenos Aires, 20 July 1989).

11. Rojas, interview.

12. General (Ret.) Tomás Sánchez de Bustamante, interview, Buenos Aires, 31 May 1989; italics mine.

13. Frondizi, questionnaire; see also Frondizi 1964, 1982.

14. Bernando Larroudé, interview, Buenos Aires, 8 April 1989; Potash 1980:276–77.

15. An important exception to this rule was Frondizi's close associate, Rogelio Frigerio. Military pressures eventually forced Frondizi to displace Frigerio as well.

16. Frondizi, questionnaire.

17. Colonel (Ret.) Luis Perlinger, interview, Buenos Aires, 9 May 1989.

18. Gen. Sánchez de Bustamante, interview, Buenos Aires, 3 June 1989; emphasis in original.

19. Gen. Sánchez de Bustamante, interview, 3 June 1989.

20. The contracts with foreign petroleum countries had formed part of Frondizi's successful plan to increase production.

21. General (Ret.) Alejandro Agustín Lanusse, interview, Buenos Aires, 2 November 1988.

22. National Defense Law, Law 16.970, Repúblic Argentina, *Boletín Oficial de la República Argentina,* no. 21,043, 10 October 1966:1–4; Repression of Communism, Law 17.401, *Leyes Nacionales,* 1967:315–20; Repression of Communism, Law 18.234, *Leyes Nacionales,* 1969:437–39.

3. Disappointments of Military Rule

1. *Revista de la Escuela Superior de Guerra,* published by the Superior War School, is probably the journal most representative of the army's official position.

2. A list by the army of the most important events in the war indicates no actions before the assassination of Aramburu. "Síntesis de los Principales Episodios de la Guerra contra la Subversion," in Ejército Argentino, *Boletín Público del Ejército Argentino,* no. 4547 (1987): Supplement. Aramburu's death also appears as the initiation of revolutionary violence in *Terrorism in Argentina,* published by the Argentine military government in January 1980.

3. According to the military's data in *Terrorism in Argentina,* of 688 deaths attributed to terrorists, 515 victims (75 percent) were members of either the military or security forces (314). Interestingly, the number of total deaths given here is actually below the CONADEP estimate.

4. The military government claimed the following about "subversion": "Despite the fact of its being the most tragic expression of the phenomenon, the most objective contempt for human rights, armed conflict is only one of its aspects. It has been proved that the former exists because, before and during its development, the ideology of death was introduced and dominated education, culture, the workers, the economy and justice" (Ejército Argentino 1980:3).

5. *Clarin Internacional,* 25–31 October 1994:1. The promotion of these officers was blocked for this reason, despite President Menem's support for them.

6. According to Varas, Centro para Estudios Legales y Sociales (CELS) claimed that they had enough evidence to convict 896 officers. Varas obtained the estimate of 1,300 from CONADEP.

7. Tucumán is a northern province in Argentina where the most direct battles occurred between guerrillas and the military.

8. *Página 12* (Buenos Aires), 26 April 1995:2–3.

9. Even Admiral Jorge Anaya, a member of one of the military juntas, claimed quite adamantly: "The military government was a failure. It was terrible!" (Interview, Buenos Aires, 18 October 1988).

10. This contrasts with the regime of 1966–73, during which only 15 percent of cabinet ministers were from the military (Ricci and Fitch 1988: table 1).

11. A lieutenant colonel casually commented to me that he had once managed to obtain a submachine gun as "war booty."

12. Admiral (Ret.) Jorge Anaya, interview, Buenos Aires, 19 December 1988.

13. Anaya, interview. While Anaya's testimony reveals the information on which the junta's decision to initiate Operación Azul may have been based, other sources differ as to when the submarines were actually sent. According to the British report on the Falklands conflict (commonly referred to as the "Franks report," the submarines were not launched until 29 March (Gamba 1984:139). On the other hand, Rear Admiral Jorge Fraga writes that information on Great Britain's launching of a submarine arrived in Argentina on 1 April (1983:134). Clearly this would not have given Argentina enough time to react by 2 April.

14. Initially named Operación Azul, the invasion of the islands was renamed Operación Rosario by Colonel Mohammed Alí Seineldín after his appeals to the Virgin of Rosario to calm the storm that he and his troops encountered en route to the Malvinas (Ruíz Moreno 1986:21). Seineldín later appeared as the leader of the December 1988 military uprising.

15. Within the region, Argentina did, however, receive aid from Peru, Venezuela, and Ecuador. Libya was also a contributor, asking only symbolic payment for the material "sold" to Argentina.

4. Quest for Control

1. Without explicitly mentioning a pact, a general at the time did indicate to me that despite the historic anti-Peronism of the army's officer corps, at the time of the elections the military leadership did expect more favorable treatment from the Peronists than from the Radicals (Hector Ríos Ereñú, interview, Buenos Aires, 15 August 1989).

2. Alfonsín's intentions of permanently breaking down the Peronists' support base were reflected perhaps even more clearly in his determination to depoliticize the unions. See, for example, Alfonsín (1983:45–46).

3. According to Mark Osiel (1986: 160–61), the strategy of focusing blame on only certain members of the armed forces in part had to do with something of a "divide and conquer" perspective. It was hoped that the military would turn against the targeted individuals, thereby publicly placing the military institution as an opponent of human rights violations.

4. Miguel Angel Toma (Partido Justicialista), interview, Buenos Aires, 22 February 1989.

5. According to San Martino de Dromi, the law was passed without the support of the Peronists because of the Radicals' unwillingness to completely eliminate the military courts from the process and because of the law's relatively early recognition of "due obedience" on the part of subordinate members of the military (1988, 2:554).

6. Luís Moreno Ocampo, interview, Buenos Aires, 7 November 1988.

7. Although the judiciary did eventually act relatively autonomously, as is later discussed, some collusion between the judiciary and the executive did occur during the early stages of the government. The executive maintained constant contact with members of the judiciary at this point, using informal relationships to further political aims (interview with Radical politician, 5 April 1991).

8. According to Sonderéguer (1985:19), in May of 1981, an advertisement

demanding that the disappeared "appear with life" was published in various newspapers, signed by the Madres and Familiares, along with SERPAJ (Servicio de Paz y Justicia), CELS (Centro de Estudios Legales y Sociales), and APDH (Asamblea Permanente por los Derechos Humanos).

9. Political differences eventually caused the Madres to divide. The more radical minority nonetheless continued to appear as the "voice" of the Madres de Plaza de Mayo.

10. *Madres de Plaza de Mayo* (Buenos Aires), August 1985:4.

11. *Madres de Plaza de Mayo*, February 1985:4.

12. *Redacción*, January 1984:14.

13. The impact of the shrinking budget may have been mitigated by the increased efficiency of having a unified budget in the Ministry of Defense (Fontana 1990:23).

14. *Latin American Weekly Report* (London), 16 August 1985:12.

15. Claudio Álvarez and Nestor Contreras (Ministry of Defense), interview, Buenos Aires, 19 October 1988. According to *La Nación* (22 April 1989:18), a large number of civilian professors teach in the military schools. For example, in the Escuela Superior de Guerra (Army War College), only nineteen of a total eighty-four professors were reported to be from the military at the time.

16. *La Nación* (Buenos Aires), 21 April 1989:7.

17. Colonel (Ret.) Ramón Orieta, interview, Buenos Aires, 8 November 1988; Miguel Angel Toma (Partido Justicialista), interview, 22 February 1989.

18. Various smaller parties, including the Christian Democrats and the Partido Intransigente, eventually were also drawn into the discussions. However, the major conservative power, the Unión del Centro Democrático (UCEDE), remained aloof from the project (Orieta, interview).

19. At the same time that the decree was passed ordering that the military leaders be tried, another decree (Decree 158) was issued ordering that several of the leaders of guerrilla organizations from the same period also be brought to trial. The "theory of two demons" was, therefore, a principle for action as much as discourse.

20. These provisions are, in essence, post factum measures in that they impose legal procedures in these cases that were not in effect at the time that the events under consideration actually occurred.

21. An interview with an officer implicated in these proceedings illustrates the lack of control stimulated by the rush. Upon being transferred to an area in which the repression had been quite intense in previous years, this officer

came across various houses and other goods that had been left unoccupied and unclaimed since the disappearance of their owners. The officer decided to take charge of returning the items to their rightful owners. Thus, due to his knowledge of some of the relevant details, once the trials began he was cited to appear as a witness in a future court case. In the rush to file cases prior to the Punto Final, however, the list on which he appeared as a future witness was submitted as a list of people to be prosecuted. In the end, he was released from his obligation to appear in court as a beneficiary of the Due Obedience law. This implicitly identified him as one of the culprits of the human rights violations.

22. According to San Martino de Dromi, this number was closer to 300 (1988, 2:563).

5. Emergence of Rebellion

1. The exception would be mercenaries, professional "guns for hire." Mercenaries may be the only true military professionals in that their loyalties are commanded solely by their professions, and their services are only loaned to the hiring organization.

2. General (Ret.) Hector Ríos Ereñú, interview, Buenos Aires, 15 August 1989.

3. This does not include the auxiliary officer corps, which is composed of medical personnel, sanitation experts, lawyers, etc.

4. Members of the infantry who obtain more specialized training, such as parachuting or commando training, are exceptions to the more general high-cost and low-reward status of this branch of the army.

5. Ríos Ereñú, interview.

6. Evolution of Military Rebellion

1. Ríos Ereñú, interview.

2. López 1988; Grecco and Gonzáles 1988; *Somos* (Buenos Aires), 22 April 1987.

3. At the time, the *carapintadas* were fairly careful about not explicitly directing their complaints against the government. However, a document published three years later clearly stated that the uprisings were a reaction against the politics of the Alfonsín administration (Movimiento por la Dignidad y la Independencia 1990).

4. La Nación, 3 December 1988:21.

5. In the event that an officer is promoted above more senior officers, as

was the case with Caridi, the officers who have been passed over generally retire.

6. *Ámbito Financiero* (Buenos Aires), 20 January 1988.

7. *Página 12* (Buenos Aires), 2 December 1988:2–3.

8. Along with a missed connection between Albatros and Seineldín at the port where Seineldín was arriving from Panama (via Montevideo), there was a failed attempt by the rebels to liberate Rico.

9. *La Prensa* (Buenos Aires), 5 December 1988:7.

10. A close ally of General Manuel Noriega, Seineldín is attributed with having helped organize the notorious "Dignity Batallions."

11. Quoted in *Página 12*, 6 December 1988:1.

12. C.M. Acuña 1988:4; *Heraldo*, 5 December 1988:4.

13. *Clarín* (Buenos Aires), 21 June 1989:3.

14. *Página 12*, 20 December 1988:1.

15. Caridi claimed at the Seineldín trial that he had already expressed his desire to retire to the president prior to the Villa Martelli uprising. He reports responding to the rebels' demand that he resign with a rather noncommittal answer, which they interpreted as an agreement.

16. The methods used to contain the attack (and the lack of wounded among the captured) triggered new concerns about human rights in Argentina. See Amnesty International 1990.

17. *La Prensa*, 2 February 1989:5.

18. *El Periodista* (Buenos Aires), 6 April 1987:8–9.

19. "Hoja Avanzada 'Nuestra Señora de Luján,'" 18 January 1989.

20. Instructions to the *carapintadas* (members of the "National" army) in the instance of a military coup were repeated along with a condensed version of the Villa Martelli agreement in several editions.

21. Testimony of Colonel Florentino Díaz Loza. The resulting plan for the new government's military and defense policy (which at this time counted with Menem's support) was published in *Destino Histírico* 4, no. 8 (March 1989).

22. *Buenos Aires Herald*, 19 November 1989:3.

23. General Anibal Laiño, interview, Buenos Aires, 20 September 1991.

24. Personal communication from an Argentine army officer, February 1990.

25. *La Nación Internacional* (Buenos Aires), 16 July 1990:5.

26. According to estimates of the army command, by November 1990, around 40 percent of officers and 77 percent of NCOs held second jobs (*La Nación Internacional*, 5 November 1990:3).

27. General Anibal Laiño, interview, Buenos Aires, 19 September 1991.

28. *La Nación*, 16 July 1990:3.

29. *Página 12,* 12 November 1989:2–3; *Gente* (Buenos Aires), 16 November 1989.

30. *Página 12,* 26 November 1989:2–3.

31. *Página 12,* 12 November 1989; *Somos,* 14 February 1990:10–14.

32. Colonel (Ret.) Julio Carretto, interview, Buenos Aires, 11 September 1991; *Latin American Weekly Report* (London), 29 March 1990:5; Chumbita 1990:260–62.

33. *Latin American Weekly Report,* 16 August 1990:12.

34. Carretto, interview.

35. *Latin American Weekly Report,* 16 August 1990:12.

36. *Latin American Weekly Report,* 1 November 1990:12.

37. *Somos,* 14 February 1990:13.

38. Quoted in *Somos,* 14 February 1990:12.

39. "Hoja Avanzada 'Nuestra Señora de Luján,'" 2 April 1989:1.

40. See *Somos,* 5 December 1990:21–28 and 17 December 1990:2–7; R. Fraga 1991:123–33; Simeoni and Allegri 1991:278–357.

41. *La Nación Internacional* (17 December 1990:1) cited military sources that reported the arrests of 628 members of the armed and security forces.

42. *Somos,* 5 December 1990:22.

43. *La Nación Internacional,* 4 December 1990:6.

44. Ratios are based on figures provided in R. Fraga (1991:140). Since Fraga provides at least two very different estimates of the number of participants (427 on p. 133 and p. 135, and 798 on p. 140), these numbers can only be taken as estimates.

45. Estimates of casualties are drawn from R. Fraga (1991:134). The *Latin American Weekly Report* places the estimate at 19 dead and around 200 injured; figures in *La Nación Internacional* (10 December 1990:1) report 8 deaths of personnel from the military and prefectura, which when combined with the 5 civilians, would raise the total to 13. The civilian casualties occurred when a tank driven by the rebels collided with a city bus.

46. *Página 12,* 19 December 1990:2–3.

47. *La Prensa,* 3 September 1991:3.

48. Laiño, interview, 20 September 1991.

7. Foundations of Chronic Interventionism

1. The term *ideology* is used relatively loosely in this chapter to refer to systems of philosophies and beliefs that are shared within the armed forces or by particular sectors of the armed forces.

2. Gen. Sánchez de Bustamante, interview, 3 June 1989.

3. Quoted in Rouquie (1982b:342) from Ejército Argentino (1967), "Reglamento para el servicio interno."

4. The military hierarchy was more successful than the government, however, as it could more subtly introduce disciplinary sanctions and interfere with career advancement.

5. Ideally, the political beliefs of military officers would be evaluated directly, rather than using the military branch as an indicator. However, such information obviously would be available only in an extremely limited number of cases. Given the scope of the comparisons attempted in this study, I am obliged to rely on such objectively identifiable factors as the military branch. However, the result is that all conclusions about political ideas based on this data can be considered only as suggestive; it is hoped they are of interest, though not conclusive.

6. Notably, the leaders of Venezuela's 1992 coup attempts also complained about the politicization of promotions.

8. Shadows of Military Rule

1. It must be emphasized that the assessments of levels of repression used in this essay are comparative, not absolute. All of the bureaucratic-authoritarian regimes used repression, and no instance of state-directed murder or torture can truly be considered innocuous or, as termed in this chapter, "moderate." However, the degree to which the general population was affected by repression does vary from one case to another.

2. Overt military rule was actually established only in 1976 in Uruguay; however, the prior three years constituted de facto military rule as civilian president Bordaberry was little more than a figurehead during this period.

3. According to Weinstein (1988), 123 people "disappeared" in Argentina and 44 in Uruguay; around 90 were tortured to death.

4. Repression by military and police forces may actually be higher in Brazil now than under the military government, although at this point it is the potential for crime that is being targeted.

5. *Washington Post*, 26 April 1993.

6. *New York Times*, 25 July 1993.

7. *New York Times*, 28 March 1991:A3.

8. *New York Times*, 8 July 1993:A10.

9. *Latin American Weekly Report*, 20 October 1994:473.

Selected Bibliography

Acuña, Carlos H., and Catalina Smulovitz. 1993. "Ajustando las FF.AA. a la democrácia: Éxitos, fracasos y ambiguedades de las experiencias del Cono Sur." Buenos Aires: Centro de Estudios de Estado y Sociedad (CEDES).

Acuña, Carlos Manuel. 1988. "Caridi pasará a retiro y Cáceres garantiza el pacto." *La Prensa* (Buenos Aires), 6 December:4.

Acuña, Marcelo Luis. 1984. *De Frondizi a Alfonsín: La tradición política del radicalismo.* Vol. 2. Buenos Aires: Biblioteca Política Argentina, Centro Editor de América Latina.

Aguero, Felipe. 1989. "Autonomy of the Military in Chile: From Democracy to Authoritarianism." In Augusto Varas, ed., *Democracy under Siege: New Military Power in Latin America,* pp. 83–96. New York: Greenwood Press.

Alexander, Yonah, and Richard Kucinski. 1985. "The International Terrorist Network." In Georges Fauriol, ed., *Latin American Insurgencies,* pp. 41–66. Washington DC: Georgetown University Center for Strategic and International Studies and the National Defense University.

Alfonsín, Raúl. 1981. *La cuestión argentina.* Buenos Aires: Editorial Propuesta Argentina.

———. 1983. *Ahora: Mi propuesta política.* Buenos Aires: Sudamericana Planeta.

———. 1986. *Inédito: Una batalla contra la dictadura.* Buenos Aires: Editorial Legasa.

———. 1987a. *Discursos presidenciales.* Vol. 15. Buenos Aires: República Argentina, Secretaria de Información Pública, Dirección General de Difusión.

———. 1987b. "La participación de los trabajadores." In Fernando Rubén Pieske, *Hombre de prensa: La actividad periodística de Raúl Alfonsín.* Buenos Aires: Editorial Plus Ultra.

———. 1987c. "Propuesta y Control." In Fernando Rubén Pieske, *Hombre de prensa: La actividad periodística de Raúl Alfonsín.* Buenos Aires: Editorial Plus Ultra.

Amnesty International. 1990. *Argentina: The Attack on the Third Infantry Regiment Barracks at la Tablada.* New York: Amnesty International U.S.A.

Anaya, Jorge (Admiral). 1988. "La defensa de nuestra soberania—1982." Published as "La historia secreta de la Guerra de las Malvinas." *Historia* 9, no. 35 (September-November 1989): 3–62.

Andersen, Martin Edwin. 1993. *Dossier Secreto: Argentina's Desaparecidos and the Myth of the "Dirty War."* Boulder: Westview Press.

Anzorena, Oscar. 1988. *Tiempo de violencia y utopia (1966–1976).* Buenos Aires: Editorial Contrapunto.

Armijo, Leslie Elliott. 1994. "Menem's Mania? The Timing of Privatization in Argentina." *Southwestern Journal of Law and Trade in the Americas* 1, no. 1:1–28.

Arregui, J. J. Hernández. 1973. *Qué es el ser nacional.* Buenos Aires: Editorial Plus Ultra.

Arriagada Herrera, Genaro. 1986. "The Legal and Institutional Framework of the Armed Forces in Chile." In J. Samuel Valenzuela and Arturo Valenzuela, eds., *Military Rule in Chile,* pp.117–43. Baltimore: Johns Hopkins University Press, 1986.

———. 1988. *Pinochet: The Politics of Power.* Boston: Unwin Hyman.

Asamblea Permanente por los Derechos Humanos. 1982. *Las cifras de la Guerra Sucia.* Buenos Aires: Asamblea Permanente por los Derechos Humanos (APDH).

Asociación Americana de Juristas. 1988. *Juicios a los militares.* Cuaderno no. 4. Buenos Aires: Rama Argentina de la Asociación Americana de Juristas.

Aurelli, Victoria. 1989. "Nace un místico en la Argentina." Pamphlet from Seineldín movement.

Barral, Patricia. 1991. "Como en casa." *Noticias,* 1 September:68.

Beltrán, Virgilio. 1987. "Political Transition in Argentina: 1982–1985." *Armed Forces and Society* 27, no. 2 (winter): 215–34.

Brysk, Allison. 1994. *The Politics of Human Rights in Argentina.* Stanford: Stanford University Press.

Buchanan, Paul G. 1987. "The Varied Faces of Domination: State Terror, Economic Policy, and Social Rupture during the Argentine 'Proceso,'

1976–81." *American Journal of Political Science* 31, no. 2 (February): 336–82.

Caputo, Dante. 1983. "Balance Provisorio." In Peter Waldmann and Ernesto Garzón Valdéz, eds., *El poder militar en la Argentina, 1976–1981.* Buenos Aires: Editorial Galerna.

Carretto, Julio (Lieutenant Colonel). 1987. *La ideología y la nueva guerra.* Buenos Aires: Círculo Militar.

Castello, Antonio Emilio. 1986a. *La democracia inestable: 1962–1966.* Buenos Aires: Editorial Astrea de Alfredo y Ricardo Depalma.

———. 1986b. "Onganía y la caída de Illia." *Todo es Historia* 19 (July): 8–27.

Castiglione, Marta. 1992. *La militarización del estado en la Argentina.* Buenos Aires: Centro Editor de América Latina.

Child, Jack. 1985. "US Policies toward Insurgencies in Latin America." In Georges Fauriol, ed., *Latin American Insurgencies,* pp. 131–60. Washington DC: Georgetown University Center for Strategic and International Studies and National Defense University.

———. 1990. "Geopolitical Thinking." In Louis Goodman, Johanna Mendelson, and Juan Rial, eds., *The Military and Democracy: The Future of Civil-Military Relations in Latin America,* pp. 143–64. Lexington MA: Lexington Books.

Chumbita, Hugo. 1990. *Los carapintada: Historia de un malentendida argentino.* Buenos Aires: Editorial Planeta.

Collier, David, ed. 1979. *The New Authoritarianism in Latin America.* Princeton: Princeton University Press.

Comisión Rattenbach. 1988. *Informe Rattenbach: El drama de Malvinas.* Buenos Aires: Ediciones Espartaco.

Comisión Nacional Sobre la Desaparación de Personas (CONADEP). 1986. *Nunca más.* Buenos Aires: Editorial Universitaria de Buenos Aires.

Congreso Argentino. Various years. *Anales de legislación argentina.* Buenos Aires: Congreso Argentino.

Consejo Supremo de las Fuerzas Armadas. 1984. Letters between Consejo Supremo de las Fuerzas Armadas and Ministry of Defense, October to November.

Cooke, John William, and Juan Domingo Perón. 1972. *Correspondencia Perón-Cooke.* Vol. 2. Buenos Aires: Ediciones Parlamento.

Corradi, Juan. 1987. "The Culture of Fear in Civil Society." In Monica Peralta Ramos and Carlos H. Waisman, eds., *From Military Rule to Liberal Democracy in Argentina,* pp. 113–30. Boulder: Westview Press.

Dabat, Alejandro, and Luís Lorenzano. 1982. *Conflicto malvinense y crisis nacional.* Mexico City: Teoría y Política.

Dahl, Robert. 1971. *Polyarchy: Participation and Opposition.* New Haven: Yale University Press.

————. 1989. *Democracy and Its Critics.* New Haven: Yale University Press.

Dassin, Joan, ed. 1986. *Torture in Brazil.* New York: Vintage Books.

de Imaz, José Luis. 1977. *Los que mandan.* Buenos Aires: Editorial El Coloquio.

de Martini, Siro. 1988. "La Causa Malvinas: Último acto de un drama." *La Prensa* (Buenos Aires), October 20.

De Mattei, José Ismael (Capitán). 1983. "Defensa nacional y teoría de la seguridad." *Revista Militar,* no. 711 (July to December).

de Naurois, Patricio. 1958. "Guerra subversiva y guerra revolucionaria." *Revista de la Escuela Superior de Guerra,* no. 331 (October-December): 687–702.

De Riz, Liliana. 1981. *Retorno y derrumbe: El último gobierno peronista.* Mexico City: Folios Ediciones.

Di Tella, Torcuato. 1971–72. "La búsqueda de la fórmula política argentina." *Desarrollo Económico* 11, nos. 42–44 (July-March): 317–25.

Diamint, Rut Clara. 1990. *La militarización de la cultura política argentina: El culto a San Martín.* Buenos Aires: Center for European–Latin American Research (EURAL).

Diamond, Larry, Juan Linz, and Seymour Martin Lipset. 1988. "Introduction: Comparing Experiences with Democracy." In *Politics in Developing Countries,* pp. 1–37. Boulder and London: Lynne Rienner.

Diamond, Marcelo. 1983. The Argentine Pendulum: Until When? Paper prepared for the Conference on Models of Political and Economic Change in Latin America, November, Center for Latin American and Iberian Studies, Vanderbilt University, Nashville TN.

Díaz Bessone, Ramón Genaro. 1988a. *Guerra revolucionaria en la Argentina (1959–1978).* Buenos Aires: Circulo Militar.

————. 1988b. "Guerra revolucionaria en la Argentina, 1959–1978." *Revista Militar,* no. 719 (January-March): 7–24.

Díaz Loza, Florentino. 1973. *Doctrina política del Ejército.* Buenos Aires: A. Peña Lillo.

Downs, Anthony. 1957. *An Economic Theory of Democracy.* New York: Harper Press.

Drake, Paul, and Ivan Jaksic, eds. 1991. "Introduction: Transformation and Transition in Chile, 1982–1990." In *The Struggle for Democracy in*

Chile, 1982–1990, pp. 1–20. Lincoln and London: University of Nebraska Press.

Druetta, Gustavo. 1988. Diputados y defensa: El poder legislativo en la política militar. Paper prepared for the Conference on Fuerzas Armadas, Estado, Defensa, y Sociedad, 26–28 October, Buenos Aires.

Duhalde, Eduardo Luís. 1983. *El estado terrorista argentino.* Barcelona: El Caballito.

Durkheim, Emile. 1933. *The Division of Labor in Society.* New York: Free Press.

Ejército Argentino. 1955. Conclusiones del Tribunal Superior de Honor que juzgó la conducta del entonces General de Ejército Juan Domingo Perón y que culminó con su descalificación.

———. 1958–1990. *Boletín Militar Público* (later published as *Boletín Público del Ejército*).

———. 1958. *Libro Negro de la Segunda Tiranía.* Buenos Aires: Ejército Argentino.

———. 1968 and 1981. *Escalafón del Ejército Argentino* (Reservado). Primera Parte: Personal en Actividad.

———. 1975–78, 1980–88. *Boletín Reservado del Ejército.*

———. 1980. *Terrorism in Argentina.* (Published by the Proceso military government).

Escudé, Carlos. 1987. *Patología del nacionalismo.* Buenos Aires: Editorial Tesis.

———. 1988. "Argentine Territorial Nationalism." *Journal of Latin American Studies* 20 (May): 139–65.

Estévez, Eduardo. 1990. "Aspectos salientes de la relación gobierno-fuerzas armadas 1983–1989." In National Democratic Institute for International Affairs, *Hacía una nueva relación: El papel de las Fuerzas Armadas en un Gobierno Democrático*, pp. 77–97. Buenos Aires: National Democratic Institute for International Affairs and Fundación Illia.

Evans, Peter. 1979. *Dependent Development: The Alliance of Multinational, State and Local Capital in Brazil.* Princeton: Princeton University Press.

Feldman, David Lewis. 1985. "The United States Role in the Malvinas Crisis, 1982: Misguidance and Misperception in Argentina's Decision to Go to War." *Journal of Interamerican Studies and World Affairs* 27, no. 2 (summer): 1–19.

Figueroa, Pío Uladimero (Lieutenant Colonel). 1984. "Ideales del Ejército Argentino." *Revista Militar,* no. 713 (July-December): 11–14.

Finer, S. E. 1962. *The Man on Horseback: The Role of the Military in Politics.* New York: Frederick A. Praeger.

Fitch, John Samuel. 1986. "Integrating the Military." *Harvard International Review* 8, no. 6: 18–19, 23–24, 28.

Fontana, Andrés. 1984. *Fuerzas armadas, partidos políticos y transición a la democracia en Argentina.* Buenos Aires: CEDES.

———. 1987a. Political Decision-Making by a Military Corporation. Ph.D. diss., University of Texas.

———. 1987b. "La política militar del gobierno constitucional argentino." In José Nun and Juan Carlos Porantiero, eds. *Ensayos sobre la transición democrática en la Argentina,* pp. 375–418. Buenos Aires: Puntosur editores.

———. 1990. "La política militar en un contexto de transición: Argentina 1983–1989." Buenos Aires: CEDES.

Fraga, Jorge A. 1983. *La Argentina y el Atlántico Sur.* Buenos Aires: Instituto de Publicaciones Navales.

Fraga, Rosendo. 1988. *Ejército: Del escarnio al poder (1973–1976).* Buenos Aires: Editorial Planeta.

———. 1989. *La cuestión militar: 1987–1989.* Buenos Aires: Editorial Centro de Estudios Unión para la Nueva Mayoria.

———. 1991. *Menem y la cuestión militar.* Buenos Aires: Editorial Centro de Estudios Unión para la Nueva Mayoria.

Frondizi, Arturo. 1957. "Industria Argentina y desarrollo nacional." *Qué* 1, no. 1 (February): 1–30.

———. 1964. *Estrategia y táctica del movimiento nacional.* Buenos Aires: Editorial Desarrollo.

———. 1982. *Mensajes presidenciales: 1958–1962.* Vol. 4, 13 November 1960 to 7 December 1961. Buenos Aires: Centro de Estudios Nacionales.

Fruhling, Hugo. 1989. El movimiento de derechos humanos y la transición democrática en Chile y Argentina." Unpublished paper.

Gamba, Virginia. 1984. *El peón de la reina.* Buenos Aires: Editorial Sudamericana.

García, José. 1978. "Military Factions and Military Intervention in Latin America." In S. W. Simon, ed., *The Military and Security in the Third World: Domestic and International Impacts,* pp. 47–75. Boulder: Westview Press.

García Enciso, Isias J.(Brigadier General). 1984. "Estado actual y posible evolución del problema malvinas," *Revista Militar,* no. 712 (January-June).

Genta, Jordan B. N.d. *Acerca de la libertad de enseñar y de la enseñanza de la libertad; Libre exámen y comunismo, guerra contrarevolucionaria.* Buenos Aires: Ediciones Dictio.

Gibson, Edward L. 1990. "Democracy and the Electoral Right in Argentina." *Journal of Inter-American Studies and World Affairs* 32, no. 3 (fall): 177–228.

González Bombal, Inés. 1991. *El diálogo político: La transición que no fue.* Buenos Aires: CEDES.

Goyret, José Teofilio (General). 1984. "Acciones del Ejército Argentino en la Guerra de las Malvinas." *Revista Militar*, no. 712 (January-June).

Grecco, Jorge, and Gustavo González. 1988. *Felices pascuas: Los hechos inéditos de la rebelion militar.* Buenos Aires: Planeta.

Guevara, Juan Francisco. 1975. *Proyecto XXI, Mañana se hace hoy.* Buenos Aires: Editorial Ancora.

Hernández, Pablo. 1989. *Conversaciones con el Teniente Coronel Aldo Rico: De Malvinas a Operación Dignidad.* Buenos Aires: Editorial Fortaleza.

Hirschman, Albert. 1970. *Exit, Voice and Loyalty.* Cambridge: Harvard University Press.

Hunter, Wendy. Forthcoming. "Politicians against Soldiers: Contesting the Military in Post-Authoritarian Brazil." *Comparative Politics.*

Huntington, Samuel P. 1957. *The Soldier and the State: The Theory and Politics of Civil-Military Relations.* Cambridge: Harvard University Press.

———. 1968. *Political Order in Changing Societies.* New Haven: Yale University Press.

International Monetary Fund (IMF). 1994. *International Financial Statistics Yearbook.* Washington: International Monetary Fund.

Janowitz, Morris. 1961. *The Professional Soldier.* Glencoe: Free Press.

Janowitz, Morris, and Jacques Van Doorn. 1971. *On Military Intervention.* Rotterdam: Rotterdam University Press.

Jowitt, Kenneth. 1987. "Moscow 'Centre,'" *Eastern European Politics and Society* 1, no. 3:396–48.

Karl, Terry Lynn. 1990. "Dilemmas of Democratization in Latin America." *Comparative Politics* 23, no. 1 (October): 1–21.

Karl, Terry Lynn, and Philippe Schmitter. 1991. "Modes of Transition in Latin America, Southern and Eastern Europe." *International Social Science Journal*, no. 128 (May): 269–84. Issue on the Age of Democracy: Democratic Transition in the East and the South.

Selected Bibliography

Kvaternik, Eugenio. 1987. *Crisis sin salvaje: La crisis político-militar de 1962–1963*. Buenos Aires: Instituto de Desarrollo Económico y Social (IDES).

———. 1990. *El péndulo cívico-militar: La caída de Illia*. Buenos Aires: Instituto Torcuato Di Tella, Editorial Tesis.

Lanusse, Alejandro A. 1977. *Mi testimonio*. Buenos Aires: Lasserre Editores.

———. 1988. *Protagonista y testigo*. Buenos Aires: Marcelo Lugones.

Leis, Hector Ricardo. 1989. *El movimiento por los derechos humanos y la política argentina*. 2 vols. Buenos Aires: Centro Editor de América Latina.

León, Ángel Daniel (Lieutenant Colonel). 1988. "¿Qué pasa en el Ejército argentino?" *La Prensa* (Buenos Aires), 14 February: 9.

Linz, Juan. 1978. *The Breakdown of Democratic Regimes: Crisis, Breakdown and Reequilibrium*. Baltimore: Johns Hopkins University Press.

Linz, Juan, and Alfred Stepan, eds. 1978. *The Breakdown of Democratic Regimes*. Baltimore: Johns Hopkins University Press.

López, Ernesto. 1987. *Seguridad nacional y sedición militar*. Buenos Aires: Editorial Legasa.

———. 1988. *El último levantamiento*. Buenos Aires: Editorial Legasa.

Loveman, Brian. 1993. *The Constitution of Tyranny: Regimes of Exception in Spanish America*. Pittsburgh: University of Pittsburgh Press.

Lubertino Beltrán, María J. 1987. *Perón y la Iglesia*. Buenos Aires: Centro Editor de America Latina.

Luna, Felix. 1972. *Argentina de Perón a Lanusse: 1943–1973*. Buenos Aires: Editorial Planeta Argentina.

Luttwack, Edward. 1968. *Coup D'Etat: A Practical Handbook*. Cambridge: Harvard University Press.

Mainwaring, Scott. 1990. Presidentialism, Multiparty Systems, and Democracy: The Difficult Equation. Notre Dame IN: Helen Kellogg Institute for International Studies, University of Notre Dame. Unpublished paper.

Malamud-Goti, Jaime. 1990. "Traditional Governments in the Breach: Why Punish State Criminals?" *Human Rights Quarterly* 12:1–16.

———. 1991. Punishment and a Rights-Based Democracy. Unpublished paper.

Ministerio de Economía [Argentina]. 1982. *Informe económico, reseña estadistica, 1978–81*. Buenos Aires: Ministerio de Economía.

———. 1983. *Informe económico, reseña estadistica, 1980–1983*. Buenos Aires: Ministerio de Economía.

Monteon, Michael. 1987. "Can Argentina's Democracy Survive Economic Disaster?" In Monica Peralta-Ramos and Carlos H. Waisman, eds., *From Military Rule to Liberal Democracy in Argentina*. Boulder: Westview Press.

Movimiento por la Dignidad y la Independencia. 1990. Convocatoria nacional de la Operación Nacional de la Operación Dignidad.

———. 1991a. *Dignidad,* nos. 1–2 (July).

———. 1991b. Pensamiento y doctrina.

———. 1991c. Resumen de la propuesta nacional.

Moyano, María José. 1991. [1989]. "The 'Dirty War' in Argentina: Was It a War and How Dirty Was It?" In Hans Werner Tobler and Peter Waldmann, eds., *Staatliche und para staatliche Gewalt in Lateinoamerica*. Frankfurt: Vervuert.

Munck, Gerardo. 1994. The Critical Juncture Framework and Argentina: The Menem Revolution in Comparative Perspective. Paper presented at the American Political Science meeting, 1–4 September, New York.

Munck, Ronaldo. 1989. *Latin America: The Transition to Democracy*. London: Zed Books.

Mustapic, Ana María. 1986. "Parlamento: ¿Acuerdo o regla de la mayoría?" In De Riz et al., eds., *El parlamento hoy*. Buenos Aires: CEDES.

Norden, Deborah. 1990. "Democratic Consolidation and Military Professionalism: Argentina in the 1980's. *Journal of Interamerican Studies and World Affairs* 32, no. 3 (fall): 151–76.

Nordlinger, Eric. 1977. *Soldiers in Politics: Military Coups and Government*. Englewood Cliffs NJ: Prentice-Hall.

Nougues, Jean. 1962. "Radioscopia subversiva de la Argentina." *Revista de la Escuela Superior de Guerra*, no. 344.

O'Donnell, Guillermo. 1973. *Modernization and Bureaucratic Authoritarianism*. Berkeley: Institute of International Studies.

———. 1988. *Bureaucratic Authoritarianism: Argentina, 1966–1973, in Comparative Perspective*. Berkeley and Los Angeles: University of California Press.

O'Donnell, Guillermo, and Philippe Schmitter. 1986. *Transitions from Authoritarian Rule: Tentative Conclusions about Uncertain Democracies*. Baltimore: Johns Hopkins University Press.

O'Donnell, Guillermo, Philippe Schmitter, and Laurence Whitehead, eds. 1986. *Transitions from Authoritarian Rule*. Baltimore: Johns Hopkins University Press.

Operación Virgen de la Valle. 1988–89. "Hoja Avanzada Nuestra Señora de Luján," nos. 1–25 (December-July).

————. 1990. Seineldín video.

Osiel, Mark. 1986. "The Making of Human Rights Policy in Argentina: The Impact of Ideas and Interests on a Legal Conflict." *Journal of Latin American Studies* 18 (May): 135–78.

Pérez Andrade, Diego. 1990. "Una historia de los sucesos que faltaba relatar." *La Nación Internacional,* 10 December: 5.

Perina, Ruben. 1983. *Ongania, Levingston, Lanusse: Los militares en la política Argentina.* Buenos Aires: Editorial de Belgrano.

Perón, Juan Domingo. 1982. *Tres revoluciones militares.* Buenos Aires: Peña Lillo Editor.

————. 1988. *Discursos Completos: 1974.* Vol. 3. Buenos Aires: Editorial Megafon.

Pion-Berlin, David. 1989a. A House Divided: Segmented Professionalism and Security Ideology in the Argentine Army, 1984–1989. Paper presented at the Latin American Studies Association 15th International Congress, 5–7 December. Miami, Florida.

————. 1989b. "Latin American National Security Doctrines: Hard- and Softline Theme." *Armed Forces and Society* 15, no. 3 (spring): 411–29.

————. 1990. "Civil-Military Relations in Democratic Argentina: An Unstable Equilibrium." Columbus: Ohio State University.

Poder Judicial de la Nación Argentina. 1991. Transcript of trial for December 1990 rebellion. Introductions of Prosecutor and Defense; Declarations of Humberto Romero, Dr. Horacio Jaunarena, General José Dante Caridi, Dr. Ricardo Raúl Alfonsín, Aldo Rico, Julio Enrique Vila Melo, General Heriberto Auel, Colonel Florentino Diaz Loza, Colonel Jorge Luis Toccalino, General Pablo Skalany, Dr. César Arias, First Lieutenant Daniel Enrique Martella.

Potash, Robert. 1969. *The Army and Politics in Argentina, 1928–1945: Yrigoyen to Perón.* Stanford: Stanford University Press.

————. 1980. *The Army and Politics in Argentina, 1945–1962.* Stanford: Stanford University Press.

Potash, Robert, ed. 1984. *Perón y el G.O.U.: Los documentos de una logia secreta.* Buenos Aires: Editorial Sudamericana.

Przeworski, Adam. 1986. "Some Problems in the Study of the Transition to Democracy." In Guillermo O'Donnell, Philippe Schmitter, and Lawrence Whitehead, eds., *Transitions from Authoritarian Rule: Comparative Perspectives,* pp. 47–63. Baltimore: Johns Hopkins University Press.

Rein, Ranaan. 1993. *The Franco-Perón Alliance: Relations between Spain and Argentina, 1946–1955*. Pittsburgh: University of Pittsburgh Press.

República Argentina. Various years. *Anales de Legislación Argentina*.

———. Various years. *Boletín Oficial*.

———. Various years. *Leyes Nacionales*.

———. 1985. *Código de justicia militar*, with commentaries by Igounet and Igounet. Buenos Aires: Libreria de Jurista.

Rial, Juan. 1990. "Las Fuerzas Armadas en los años 90: Una agenda de discusión." Montevideo: Sociedad de Análisis Política (PEITHO).

Ricci, María Susana, and J. Samuel Fitch. 1988. Military Regimes in Argentina: 1966–1983. Paper presented at the Conference on Civil-Military Relations and Democracy in Latin America, sponsored by American University and PEITHO (Uruguay), 16–20 May, Washington DC.

———. 1990. "Military Regimes in Argentina: 1966–1973 and 1976–1983." In Louis Goodman, Johanna Mendelson, and Juan Rial, eds., *The Military and Democracy: The Future of Civil-Military Relations in Latin America*, pp. 55–74. Lexington MA: Lexington Books.

Riker, William R. 1962. *The Theory of Political Coalitions*. New Haven and London: Yale University Press.

Rizzi, Fernando. 1990. "Arturo Illia, el docente." In Pablo Eugenio Batalla and Fernando Rizzi, eds., *Arturo Illia*. Buenos Aires: Fundación Arturo Illia para la Democracía y la Paz.

Rock, David. 1975. "Radical Populism and the Conservative Elite, 1912–1930." In Rock, ed., *Argentina in the Twentieth Century*. Pittsburg: University of Pittsburg Press.

———. 1987. *Argentina 1516–1987: From Spanish Colonization to Alfonsín*. Berkeley and Los Angeles: University of California Press.

Rodríguez Zía, Jorge. 1987. *El punto fatal: La obedencia indebida*. Santa Fe de la Vera Cruz.

Rouquie, Alain. 1975. *Radicales y Desarrollistas*. Buenos Aires: Schapire.

———. 1981. *Poder militar y sociedad política en la Argentina*. Vol. 1. Buenos Aires: Emecé.

———. 1982a. "Hegemonía militar, estado y dominación social." In Rouquie, ed., *Argentina, hoy*, pp. 11–50. Mexico City: Siglo Veintiuno.

———. 1982b. *Poder militar y sociedad política en la Argentina*. Vol. 2. Buenos Aires: Emecé.

———. 1987. *The Military and the State in Latin America*. Berkeley and Los Angeles: University of California Press.

Rueschemeyer, Dietrich, Evelyne Huber Stephens, and John D. Stephens. 1992. *Capitalist Development and Democracy.* Chicago: University of Chicago Press.

Ruíz Moreno, Isídoro. 1986. *Comandos en acción: El Ejército en Malvinas.* Buenos Aires: Emecé.

Sacheri, Carlos A. 1980. *El órden natural.* Buenos Aires: Ediciones del Cruzamante.

San Martino de Dromi, María Laura. 1988. *Historia Política Argentina (1955–1988).* 2 vols. Buenos Aires: Editorial Astrea.

Sánchez de Bustamante, Tomás (General). Diario de guerra del Regimiento 10 de Tiradores Blindados, 1962–1963. Unpublished diary.

Sancinetti, Marcelo A. 1988. *Derechos humanos en la Argentina postdictatorial.* Buenos Aires: Lerner Editores Asociados.

Scenna, Miguel Angel. 1980. *Los militares.* Buenos Aires: Editorial Belgrano.

Schmitter, Philippe, and Terry Lynn Karl. 1991. What Kind of Democracies Are Emerging in South America, Central America, Southern Europe and Eastern Europe? Paper presented at international colloquium, Transitions to Democracy in Europe and Latin America, 21–25 January, University of Guadalajara and FLACSO, Mexico.

Scully, Timothy. 1992. *Rethinking the Center: Party Politics in Nineteenth- and Twentieth-Century Chile.* Stanford: Stanford University Press.

Seineldín, Mohamed Alí. 1990(?). Bases para un Proyecto Nacional. Pamphlet.

Sheetz, Thomas. 1994. "Gastos militares en América del Sur." In *Proliferación de armamentos y medidas de fomento de la confianza y la seguridad en América Latina.* Lima: Centro Regional de las Naciones Unidas para la Paz, el Desarme y el Desarrollo en América Latina y el Caribe.

Sigmund, Paul E. 1977. *The Overthrow of Allende and the Politics of Chile, 1964–1976.* Pittsburgh: University of Pittsburgh Press.

Simeoni, Hector Ruben, and Eduardo Allegri. 1991. *Linea de fuego: Historia oculta de una frustración.* Buenos Aires: Editorial Sudamericana.

Skidmore, Thomas. 1988. *The Politics of Military Rule in Brazil, 1964–85.* New York: Oxford University Press.

Smith, William. 1989. *Authoritarianism and the Crisis of the Argentine Political Economy.* Stanford: Stanford University Press.

Snow, Peter. 1971. *Political Forces in Argentina.* Boston: Allyn and Bacon.

Sonderéguer, María. 1985. "Aparición con vida: El movimiento de derechos humanos en la Argentina." In Elizabeth Jelin, ed., *Los nuevos movi-*

mientos sociales, pp. 7–32. Vol. 2. Buenos Aires: Centro Editor de América Latina.

Spitta, Arnold. 1983. "El 'Proceso de Reorganización Nacional' de 1976 a 1981: Los objetivos básicos y su realización práctica." In Peter Waldmann and Ernesto Garzón Valdéz, eds., *El poder militar en la Argentina: 1976–1981.* Buenos Aires: Editorial Galerna.

Stepan, Alfred. 1971. *The Military in Politics: Changing Patterns in Brazil.* Princeton: Princeton University Press.

———. 1973. "The New Professionalism of Internal Warfare and Military Role Expansion." In Stepan, ed., *Authoritarian Brazil: Origins, Policies, and Future.* New Haven: Yale University Press.

———. 1988. *Rethinking Military Politics: Brazil and the Southern Cone.* Princeton: Princeton University Press.

Stepan, Alfred, and Michael Fitzpatrick. 1985. Civil-Military Relations and Democracy: The Role of the Military in the Polity. Paper prepared for project, The Role of Political Parties in the Return to Democracy in the Southern Cone, Woodrow Wilson Center, Washington DC, July.

Teissere, Germán R. (First Lieutenant). 1953. "Influencia del Ejército en el desarrollo de los valores materiales y morales del Pueblo Argentino." *Revista de la Escuela Superior de Guerra,* no. 617 (January).

Terragno, Rodolfo. 1974. *Los 400 días de Perón.* Buenos Aires: Ediciones de la Flor.

Train, Harry. 1987. "Malvinas: Un caso de estudio." *Boletin del Centro Naval* 105, no. 748 (January-March).

Turner, Frederick C. 1983. "The Aftermath of Defeat in Argentina," *Current History,* 82 (February): 58–61.

Unión Cívica Radical (UCR). 1973. *Plataforma de gobierno.* Buenos Aires: El Cid Editor.

United Nations. *United Nations Statistical Yearbook, 1979/1980.* New York: United Nations.

———. *United Nations Statistical Yearbook, 1983/1984.* New York: United Nations.

Valenzuela, Arturo. 1985. "A Note on the Military and Social Science Theory." *Third World Quarterly* 7, no. 1 (January): 132–43.

Valenzuela, Samuel. 1992. "Democratic Consolidation in Post-Transitional Settings: Notion, Process, and Facilitating Conditions." In Scott Mainwaring, Guillermo O'Donnell, and J. Samuel Valenzuela, eds., *Issues in Democratic Consolidation: The New South American Democracies in*

Comparative Perspective, pp. 57–104. Notre Dame IN: University of Notre Dame Press.

Valenzuela, Samuel, and Arturo Valenzuela, eds. 1986. *Military Rule in Chile: Dictatorships and Oppositions*. Baltimore: Johns Hopkins University Press.

Van Doorn, Jacques. 1965. "The Officer Corps: A Fusion of Profession and Organization." *European Journal of Sociology* 6:262–82.

Varas, Augusto. 1989. "Democratization and Military Reform in Argentina." In Varas, ed., *Democracy under Siege: New Military Power in Latin America*, pp. 47–64. New York: Greenwood Press.

Verbitsky, Horacio, ed. 1987 [document dated 24 March 1976]. "Acta fijando el propósito y los objetivos básicos para el Proceso de Reorganización Nacional." In *Medio siglo de proclamas militares*, pp. 145–46. Buenos Aires: Editora/12.

Verone, Mario Antonio. 1985. *La caída de Illia*. Buenos Aires: Editorial Coincidencia.

Waisbord, Silvio. 1991. "Politics and Identity in the Argentine Army: Cleavages and the Generational Factor." *Latin American Research Review* 26, no. 2:157–70.

Waldmann, Peter, and Ernesto Garzón Valdés, eds. 1983. *El poder militar en la Argentina: 1976–1981*. Buenos Aires: Editorial Galerna.

Wallerstein, Michael. 1980. "The Collapse of Democracy in Brazil: Its Economic Determinants." *Latin American Research Review* 15, no. 3:3–40.

Weinstein, Martin. 1988. *Uruguay: Democracy at the Crossroads*. Boulder: Westview Press.

Welch, Claude. 1976. "Civilian Control of the Military: Myth and Reality." In Welch, ed., *Civilian Control of the Military*, pp. 1–42. Albany: State University of New York Press.

———. 1987. *No Farewell to Arms?* Boulder: Westview Press.

Wilkie, James W., and Carlos Alberto Conteras, eds. 1992. *Statistical Abstract of Latin America*. Vol. 29. Los Angeles: UCLA Latin America Center Publications.

Wilkie, James, David Lorey, and Enrique Ochoa, eds. 1988. *Statistical Abstract of Latin America*. Vol. 26. Los Angeles: UCLA Latin American Center Publications.

Wilkie, James, and Adam Perkal. 1984. *Statistical Abstract for Latin America*. Vol. 23. Los Angeles: UCLA Latin America Center Publications.

World Bank. 1983. *World Tables*. Vol. 1. Washington DC: International Bank for Reconstruction and Development.

Wynia, Gary W. 1992. *Argentina: Illusions and Realities,* 2 ed. New York: Holmes and Meier.

Interviews

In order not to endanger or otherwise prejudice those individuals who have opted to help me, many of the interviews conducted (as well as some of the information tendered) will have to remain confidential. In some cases, this is in response to the explicit request of the informant. In other cases (particularly in regard to active-duty military officers), I have decided to lean toward caution and omit the names of those whose collaboration may, in some way, cause them problems.

Claudio Alvarez and Nestor Contreras (Ministry of Defense). Buenos Aires, 19 October 1988.
Admiral (Ret.) Jorge Anaya. Buenos Aires, 19 December 1988.
Colonel (Ret.) Julio Carretto. Buenos Aires, 11 September 1991. (Carretto was a lieutenant colonel during our first two meetings).
Navy Captain (Ret.) Siro de Martini. November 1988.
General Fiorda. Buenos Aires, 5 April 1989.
Rosendo Fraga (Centro Union por la Nueva Mayoria). Buenos Aires, 14 Nov. 1988; 21 Nov. 1988.
Arturo Frondizi. Written response to questionnaire. May 1989.
Horacio Jaunarena (Minister of Defense). Buenos Aires, 3 August 1989.
General Anibal Laiño. Buenos Aires, 19 and 20 September 1991.
General (Ret.) Alejandro Agustín Lanusse. Buenos Aires, 2 November 1988.
Bernardo Larroudé (Frondizi government). Buenos Aires, 18 March 1989; 8 April 1989.
Jaime Malamud Goti (adviser to Alfonsín). Washington DC, 5 April 1991.
Luís Moreno Ocampo (federal prosecutor). Buenos Aires, 7 November 1988.
Colonel (Ret.) Ramón Orieta. Buenos Aires, 8 November 1988.
Hernán Patiño Meyer (Partido Justicialista). Buenos Aires, 1 February 1989.
Colonel (Ret.) Luis Perlinger. Buenos Aires, 9 May 1989.
Lieutenant Colonel (Ret.) Luis Polo and Lieutenant Colonel (Ret.) Dario Fernandez Maguer. Buenos Aires, 27 July 1989.
Lieutenant Colonel (Ret.) Aldo Rico. Buenos Aires, 19 September 1991.
General (Ret.) Hector Ríos Ereñú. Buenos Aires, 15 August 1989.
Admiral (Ret.) Isaac Rojas. Buenos Aires, 20 July 1989.

Dr. Tomás Sánchez de Bustamante (Partido Radical). Buenos Aires, 31 January 1989.

General (Ret.) Tomás Sánchez de Bustamante. Buenos Aires, 26 April 1989; 31 May 1989; 3 June 1989.

Eduardo Tholke (Ministry of Interior). Buenos Aires, 22 June 1989.

Miguel Angel Toma (Partido Justicialista). Buenos Aires, 22 February 1989.

Index